Studien der Hessischen Stiftung Friedens- und Konfliktforschung
Studies of the Peace Research Institute Frankfurt

Ernst-Otto Czempiel, Gert Krell, Harald Müller,
Reinhard Rode (Eds.)

United States Interests and Western Europe: Arms Control, Energy, and Trade

Campus Verlag
Frankfurt/New York

Published with the support of the Volkswagenwerk Foundation

CIP-Kurztitelaufnahme der Deutschen Bibliothek

*United States interests and Western Europe: arms
control, energy, and trade* / Ernst-Otto
Czempiel ... (Eds.). – Frankfurt [Main] ; New
York : Campus-Verlag, 1981.
  (Studien der Hessischen Stiftung Friedens- und
  Konfliktforschung)
  ISBN 3-593-32914-X

NE: Czempiel, Ernst-Otto [Hrsg.]

Contents

Foreword

In spite of its relevance United States policy towards Western Europe seldom has been analysed. There are many studies dealing with NATO and alliance matters, of course. But European politics of the United States comprehend much more than military security only. It is, as all politics, based on three dimensions with security being one of them, economic well-being and rule the two others. All three have to be considered if foreign policy and international politics shall be analysed properly.

Even less known is the fact that American-European relations are a problem of peace. Peace does not only mean to avoid war. This is only the first step. Peace, in its developing stage, means fostering and promoting cooperative and harmonious patterns of relationship. From this vantage point United States-European relations pose one of the most important peace problems. That means that peace depends to a large extent on American policy towards Europe (and on European responses). It could be argued that with regard to peace this relationship is more important than the East-West-conflict.

In addition to that, American policy towards Western Europe is an important parameter for the foreign policy of Western European states, above all the Federal Republic of Germany. European states are middle powers. Their range of action is limited, is being described by the behavior of the superpowers. The closer the relationship between a superpower and a middle state the more acts the former as a political condition for the latter.

It is for those reasons that the "Research Group USA" within the Hessische Stiftung Friedens- und Konfliktforschung, Frankfurt, since 1976 has analysed extensively the United States policy towards Western Europe. There have been two larger research projects covering not only foreign but domestic problems as well. Finishing the first research project the research group has arranged in December 1980 an international conference at Bad Homburg dealing with "Trends and Perspectives in United States Economic and Security Policy towards Europe".

Topics have been American European policies in the field of arms control, trade and energy. The idea has been to combine some issues within the dimension of security and economic well-being. The research group has presented to the conference its main findings and had invited from the United States and European countries distinguished experts in the respective fields to produce their own results.

This volume contains six papers presented to the conference and an introductory analysis of the somewhat larger U.S.-European-Soviet Union context within which American policy towards Western Europe has to be seen.

The research group is very much obliged to the Stiftung Volkswagenwerk, Hannover, for a grant financing the project as well as the conference. The Werner-Reimers-Foundation kindly lent hospitality to the conference in Bad Homburg. We thank our foreign collegues who have presented papers and/or comments to the conference. The volume documents the front of research in the countries and disciplines concerned. But it is not only directed towards the academic community. Decision-makers are bound to know as exactly as possible the environment within which they have to operate. With regards to them the volume hopes to produce partial enlightment of their operational environment.

Frankfurt, Spring 1981
E.-O. Czempiel, Gert Krell, Harald Müller, Reinhard Rode

Ernst-Otto Czempiel

United States-Western European Relations in a Global Perspective. An Introduction

1. The analysis of American interests in Europe is a timely and important subject. American-European relations are the corner-stone of the West. They are, on the other hand, no more the undisputed relations they used to be in the past. There are differences on both sides of the Atlantic, divergent political, economic, and military interests. There is, what is more important, an ongoing discussion of those divergencies. This discussion is not always helpful. Sometime it puts oil into the flames, sometimes it even invents problems or magnifies them. The articles collected in this volume try to put solid rock under this discussion. They analyze American interests in Western Europe within the fields of arms control, energy, and trade. Interests are the basis of politics. Perceptions vary, interests remain. They are stable, but they are not static. And they are not completely independent. Although American interests in Europe are one of the great pillars of the East-West conflict, they are not unaffected by this conflict. The United States guarantee European security for several reasons, the most reliable being American interests in the old continent. Great nations, Kissinger used to say, do not have friends, but interests.

These interests must be defined within the context of the East-West conflict. Each of the following articles reflects in its own realm the relationship between this conflict and the figure of American interests. It is evident that the emphasis lies on those interests, not on the East-West conflict. It seems, therefore, appropriate, if not necessary, to introduce into this volume by putting the emphasis on this conflict. It contains the political constellation of which American interests in Europe are a part. They belong to the larger issue of American-Soviet relations and their development over the years. This connection is evident only with regard to arms control. It is related to the military confrontation between Washington and Moscow, which is one of the important parts of the conflict. The issues of energy and trade do not easily demonstrate their connection with the East-West conflict but it is present. As far as energy is concerned the relationship emerges slowly but dangerously in the region of the Middle-East. With regard to trade it had been Henry Kissinger who in 1974, the Year of Europe, underlined the relationship between European security interests on the one hand and American economic interests in Europe on the other. Since then, at least, the Jackson/Vanik amendment as well as the grain embargo and its lifting have made visible the close relationship between American trade interests in Europe and the development of the East-West conflict.

The proper context of those American interests is larger than the field of the East-West conflict. Relationships with Japan and China have to be considered; American/European interests in the Third World play a dominant role. These aspects are being touched upon within the respective articles. It would be tempting to include them into the introduction, to write the history of world politics in order to present the adequate context for the analysis of American interests in Europe. It goes without saying that this is impossible, for reasons of time and space. The introduction, therefore, concentrates upon the East-West conflict. It is not the only the proper surrounding of those interests, it underlies them. Whether arms control, energy, or trade is concerned the development of the East-West conflict is one of the factors determining the issues. At the same time it is being affected by these issues. The fate of détente depends to a large extent on the fate of arms control and trade, on the securing of energy resources. Détente would be better off if the Soviet Union would not have to add energy as one of their interests in the Middle East. The outlook for arms control would be much more optimistic if the goal of détente still would dominate American policies towards the Soviet Union. Generally speaking, the development of American-Soviet relations is of utmost importance for American interests in Europe. At the same time these interests influence considerably the development of this relationship. For the Europeans, finally, the development of American-Soviet relations is of major importance. They are more or less dependent on foreign energy resources; their survival depends on arms control and their well-being on peace as a pre-condition for trade. They observe with apprehension the development of American-Soviet relations in the 80's, they are interested in the pursuit of détente. Everything will change if détente fails. Détente, therefore, is the overall parameter of American interests in Europe. Nobody doubts that at the beginning of the 80's détente is very much in danger. A closer and more analytical look, however, implies that the basic condition of détente still is intact. The structure is still there but the ongoing processes are disturbing. The question is: What will American interests in Europe contribute to the future of détente? And the other question is: How will the development of American-Soviet relations affect American interests in Europe?

2. Structurally speaking there are no causes for a serious and deep deterioration of détente. With its center in Europe the East-West conflict reached its first point of transformation in 1955. The division of Germany was completed (with the exception of Berlin); so was the division of Europe. It may not have been the best solution possible but it was a solution with which both sides could live. Therefore, tensions were lowered. Nobody knew this better than Konrad Adenauer, who felt correctly in those days that the détente between Washington and Moscow was the end to all aspirations for German reunification.[1] Neither Khrushchev's Berlin ultimatum of 1958, nor the Berlin Wall, nor the Cuban

missile crisis of 1962 changed the basic interests in Washington and Moscow. On the contrary, the missile crisis demonstrated the urgency and the necessity to continue détente. In illustrating the alternative development: the direct confrontation between the two superpowers, the Cuban missile crisis in both capitals re-enforced the interest in avoiding tensions of this kind, in continuing and enhancing détente.[2]

That interest was active already in 1956 at the Suez-Canal; since then it has dominated the behavior of the two superpowers even in the Third World. When one of them intervened and, in doing so, indicated her vital interest, the other abstained. This was valid in the Middle East as well as in the Far East, it was true also for Europe, where the Soviet Union could intervene militarily in Hungary 1956 and in Czechoslovakia 1968 without provoking more than verbal opposition from the United States. Czechoslovakia slackened the process of détente but did not stop it. Nor did Afghanistan 1979. France and Germany indicated that détente would not survive another blow of this kind. But the threat of Western retaliation against a Soviet intervention in Poland did not include military means. And correctly so. As Henry Kissinger always emphasized: There is no alternative to détente, at least not a meaningful alternative.

According to Richard Nixon détente started in 1970.[3] This is not verbally true, as we have seen. But détente was certainly enhanced by the Nixon administration. Insofar, 1970 really was a year of watershed. Again it was a European problem, the solution of which opened the way to more détente between Washington and Moscow. After the Four-Power-Agreement on Berlin the way was free for Nixon's visit in Moscow, 1972, and Breshnev's visit in the United States, 1973. In addition to the SALT I treaty several agreements were signed, the two most important ones dealing with the mutual relationship and the avoidance of nuclear war.

The two agreements are important not only because of their value for the American-Soviet relationship. They are important also because they reveal the underlying basic interests of this relationship. They described fairly exact the contents of détente.

Détente does not touch the substance of the conflict, but only the means of its resolution. The American-Soviet agreements of this time demostrate clearly the interests of both sides to avoid military means. The conflict remained the same; but it articulated itself less in military but in political, economic, and ideological terms. This did not mean that the military conflict did not matter. It still was the most important, the most dangerous expression of the competition. But because of its dangers the superpowers developed interest in lowering the military confrontation and in transforming the conflict from a purely military one into a mixed one. Only this is the proper content of détente. It does not mean that the conflict has ended or has improved substantially. In fact, the conflict still is the same. Détente means only to lower military tensions and to avoid a military solution of the conflict.

The agreements of 1972/73 gave ample evidence to this. SALT I was the logical outcome of this interest; it followed the Non-proliferation Treaty of 1968 and the Test Ban of 1963. At the same time SALT I opened the perspectives to SALT II. The underlying logic is cogent: A nuclear holocaust between the Soviet Union and the United States would do tremendous damage to both of them, would perhaps erase them completely from the political landscape.

Certainly, the strategic balance has shifted. In 1972 both superpowers possessed an assured second strike capability. This is still true in 1981 but it may change soon because of a new generation of weapons. They are more precise, they are capable of pre-emptive strikes. Therefore, they could provoke the temptation to strike first in order to destroy the weapons of the enemy. But given the fact that for the foreseeable future it will not be possible to destroy with a first strike all retaliation capability of the other side the nuclear balance sheet still demonstrates that who strikes first will die second. What kind of rational interest should lead Moscow and Washington to emphasize again the military means in their conflict? Even if the new generations of nuclear weapons are more precise and, therefore, can be used more selectively — would they really open up more options for their use?

Obviously, this is behind the new strategies which are developing in the United States — and probably in the Soviet Union as well.[4] The intricacies of the strategic debate shall not be discussed here. The articles by Coffey and Krell enlarge the relevant aspects. But since no specialist can guarantee that a nuclear exchange on a low level can be controlled and can be kept from escalating the ladder of higher niveaus, the basic interest in détente still is the same. Nuclear war cannot be won, can only be avoided. When the NATO council met in Washington, May 1978, it found that "in general, the foreign and other policies of the Soviet Union, including its concept of détente, are not likely to undergo any fundamental change in the period under review". Under these conditions the council stressed the "continuing validity of the two complementary functions of the alliance, identified in the Harmel report of 1967: maintenance of military security and the pursuit of détente".[5] The NATO members agreed that it was necessary to match the arms build-up of the Warsaw Pact and they resolved to do so. But NATO kept alive its traditional dual of security and détente.

3. If in European eyes the raison d'être of détente is still intact, the NATO meeting of 1978 obviously was one of the last occasions which produced a common Western view of American-Soviet relations. One year later, December 1979 in Brussels, there were substantial deviations. The American proposal to modernize the theatre nuclear forces met with considerable reluctance on the part of Western European NATO members. They did not accept President Carter's view that the Soviet intervention in Afghanistan was the worst crisis since 1945 and they agreed only slowly to the Olympia boycott. Western Eu-

12

rope watched with some apprehension the election campaign in the United States and the outcome which brought to power in Washington a president and an administration who put détente in the backyard and emphasized military strength instead. Western Europe pressed hard for the American ratification of SALT II only to see a long agony and finally the death of this treaty before the American Senate.

On the other hand, Western Europe had to see the Soviet Union intervene militarily in a country of the Third World, surpassing for the first time after 1945 its zone of influence. This military intervention surprises all the more since Moscow must have anticipated the reaction of the West, shortterm as well as longterm. Afghanistan is neither Vietnam nor the Dominican Republic. It is part of the Middle East, the region most sensitive to the West in terms of oil and security. Why did Moscow pay such a tremendous price for such a minor value, the ideological obedience of Afghanistan?

The military intervention in Afghanistan shed a new light on a hitherto silently accepted development: the massive military build-up of the Warsaw Pact and, above all, the Soviet Union. It started, as mentioned, in 1963, and the West was ready to accept it. The Nixon administration even favored the trend which would lead Moscow into the elevated position of a superpower constraining it at the same time to the obligations and behavioral limits which come with such a position. As Afghanistan demonstrates, this assumption was wrong. Soviet foreign policy was not constrained but enhanced. It showed up demonstratively on many points of the world outside its traditional range notably in Africa. Of prime importance was the enlargement of Soviet naval forces. In the decade from 1968 to 1978 Moscow lifted the number of missile destroyers and fregates from 29 to 110. Moscow, therefore, was able to assemble in the Persian Gulf and in the Indian Ocean as many ships as the West. With the demonstration of the Afghanistan intervention Western Europe became very much upset about Soviet intentions. What is Moscow up to? Is it still heading towards détente and co-existence? Or is it preparing an aggressive foreign policy leading towards the military implementation of imperialistic goals?

It is true that the turning point in American-Soviet Relations was not the intervention in Afghanistan. It happened earlier, already in 1978, probably already in 1976. It is difficult to give exact dates for political changes. They happen over time, slowly. It is even more difficult to find out the reasons for those changes. Western Europe still is somewhat puzzled about what happened in American-Soviet relations and why. Since relations of this kind are patterns of interactions which develop over time and are supported by countless actions and reactions it is extremely difficult to isolate chains of causes and consequences. On the other hand, it is necessary to decipher those developments in order to find out whether interests have changed. Nothing can be said for the Soviet Union. Moscow does not permit a view into her decision-making processes. But even for the United States with her open information policy an answer can be given only with great caution.

4. It is not easy to find out what turned around the American position toward SALT II, a treaty which had been prepared by at least three administrations. Why was President Carter unsuccessful – and why is President Reagan unwilling – to bring the treaty through Congress although two Republican presidents had worked out its essentials? According to Klingberg's cyclical theory of American foreign policy a change was due in 1979 and 1980.[6] Such explanation is not without value since there are changing popular moods. After the Vietnam war a technical reaction was to be expected emphasizing again the power posture of the United States. On the other hand, explanations of this kind are not sufficient. The foreign policy of a liberal democracy is not an outcome of public opinions and their movements. The opinion of a liberal society acts more like a permissive parameter not as a deciding element. Consequently, one has to look for other developments explaining what happened in American foreign policy.

To cut short an otherwise complex story,[7] what happened in the United States after the end of the Vietnam war was that the traditional elite which had led the country through the period of the Cold War reacted towards the possibility of a profound change in American priorities. Fundamentally, the liberal democratic society of the United States is oriented towards profits, not power. It was obliged to change its traditional behavior when Hitler, and after 1946 the conflict with the Soviet Union, forced upon it a certain preference for power and the build-up of a pertinent elite. Since then, there are two elites in the United States, one oriented towards détente and commerce, and the other towards security and power.[8] These "two cultures", as Hughes called them,[9] are not completely antagonistic. They are complementary, at least to some extent. But they emphasize different priorities. Until 1972 it has been the security-culture, which dominated American foreign policy-making. It had accepted détente with the Soviet Union on the basis of American strength and, if possible, superiority. This securty-elite was capable of combining both aims as long as the Vietnam war went on, justifying its existence and leadership. There was not the slightest intention on the part of Nixon and Kissinger to deny this elite its prerogative. But the perspective of this denial became apparent, when Nixon succeeded in bringing the Vietnam war to an end. At this point détente could get a new meaning. Why should the United States keep a huge military build-up and a security elite in power if there was no war to wage and if there was détente with the leading enemy, the Soviet Union? Consequently, an extended discussion about the national priorities which had began earlier[10] could have led to a new, and different, distribution of influence and power within the United States.

It was this perspective, obviously, which stimulated the security-elite to react. Significantly, its campaign started in 1974, the year when the Vietnam war ended. At this time, Committees like that of the Present Danger and other groups began to work. Two years later, in 1976, President Ford was already pressed by his competitor Ronald Reagan to drop the word détente altogether. In 1976 Jimmy Carter with his commitment to détente and arms control won the election, if only by a small margin. But it was evident at this time already that the equity-culture, which Carter represented, was not strong enough to prevail over the security-culture. The more the memory of Vietnam faded away the stronger the memory of American strength and leadership became, the stronger became the impression that both were lost in the wake of the Vietnam war.

The impression was not an artificial one. Whereas the United States, in fact, reduced their armaments since 1974 in absolute and in relative terms, the Soviet Union stepped up their armaments. The hint toward the "Cuban brigade" in 1979 probably was only a tactical gimmick, directed against the SALT II treaty. But its reception in Congress and in the United States in general demonstrated a certain sensitivity against a relative shift in military power. With the United States retreating from power the Soviet Union obviously was augmenting it and was shifting gears. Nixon and Kissinger had hoped to combine their policy of détente with some sort of self-containment of the Soviet Union. This was the famous "linkage". If it was too optimistic, if not naiv, to assume that the Soviet Union would resist all temptations to enlarge its influence in the world, it was rather safe assumption that the Soviet Union would respond in kind towards the relative disarmament which took place on the part of the United States. But Moscow did not answer. On the contrary, it gave ample evidence to the argument of the security-culture that the Soviet Union used its newly gained strength (and the relative weakness of the United States) to expand its empire and influence. When Brzezinski argued that the SALT II treaty died in the "sands of Ogaden" so was this a pars pro toto. But within this limit it captured the attention of many Americans and it certainly reflected the assessment of the security-elite.

If one more proof was needed, Iran forwarded it. There is no connection between Teheran and Moscow, no invisible Soviet hand in the fall of the Shah. In a precise anlaysis, there is even no sign of American weakness in the fact that Iranian revolutionaries captured 52 hostages. No nation of the world, whatever her power base, would have been able to enforce their release upon the Iranians. But in politics perceptions, not facts, are relevant. And there is no denying the fact that the combination of the hostages in Teheran and the Soviet intervention in Afghanistan paved the way for the election of Ronald Reagan with his campaign slogan "let's make America great again".

As is natural with all dialectic developments, the Reagan administration is an ultra-security establishment. In its reaction towards its opposite number, the Carter administration, the Reagan administration is "more conservative, . . . more militaristic, more outspoken, more social and more relaxed than its immediate predecessors. . . . It is also less centralized, less experienced, less pessimistic, and less interested in the poor at home and abroad".[11] It is not only interested in security but in re-establishing the American leadership.

In reacting towards the détente policy of Nixon and Kissinger, in honoring the non-honoring by the Soviet Union of the American readiness to accept her on an equal, but not as superior, footing the American society has installed an administration which with historic necessity put the emphasis not on détente but on military strength.

When this development began, probably in 1974 and certainly in1976, the United States deviated from the path of détente. She did not abandon détente but put it in the backyard in order to give priority to the goal of re-gaining strength, if not superiority. For almost 30 or 40 years the United States had been the leading superpower in the world and it is understandable that the re-establishment of this positon, at least the keeping of absolute parity with the Soviet Union, dominates American foreign policy. After she will have reached this position the United States will be prepared again to accept détente as the most eminent goal in its relationship with the Soviet Union. It is doubtful whether the Reagan administration will lead the way towards this development. But the working time for an American administration is only four years, and there are many shifts in between.

Anyhow, Europe sees the United States in the foreseeable future neglecting the goal of détente and pushing the goal of military balance, parity and/or superiority. Western Europe, more or less, agrees to this development. There are differences in emphasis, though. In general, centrist and conservative parties favor the shift in American behavior; social democratic parties are ready to go along. But nobody denies the necessity for the United States to recover some military strength, to fill some gaps, to keep abreast with the Soviet Union. European apprehension starts with regard to the middle-run future. What will happen if the new course of American foreign policy leads toward new interests, toward the neglecting of détente altogether? We shall return to this point later on.

5. If American motives and movements are somewhat plausible, the same could be said about the Soviet Union, although with great caution. Given the uncertainty which Moscow offers to its international environment and given the difficult and complex competition within the Communist party no explanations but only hunches are possible. In 1962 Moscow got a striking proof of its military inferiority. In its wake, Khrushchev fell and a new leadership took over. Drawing consequences from this experience, the Soviet Union has slowly but continuously stepped up it armaments. Given the inflexibility of the Soviet bureaucracy, it is understandable that such a policy, once set in motion, continues to move without checking its appropriateness. Having lagged behind in nuclear technology the Soviet Union had to invent MIRV's as well as the SS–20. Having been a continental power for most of its history, Moscow had to establish a fleet. It could be calculated at what point in time the Soviet Union would reach parity with the United States, would even gain superiority if Moscow decided to continue this way. The Western European know (as did Nixon and Kissinger) that Moscow's arms build-up could be stopped only by agreement, not by force. This is why they pressed hard upon the United States for the ratification of SALT II and – perspectively – for SALT III.

Looking down the years until the late 60's, one finds only continuity in the Soviet arms build-up, no alarming excesses. One finds, however, Soviet anxieties and, in their consequence, a shift in Soviet foreign policy. In the autumn of 1979 signals came from Moscow that the Soviet Union was re-assessing its policy towards détente.[12] Again it is not easy to give the reasons for this. One of them certainly has to be found in the general shift of attitudes in the United States. Another one, perhaps a more important one, came with President Carter's China policy. Unitl 1978 Carter had continued the balance policy towards China which Ford and Nixon had maintained. This policy was changed towards recognition and closer cooperation when China and the United States exchanged ambassadors in the spring of 1979. The triangle relationship between Washington, Bejing and Moscow was seriously affected. Not facts, but perceptions provoked in Moscow the feeling of a new "encirclement". NATO's modernization plans of December 1979 added to this feeling. There are European voices which assume that the new American China policy as well as the TNF modernization belong to the main reasons for the Soviet invasion of Afghanistan.[13]

If for the different reasons, there does exist obviously within the Soviet Union an ambiguity comparable to the equivocality which can be found in the action/reaction syndrom of the United States. It is evident that the Soviet Union will not abandon détente, that she will continue détente but only on her own terms. Having become much stronger than a couple of years ago the Soviet Union obviously is inclined to give détente a new meaning, to subordinate it to security and military power posture. To some extent, Moscow mirrors what has been going on in the United States. The Soviet Union is interested to continue détente, but she is obviously more interested to guarantee her own security by a superior military capability and by subordinating to this capacity all demands which might come with a definite pursuit of détente. If, for different reasons, détente has taken the same second place in the rank order of Soviet foreign policy goals, which has been awarded it in the United States.

This is what disturbs Western Europe these days. Neither the behavior of the United States nor that of the Soviet Union can be explained completely within realms of the East-West conflict. With its traditional center in Western Europe this conflict would have demanded — and permitted — a continuing détente policy, expressed in terms of the reduction of military tensions. Arms control, not re-armament, would have been the leading goals of such a policy. Since they cannot be found in the behavior of the two superpowers, their policy orientation must have shifted. Western Europe is anxious that it is not anymore the

Western Europe is anxious that it is not anymore the East-West conflict which determines the behavior of the superpowers but a global rivalry between them for which the East-West conflict is the only one small, if important theatre. If this proves to be correct, American interests in Europe certainly will be affected. They will probably not shift, but they will get another place on the rank order of American goals. On the other hand, Western Europe will be led to define its relationship to the United States in the light of those new circumstances.

17

6. There seems to emerge a break in the perceptions of the conflict. For Western Europe it is still the old East-West competition with Central Europe at its center and with the Soviet Union nowadays trying to reach out into the world. Western Europe watches carefully what the Soviet Union is trying to do in the Middle East, in Africa, and elsewhere. But it is far from holding the Soviet Union responsible for all and everything which is happening in the world. In Latin America, for example, the cause for unrest is not the Soviet Union but social injustice and political repression. Of course, the Soviet Union tries to exploit the turmoil in El Salvador. But Western Europe is far from believing that she adds more than a sideline to the conflict.[14] Its roots do not lie in the rivalry between liberalism and communism but in the peculiar tradition of conservative rule in Latin America. Even Cuba, Moscow's foothold in the Caribbean, is of no importance to this conflict. Castro has been so disappointed about his inability to export the Cuban model to his Latin American neighbors that he exported the model and the Cuban influence to Africa. In the Caribbean basin Cuba for the time being is without great influence. Of course, if the repression in El Salvador goes on it will strengthen the Marxist wing of the guerill movement and could, should this wing finally prevail, bring Marxist and Cuban influence to El Salvador. Even this would not mean that such a country would be totally lost for the West. As the United States certainly has lost control over developments in Latin America, the Soviet Union will not be able to gain it. The world of the 1980's, in Europe's view, is not the world of the 1950's. Particularly in Latin America the influence of the United States has diminished, the relevance of regional powers as Mexico, Venezuela, Brasil, and Argentina has been augmented. With the growing complexity within the Third World the causes for political change have become more complex, too.

A similar relationship is seen by Western Europe in Africa. Nobody denies the fact that Moscow has won access to this continent, notably in the Horn of Africa and, at least to some degree, in Angola.[15] The renversement des alliances which took place in Somalia and Ethiopia demonstrates clearly the volatility of the situation, the minor role ideology and political obedience play in Africa. For Western Europe it is evident that the major problems disturbing the continent still are the remnants of colonialism expressed in Namibia and (if in different shape) in the Republic of South Africa.[16] This is why Great Britain pressed hard for a solution in Zimbabwe.[17] If the United States would recognize Angolan government, the Cubans might leave the country immediately. If the West would be adamant with regard to Namibia, the SWAPO probably could be held in the Western camp. The Soviet Union has declared herself the great protector of the national liberation movements. But history points out that those movements definitively would prefer help from Western countries. If it would be given, Soviet influence would diminish and could perhaps be banned completely. It is not the cause of the conflict in the Third World but belongs in most cases to the temporary consequences of unresolved conflicts.

Western Europe does not neglect the political impact of military power, in particular of naval power. It watches with apprehension the enlarging presence of Soviet navy in the Indian Ocean[18] and the political influence which comes with such a presence. After the invasion of Afghanistan the Middle East and the region from Turkey to Indochina has certainly gained a new military sensitivity.[19] The problems of this region, however, are not military in nature. Particularly in the Middle East, the problems are political, social, and economic. The Arabian states live through a period of social destabilization because of rapid transformation. Their systems of government, their social organization have not kept abreast of those developments. For Western Europe, the Iran is a striking example for (next to many other faults) the clashes originating when a feudal regime tries to control a modernizing society. Problems of this kind in the Middle East are being enhanced by the main conflict facing the Middle East: the conflict between Israel and the Arabian states.[20] Compared with this problem the influence of the Soviet Union and Marxism certainly belongs to the quantitées negliables. A successful American policy drew Moscow out of Egypt and the chances are that it will not return at least before the reign of Sadat ends. Even afterwards, the Soviet Union can be kept from the region if the West succeeds in solving or at least weakening the Israel-Arabian conflict. This is why in Venice[21] the Europeans pointed towards the legitimate claims of the Palestinians. The strategic advantage in the region which Moscow has gained by its intervention in Afghanistan must be taken care of militarily. This advantage will lead to nothing if the political and socio-economic problems of the region can be solved. This is not a military but a political task. In the European view the conflict in the Middle East is still a regional one with elements of the East-West conflict only superseding it. The correctness of this analysis is of vital importance to the Europeans. They depend to a very large extent on Middle East oil. As the articles of de Carmoy and Müller point out Europe observes with apprehension the development of American energy interests in the Middle East as well as in Europe.

Finally, if it comes to Asia,[22] the Soviet Union certainly won a military stronghold in Vietnam. But this advantage is more than compensated for by the Sino-Soviet conflict which binds more than a third of the Soviet army and is probably more disturbing Moscow than its East-West counterpart. China is the third superpower, if only in coming, the Chinese-American relationship[23] will be at least as important for the region as the Soviet-American one. As far as the smaller countries are concerned, development is their main problem, not Soviet influence.

7. Seen from Europe, the East-West conflict does not dominate the world but only the old continent and the related antagonism between East and West. In all parts of the so-called Third World social and political conflicts dominate the scene and they are not originally related to the dichotomy between liberalism and communism.[24] Of course, the superpowers try to intermingle and to

19

enlarge their influence. But they will not succeed because of the autonomy of those regions and their internal problems. To define them within the East-West relationship is a last outcome of a Euro-centric view of the world. It is interesting that this view is not being held anymore in Western Europe but probably in the Soviet Union and the United States. For Western Europe détente, as the calming-down of the military aspect of the East-West rivalry, it is a necessary precondition for a clear view upon what is going on in the world. In Europe, the military conflict should be impossible because of its devastations. In the Third World the military conflict between East and West is unnecessary because of its unrelatedness.

It seems as if the United States has abandoned this view of the world which she had shared with the Europeans until the mid-70's. Since then another view appeared in the United States. More and more Washington begins to perceive a global bipolar American-Soviet conflict in the world. This new conflict incorporates the old East-West conflict, but surpasses it. It is a conflict between two superpowers and it comprehenses the whole world. The genesis of this new conflict obviously has to do with the rise of the Soviet Union into the position of a global power.

Until the late 70's the United States had been the sole real global power in the world. The Soviet Union was a superpower only in certain geographic regions. Since the late 70's the Soviet Union has reached more or less strategic parity with the United States and has become the second real global power. Washington's sensitivity for this development was much greater than that of Europe. When General Haig at his first press conference as the American Secretary of State stressed the global nature of the Soviet threat, he reflected exactly this new, and different, view of the world. Because of the dominant military position of the United States during the Nixon administration, Henry Kissinger could stick to his linkage-concept which tried to trade arms control benefits for the Soviet Union against her well-behavior in the Third World. This concept is gone, now that the Soviet Union has reached parity. There are no bargains to strike on the basis of benefits. There is a competition which probably has become worldwide as far as Washington and Moscow are concerned. Even if their conflict has nothing to do with the conflicts in the respective regions of the world, it might in itself have become a global conflict. It might become even a global military conflict. With two superpowers competing against each other all over the world the possibility of military clashes cannot be excluded. This possiblity has to be taken care of. From hence the newly emerged American interest in stepping up their armaments; from hence perhaps the Soviet interest in building a global military capacity.

8. If this assessment is a correct one American interests in Europe certainly will be affected by the new situation. The suspension of détente will become logical, if only temporarily. There will be probably no hot war since the foundations of deterrence still are stable, the perspectives of a nuclear holocaust too

terrific. But military means will play a more dominant role with consequences for American interests in arms control. With détente dwindling Western Europe will become more dependent on the United States. This, certainly, will have consequences in the fields of energy and, above all, trade. Western Europe will need the United States in order to secure the energy supply, to protect the production and the transportation of oil. Accordingly, the relevance of trade will diminish. The economic interests of the United States and Western Europe are, as the articles by Kline and Rode point out, complementary. The basic structures of commercial exchange are stable and will probably remain in this status. But with the global rivalry between the Soviet Union and the United States Washington will become more and more interested in winning this competition and it will subordinate all other interests to this one.

It is impossible to predict the consequences for American interests in Europe and for the resulting European-American relations. Prophecies are not the business of the political scientist. But it is important to know that the overall constellation within which American interests in Western Europe are to be defined probably is within a process of change. The developing global rivalry between the Soviet Union and the United States alters the parameters of American interests in Europe. In themselves these interests are stable, as the analyses by all authors in this volume bear out. Confined to the narrow American-European context there are no differences of interest, no major clashes ahead. The American-European relationship within the fields of arms control, energy, and trade is intact. Interdependence works, and it works well. But the global configuration is about to change. It will be the task of the United States as well as of Western Europe to see to it that their relationship will not change even as the global circumstances do.

Notes

1 Konrad Adenauer, Erinnerungen 1955–1959, Stuttgart 1967.
2 Cf. H. S. Dinerstein, The Making of a Missile Crisis: October 1962, Baltimore, Johns Hopkins Press, 1976.
3 Cf. Richard Nixon, U.S. Foreign Policy for the 1970's. The Emerging Structure of Peace. A Report to the Congress, 9th February, 1977, p. 2 ff.
4 Cf. D. Ross, Rethinking Soviet Strategic Policy: Inputs and Implications, in: The Journal of Strategic Studies I, No. 1, May 1978, p. 3 ff. J. Kruzel, Arms Control and American Defense Policy: New Alternatives and Old Realities, in: Daedalus, 110, 1, Winter 1981, p. 137 ff.
5 Alliance Study of East-West Relations, in: Wireless Bulletin 102, 2nd June, 1978, p. 1–2.
6 F. L. Klingberg, Cyclical Trends in American Foreign Policy Moods and Their Policy Implications, in: C. W. Cagley and P. J. McGowan (eds.), Challenges to America. United States Foreign Policy in the 1980's, London 1980, p. 51 ff.

7 Cf. E. O. Czempiel, Die Vereinigten Staaten von Amerika und die Entspannung, in: Aus Politik und Zeitgeschichte, B 27/77, 17th September, 1977. p. 3 ff.

8 Cf. E. O. Czempiel, Amerikanische Außenpolitik, Stuttgart 1979.

9 See Th. L. Hughes, The Crack-Up, in: Foreign Policy 40, Fall 1980, p. 50.

10 Cf. United States Congress, Joint Economic committee, Changing National Priorities, Hearings, 2 vols., Washington 1970; and: National Priorities. The Next Five Years, Hearings, Washington 1972.

11 J. Reston, The Reagan Show's Dress Rehearsal, in: International Herald Tribune, 2nd February, 1981, p 4.

12 St. Talbott, U.S.-Soviet Relations: From Bad to Worse, in: Foreign Affairs, 58, 3, 1980, p. 515 ff.

13 See H.-G. Wieck (former German ambassador to the Soviet Union), Die Sowjetunion in den achtziger Jahren, Bonn, Deutsche Gesellschaft für Auswärtige Politik 1980, mimeo.

14 For a contrasting American view see Robert S. Leiken, Eastern Winds in Latin America, in: Foreign Policy, 42, Spring 1981, p. 94 ff.

15 For a critical review of American African policies see Helen Kitchen, Eighteen African Guideposts, in: Foreign Policy 37, Winter 1979/80, p. 71 ff. For the new approach of the Reagan Administration cf. J. Power, Angola, Namibia, and the U.S., in: International Herald Tribune, 3rd April, 1981.

16 This view is to some extent shared by officials of the Reagan Administration, cf. Chester A. Crocker, South Africa: Strategy for Change, in Foreign Affairs, 95, 2, Winter 1980/81, p. 323 ff.

17 See Xan Smiley, Zimbabwe, Southern Africa, and the Rise of Robert Mugabe, in: Foreign Affairs, 85, 2, Summer 1980, p. 106 ff.

18 Early warnings came from Great Britain. See P. Wall (ed.), The Indian Ocean and the Threat to the West: Four Studies in Global Strategy, London, Business Books, 1975.

19 It is rather an old one, cf. H. B. Ellis, Challenge in the Middle East: Communist Influence and American Policy, New York, Ronald Press Co., 1966.

20 The problems involved are listed in: Congressional Quarterly: The Middle East, Israel, Oil, and the Arabs, 4th ed., Washington, July 1979, p. 89 ff.

21 See the Declaration of June, 1980, in: Bulletin of the European Communities 6–1980, No. 1.1.6.

22 Cf. J. Yung-hwan (ed.), U.S. Foreign Policy in Asia: An Appraisal, Santa Barbara, Clio, 1978.

23 See W. J. Barnds (ed.), China and America. The Search for a New Relationship, New York, New York University Press (for the Council on Foreign Relations) 1977.

24 See the (European dominated) Report of the Brandt Commission, North-South: A Program for Survival, Cambridge, Mass. MIT Press, 1980.

Gert Krell

The SALT II — Debate in the U.S. Senate

1. SALT II: The Context of the Debate

There can be no doubt that the 1970's have seen severe changes in the domestic and international context of U.S. foreign and defense policies. Among these are the definitive loss of nuclear superiority and a more general decline of U.S. military power vis-a-vis the Soviet Union, the gradual deterioration in U.S.-Soviet relations, a deep and lasting crisis of economic performance and stability, and a further weakening of America's political and economic predominance over Third World countries. With these changes the perceptions and definitions of U.S. status, power, and policies changed, and also the setting and the strengths of the various forces in the political system that define situations and raise demands. In the first half of the 1970's the strongest challenges to military expenditures and weapon procurement in the post-World War II history had been brought forth, and as late as 1975/76 sizeable minorities in the Senate asked for measures of unilateral restraint in armaments.[1] Under President Carter, liberal criticism of military expenditures continued to slow down. While this may be attributed at least in part to Carter's initial moderation in defense policy, factors such as the quantitative decline of the liberal element in the Senate and above all the change in the public and official mood finally led to a new pro-defense consensus much more in line with the general post-war trend. The 55:42 vote for part 2 of the Hollings amendment of September 1979, calling for a 5 % real increase in military expenditures for fiscal years 1981 and 1982, over the opposition of the Armed Services Committee Chairman Senator Stennis, before Afghanistan, and long before the newly elected Reagan Senate, is the most vivid expression of the 1970's turn-about from the "national priorities" debate to a broad support for a new phase of real growth in defense budgets.[2]

Conservative opposition against the SALT process and the perceived weakening of America's military posture had begun forming towards the end of the Kissinger era, with the founding of the Committee on the Present Danger in 1976 and the new nationalism evident in the 1976 election as clear indicators of things to come. In March 1977 40 Senators voted against Paul Warnke's nomination to head the U.S. SALT delegation, a warning that SALT II, if it could be negotiated after all, might run into domestic difficulties.[3]

The general direction of the domestic mood, the coming elections with their unavoidable sharpening of partisanship, and the chill in U.S.-Soviet relations would have reflected on the ratification of any SALT II treaty. The conservatives determined the character of the debate and they used it and their veto power for an assault on Carter's defense and foreign policies. The administration concentrated on the military advantages of the treaty, detente and arms control considerations played only marginal roles. Thus the Secretary of Defense and the Joint Chiefs of Staff bore the greatest burden of defending SALT, while Paul Warnke had even resigned before the end of the negotiations in order to appease the critics. This time, the famous "assurances", which the military usually get for their support of arms control treaties, were requested by the Senate Foreign Relations Committee. In one of the understandings connected with its support of SALT the Committee asserted the Senate's intention to authorize and fund all nuclear weapons necessary to assure essential equivalence with the Soviet Union, including seven specifically named programs.[4] This was not a tactical amendment, and hopes of appeasement proved futile anyway.

In essence, it was a debate between the political center and some moderate conservatives on the one hand, and the hard-line defense conservatives on the other, with several other moderates undecided, in this quite similar to SALT I. But the SALT I debate had been much shorter, and the stakes much lower. This time the opposition was stronger and more assertive, the center less sure of itself, and many from the left — which was no longer a serious counterweight — shifted to the arguments of the center. Not even the Foreign Relations Committee, which in 1979 was still more liberal than the Senate as a whole, could muster a two thirds majority when it reported the treaty to the floor. In the Armed Services Committee 10 Senators (7 Republicans, 3 Democrats) out of 17 voted against SALT II[5].

Latent opposition among the military hierarchy was strong, at least one of the Chiefs of Staff whose terms had come to an end under Carter opposed the treaty.[6] Critical was the defection of General Rowny, who had represented the Joint Chiefs on the SALT delegation. He had been kept on board, again with appeasement in mind. But when SALT was finished, Rowny resigned. He had accumulated any knowledge about delicate internal differences within the administration and about the negotiating process that the opponents might wish to have. Open opposition came from many high-ranking retired military people,[7] and also from major former civilian officials. Paul Nitze's objections were predictable. He had resigned in protest from the SALT delegation as early as 1974, had co-founded the Committee on the Present Danger, and had voiced his political and personal hostility to the Carter administration during the Warnke nomination hearings in early 1977.[8] That it may be inherently more difficult for a Democratic administration to get arms control treaties (or other non-nationalistic treaties such as the Panama Canal Treaty) ratified, is demonstrated by the long list of Nixon/Ford officials who testified against SALT II: Thomas Moorer, former chairman of the Joint Chiefs of Staff; Fred Charles Iklé, Director of

ACDA; Ronald Rumsfeld, Secretary of Defense. Henry Kissinger and General Haig voiced serious concerns and demanded conditions, but stopped short of a rejection that would have made renegotiation necessary.

Most of the testimony from party and political action groups came as no surprise. One would expect the Coalition for Peace Through Strength, the American Security Council, and the Committee on the Present Danger to come out against SALT II, as well as the American Legion and the American Conservative Union. The statement by the Ripon Society was as far apart from that of the ACU as one can imagine, demonstrating the broad spectrum of the Republican Party. Senator McIntyre, the former chairman of the Subcommittee on Research and Development, testified on behalf of "Americans for SALT". AFL-CIO came out in favor of the treaty, but also of more arms. Several Protestant denominations, the Catholics, and the Jews supported SALT II. Some old hands such as Averell Harriman and Edward Teller, who had been in American politics and in arms control controversies from the beginning of the nuclear age, also testified on their respective sides of the fence.

The way people looked at SALT II was heavily influenced by their general political philosophy. But the SALT debate brought into focus objective problems of arms control and US-Soviet relations as much as it presented different perceptions of the military balance and the role of nuclear weapons in foreign policy. The opposition was by no means homogeneous. The level of objections varied greatly, ranging from the fundamentalist and autistic or pathological over the unbalanced and inconsequential to the genuine and serious argument. This shall now be discussed in detail.

2. SALT II and Equity

There exists a general consensus between the negotiating parties that a SALT treaty should grant equality to both sides. The problem is how to measure equality between two military postures that are vastly different in composition and are grossly asymmetrical in several quantitative and qualitative aspects. While the Soviets have often used the term "equal security", thus referring to their perceived disadvantage in nuclear geopolitics, the famous Jackson amendment to the SALT I Interim Agreement had stipulated that the US must have equality in intercontinental strategic weapons in a future SALT agreement, although the legislative record does not show that this means equality in throw-weight, as Jackson claimed in the SALT II debate.[9] So SALT II should establish some kind of symmetry in those weapons that are part of the treaty. Obviously, this does not by itself solve the problem, where to draw the line between those weapons that are being negotiated and those that are not, and how the exclusion of other weapons and other imbalances reflects on the balance that is being negotiated. It is clear that any agreement on equality demands a certain amount of political judgement. Arms control can never level all asymmetries.

Both sides will try to chip away from the other side's programs and advantages which it considers most threatening, while at the same time trying to protect its own. There have to be trade-offs. It is natural that détente sceptics in the US will focus on the concessions the US has made and on remaining imbalances that favor the Soviet Union. A fair judgement as to the treaty's equity must answer the following questions: 1) What is the total picture of the various trade-offs? 2) How relevant are the remaining asymmetries within and outside the treaty?[10]

With the material in the Senate Foreign Relations and the Armed Services Committee Hearings and with Talbott's Book[11] about the history of the negotiations, a fairly detailed record of the various concessions and trade-offs can be established. This record allows an early dismissal of some statements from the right as autistic or propagandistic. Admiral Zumwalt's theory that the Soviets simply stick to their original positions while the US gradually move towards them, can be safely classed among the former; and Senator Jackson's outcry about "a flow of one-sided concessions" from the United States belongs to the latter category.[12] Administration spokesmen including the military have often suggested that in fact the Soviets made more concessions, and have provided a number of lists to prove the case.[13] The opponents have challenged this view, of course. Much of the controversy arises from the fact that it may be difficult to determine what a real concession is.

Throughout the SALT process one of the major Soviet concerns have been American so-called forward-based systems (FBS) — but also British and French delivery vehicles and warheads — that can reach the Soviet Union from Europe, including the Mediterranean Sea. Apart from these, Soviet negotiating strategy has concentrated on new American technologies, in SALT II chiefly the cruise missiles, but also the MX and Trident II ballistic missiles. American concerns (apart from verification issues) focused on the biggest and most dynamic element of Soviet strategic weapons, i.e. ICBMs including heavy ICBMs. The other main problem, the Backfire Bomber, was clearly secondary to the ICBM issue. Four and a half major (and several minor) trade-offs were negotiated in SALT II:[14]

1. The Soviets accepted equal aggregates for central systems (i.e. heavy bombers, ICBMs and SLBMs),[15] thus finally giving up attempts to gain other compensations for FBS. In exchange the US granted the Soviets their advantage of 308:0 in modern large ballistic missiles. Although the deal was originally made by Kissinger around Vladivostok in 1974, the Carter Administration still tried very hard to reduce the number of Soviet MLBMs, first to 150, then to 190, finally to 250. The Soviets refused to compromise, it seems that Breshnev had to fight hard to even get the Vladivostok deal accepted in Moscow.

2. The Carter Administration agreed to count all bombers with long-range ALCMs as MIRVed systems (but not to count each ALCM as one intercontinental missile), in exchange the Soviets accepted the subceilings on MIRVed ICBMs (820) and on MIRVed missiles (ICBMs plus SLBMs = 1200).

3. The Soviets accepted fractionation limits on their deployed ICBMs (4 RV's for the SS–17, 6 RV's for the SS–19, 10 RV's for the SS–18) and accepted the one new ICBM allowed to be a MIRVed one with up to 10 RV's; they had preferred a non-MIRVed type. In exchange the US agreed to limit the numbers of cruise missiles to 20 on their existing heavy bombers and to 28 on average on a possible new cruise missile carrier.

4. At one point in the negotiations the US had asked for the most stringent limits on ICBM modernization, including guidance hardware, to prevent further increases in accuracy. These proposals encountered the resistance of the Joint Chiefs and of OSD, who wanted to protect advances in MIRV and MaRV technology, and from the Soviets, who wanted to protect their fifth generation of ICBMs under development and demanded strict limitations on bomber and SLBM modernization in turn. The original US plan also had other weaknesses. Soviet ICBMs were already accurate enough to threaten Minuteman, and some of the items on the list were not verifiable. US and SU compromised on a much shorter list of 6 parameters which may be changed 5 % in either direction or – as with the number of stages and the type of fuel for the booster – not at all.

Criticism in the United States was strongest about the MLBM imbalance and the exclusion of the Backfire bomber.

FBS and MLBMs

SALT II opponents such as Nitze and Iklé certainly have a point to make when they protest that the exclusion of the forward based systems should not be regarded as a Soviet concession.[16] Americans and especially West Europeans have long since considered the FBS not to be central strategic systems, but rather theater systems that ought to be compared to Soviet nuclear systems directed against Western Europe. Most people agree that the Soviets are superior in long- and medium-range TNF,[17] so the exclusion of forward-based systems *and* Soviet LRTNF/MRTNF may well be regarded an advantage for which the Soviets, if anybody, should have paid. It is the US which assigns an albeit small number of its SALT-accountable SLBM-RV's to the European theater in order to at least ameliorate the imbalance there.

The numbers game with LRTNF and MRTNF is only part of the story, however. While the Soviet Union has a double nuclear threat against NATO (one against the US and one against Western Europe and US forces stationed there), the West has two nuclear options that threaten the Soviet Union. The fact that the US can posit medium-range nuclear weapons on third party territory to reach targets in the Soviet Union, including some of its central strategic systems, while the Soviet Union cannot (Cuban missile crisis!), is not taken lightly by the Soviets. More than anything, the FBS issue is a symbol of the sensitive geostrategic position of the Soviet Union, which counts three nuclear powers among its enemies that are to date not part of SALT. In addition to that, the US may transfer nuclear weapons to its allies, even those systems which are numerically limited by the treaty.

The other part of the Vladivostok deal, the imbalance in MLBMs (the Soviets are allowed 308 modern large ballistic missiles, while the US only has 54 old and unreliable Titan II's on the border-line between light and heavy missiles and may not convert any "light" launchers into heavy missiles launchers) again has great psychological impact. Although Soviet "light" ICBMs alone (MIRVed SS-17's and especially MIRVed SS-19's) raise the problem of Minuteman vulnerability, the 10-warhead SS-18 is the strongest symbol of Soviet strategic power vis-á-vis the US. Soviet MLBMs alone have more warheads than the entire US ICBM force and more megatonnage than US ICBMs and SLBMs combined. Some treaty opponents have insisted that the US should be granted an equal right to 308 MLBMs, even if they did not want to build them. Others suggested that each SS-18 be counted as two MIRVed ICBMs.[18] The problem is that the US military does not want heavy missiles, because the US does not need them. US ICBMs are more efficient, and the "light" MX with 10 warheads (the original preferred configuration was 6 to 8 warheads, but it was raised to 10 in order to satisfy psychological needs)[19] will have as much destructive power as the "heavy" SS-18, as long as the fractionation limit on the SS-18, which prevents a full exploitation of the missile's throw-weight, remains in place. The US pressed for and got a ban on mobile heavy ICBMs (and on heavy SLBMs and ASBMs), which again proves that the US does not even consider heavy *mobile* ICBMs a useful option for the future. To build new fixed-site heavy IBMs would not make sense anyway, and in the late 1980's the only heavy missiles deployed will be fixed-site SS-18, and they will then be vulnerable.

Backfire

The Backfire issue is a telling example of the difficulties that arms control has with the classification, categorization, and balancing of weapons systems. Its parameters set the Backfire between the FB-111, which is considered at least semi-strategic even by the Americans, and the B-52's and the B-1. Although its true range is a matter of controversy in the intelligence community, it may in fact be greater than that of the older B-52 D models. Donald Brennan suggested that only one third of US bombers, i.e. the B-52 G and H models, have a greater range than the Backfire.[20] While the Backfire is not counted in the SALT ceilings, all B–52's and the 4 B–1 prototypes are SALT-accountable. The number of 573 US bombers in the data memorandum no doubt is very generous. Two of the B-1 prototypes are not flying any more, and the other two are not equipped for combat. Of the 569 B-52's only 351 are in the active category, most of the bombers in storage have been deactivated and can no longer be used.[21] This is the basic reason why the US has only 2060 operational strategic launchers, while the Soviets have about 2500.

Admiral Moorer has stated that the Soviets would not care for the Backfires and send them on one-way missions, if they decided to attack the United States.[22] This belongs to the autistic variety of arguments that cannot be taken serious, although it may carry some weight with the extreme right. The real problem is that Backfire could in some flight profiles reach the United States and either land in friendly territory or even return to the Soviet Union. This depends on basing (Arctic basing, e.g.), on the altitude and speed of flight, on refueling, and on the possibility to land in a country near the United States (i.e. Cuba). On the other hand, almost all knowledgeable people in the field seem to agree that Backfire's primary mission is in the theater and against sea-lines of communication. It is true that the B-52's also need refueling for a round-trip mission, but the US Air Force has extensively trained refueling and has a fleet of about 600 tankers. Soviet refueling capacity is small in comparison, and the Backfire has never been exercised in a strategic role. To give Backfire a reliable international capability would require changes in construction, deployment or flight training patterns. Its intercontinental capability is marginal and inefficient.

There are a number of systems outside the SALT definition that could in theory be used against the US. The SS-20 in the Soviet Far East, the Backfire, Blinder, and Badger bombers in certain deployments, and the SS-N-4 and SS-N-5 could be employed against Alaska. The Soviets could also attack targets on the East Coast with their old SLCMs on surface ships or on submarines. Of course, the US also has several systems whose primary mission are not targets in the Soviet Union, but which could be used in such a fashion. These are not only the forward-based systems in Europe, but also aircraft in Korea or on ships in the Pacific.[23] Some decisions have to be made as to which systems are central among the strategic forces and which are not. While old Soviet cruise missiles – a point again and again raised by Senator Warner[24] – seem to be a non-issue in this context, the categorization of Backfire obviously is a more serious question. But SALT opponents cannot argue that modern US cruise missiles were limited while the Backfire was not. The protocol, which covers ground-launched cruise missiles, is absolutely meaningless. The United States has stated so repeatedly, and the point was demonstrated to the Soviets ad oculos by the NATO decision of December 1979 about Pershing II and GLMs to be stationed in Europe in 1983–1988.

It is no small irony that SALT II might have been concluded much earlier, if both sides had agreed right at the beginning to leave Backfire and GLCMs for

SALT III. Backfire versus GLCMs is another at least implicit trade-off; both types of weapons systems are only symbolically included in SALT II, both are not counted, and development can go along as planned. The restrictions are only tokens, sweeteners for internal consumption.

Strategic defense

There remains one serious point of discussion, i.e. the general exclusion of strategic defense systems.[25] Conservatives claim that this is another big US concession without compensation. The following list of the "balance" in strategic defense should be regarded as fair:

	US advantage	Soviet advantage
civil defense		X
air defense		X
ASW	X	
ABM	status uncertain, restricted by ABM-Treaty	

In fact, if not in purpose, the US in SALT II was compensated for Soviet air defense superiority. The US can have 120 heavy bombers with long-range cruise missiles, a system that the Soviets will not be able to build before the end of SALT II (and may not need at all), and thus will reach the full number of 1320 MIRVed launchers, while the Soviets will remain within the 1200 ceiling for MIRVed ICBMs + SLBMs. If the US wants civil defense and air defense to be included in future negotiations — the Soviets so far have refused to even talk about it — then they must be prepared to discuss ASW as well, which they declined to do in at least one instance.[26] Unless one does not subscribe to the more extreme estimates of Soviet civil defense protection, exclusion of strategic defense does not seem to infringe critically on the equity of SALT II.

Other Systems

One final remark in connection with the treaty's balance is in order. The Soviets fought hard against reductions, but finally they agreed to the slightly reduced ceiling of 2250 strategic nuclear delivery vehicles. They must scrap about 250 operational systems, while the US only needs dismantle 33 inactive bombers. And the Soviets gave up two systems entirely, for the sake of arms control, namely the SS-16 and the fractional orbital bombardment system. Both were not very "good" systems, that is true, but the right may no longer claim that the Russians never give up anything they have.

30

3. SALT and the Military Balance

It would have been much easier for the administration to get SALT II ratified, had the military balance been what it was in 1972. At the time of the Interim Agreement SALT supporters could point to many advantages which the United States held, especially in the number of warheads. However, with the introduction of its MIRVed ICBMs during the second half of the 1970's, one of the most dramatic build-ups of strategic power in the course of the nuclear arms race, the Soviets have begun to close the gap in warhead numbers. Their advantage in throw-weight had not just been a sign of technological backwardness, as the left had argued. Combined with increases in accuracy, the Soviets have turned it into a big advantage in time-urgent hard target counterforce capability, an embarrassing development for arms controllers in the United States.[27] Much of the SALT II debate concerned the present and the future state of the military balance between the United States and the Soviet Union. A balanced judgement is impossible without an answer to the following questions:

1. What is the overall picture of the military balance and what are the trends?
2. In which way has the arms control process influenced the trend and the balance, if at all?
3. How does the SALT II Treaty affect the military balance?

There have been statements in the debate about the military balance which are blatantly false. Senator Pell from the liberal wing of the Senate was wrong, when he suggested the US was 6:1 superior to the Soviets in forward-based systems, as was Jesse Helms from the right, when he said that megatonnage was the most important indicator of strategic power and of Soviet superiority, and that it was still going up.[28] Other "arguments" may even be called an insult to America's allies as well as to the general level of the debate. Thus, Admiral Moorer pointed out that the Third World wanted to know who is number one. People did not understand MIRVs and nuclear weapons. But they could count, and when they were told that the Soviets had 1500 ICBMs and the US only a thousand, some of the friends of the US got worried.[29]

Leaving out of account these and other similar contributions, there *is* a legitimate margin of controversy about the military balance between the US and the Soviet Union or NATO and WTO. One of the basic difficulties of all force comparisons are uncertainties in the data base and the assumptions that have to be made, especially in dynamic scenarios. Whatever the correct numbers and relations may be, there is no denying that the general trends in the 1970's have been adverse to the United States. The Soviets have reached (almost or at least) full equivalence in strategic nuclear weapons, and they have widened their lead in long-range TNF and conventional forces. SALT critics stressed Soviet advantages in SNF indicators such as (equivalent) megatonnage, throw-weight, and prompt countermilitary potential. Supporters of SALT stressed the (decreasing) warhead advantage, and better accuracy, reliability, and diversity of US forces. The following list may establish some common ground:[30]

1. The large US advantage in the number of warheads began to decline in the early 60's; the decline was reversed in the early 70's when the US started deploying MIRVs on ICBMs and SLBMs. The ratio was about 3.4:1 in 1975, when it began to decline again. The US were still clearly "ahead", when SALT II was signed, but the Soviets have continued to narrow the gap. Many analyses still predict a slight "advantage" for the US even in 1985, but the United States and the Soviet Union will soon be fairly close in warhead numbers.

2. The Soviets have long been superior in the throw-weight of their strategic missiles, but the US has always had a bomber payload advantage. Soviet throw-weight advantage will peak in the early 80's and then slow down due to MX deployment. US bomber payload advantage will increase sharply with the introduction and build-up of cruise missiles.

3. As with warheads, the Soviets had been clearly behind in equivalent megatonnage during the 60's, but they closed the gap in the early 70's and are now and will continue to be slightly superior to the United States.

4. The Soviets have also closed the gap in hard target kill potential, there will probably be rough parity in this indicator during the 80's. Since about 1977 they lead the US in prompt countermilitary potential against hard targets, a lead that will increase, until the MX will be deployed and start reversing the trend.

Although the trends do favor the Soviet Union, it must be said that the Soviets have generally come from behind, and much of Soviet growth was "necessary" in order to catch up with the United States. Viewed as a whole, the balance in strategic nuclear forces is not out of joint. While the Soviet Union now has a much stronger ICBM force than the US, the US is still ahead both in submarine and bomber technology as well as in SLBM- and bomber warheads. These advantages are hardly ever mentioned by the treaty opponents.

Much of the criticism of SALT II concentrated on the so-called counterforce gap, the fact that the Soviets will soon be able to "kill" US ICBMs with their ICBMs, while the US cannot do the same vice versa, before the MX is fully deployed in the late 1980's. This is said to give the Soviets a significant advantage in case of nuclear war, and especially a political advantage in crisis diplomacy. The critics assume that the Soviets might threaten to destroy the Minuteman force and leave the United States with a countercity-only second-strike option, which the Soviets would "counter-deter" with their large ICBM/SLBM reserve. Nobody can know for sure, if the Soviets consider their ICBM counterforce advantage to really provide them with bargaining leverage in a crisis. It could be that the Americans are simply projecting latent desires onto their chief nuclear rival. It once was explicit US strategic policy to be able to force the enemy into a position from which he could only escape through total war, while the US at the same time prevented him with its superior retaliation forces from taking this step.[31] In any case, counterforce scenarios are abstractions from a very complex web of military and political factors with known unknowns and unknown unknowns, which means high political and military risks. US forces today are much more sophisticated and diversified than Soviet forces were in the 1950's and early 60's. While the US cannot *equal* Soviet *rapid* counterforce potential in the 80's, it does have quite a considerable countersilo potential in its own ICBMs, which could be used against Soviet MIRVed ICBMs, and the US will soon have a large countersilo potential in heavy bombers with cruise missiles. US bomber and SLBM capabilities will increase, and they will still be far more capable than Soviet bombers and SLBMs in 1985. Even after an attack on US ICBMs the US has now and will in the future have flexible "options", including "options" against military targets. The complaint of some of the critics, the US followed a minimum deterrence strategy, is not based on fact but on fiction. While the Soviets do emphasize war-fighting in their deterrence posture, the US has never had a pure mutual assured destruction countercity strategy. The target lists for US strategic nuclear forces have *always* included a large number of Soviet military targets. General Jones, Chairman of the Joint Chiefs of Staff, and the SAC commander Ellis were quite outspoken about this, when they confirmed in the SALT hearings that MAD has never been the basis of US strategy, and that the implementation of targeting has essentially stayed the same since the 1950's.[32]

A Soviet planner looking into the 1980's may well come to the conclusion that the counterforce balance is in fact turning to the advantage of the United States. Soviet strategic nuclear submarines are less capable and more vulnerable than American SSBNs, as are Soviet heavy bombers. Soviet ICBMs will become vulnerable, too, and the Soviets have concentrated their strategic power much more on ICBMs than the US, which has a well balanced and diversified triad.

Concerns about the general trend of US military power vis-a-vis the Soviet Union are not limited to the conservative camp and the military. They comprise the political center and even a large part of the liberal factions. But while there is a majority consensus that the US must increase military expenditures to "maintain essential equivalence" — with disagreement as to *how much* the US should do in defense —, there exist sharply divergent views about the role of arms control and SALT II in the development of the military balance. Treaty opponents see a connection between the whole SALT process and the "deterioration" of the military balance. In this view arms control has had a "tranquilizing" effect on the public and on Congress, leading to a neglect of the national defense. Typical of this line of thought is a statement by Fred Charles Iklé, who said that SALT correleated with a period of US restraint and of Soviet military build-up, leading to a vast transformation of the global military balance, second only to that of the 1930's. US restraint had been caused at least in part by its expectations of strategic arms control.[33] Many SALT critics, especially the military – including those who support SALT II –, date the beginning of the change in the military balance back to the 1960's.[34] Talking about the 60's as a starting point may be a late expression of conservative and military unhappiness with the McNamara Department of Defense and its strong commitment to arms control. Others concentrate on the deferrals and cancellations of military programs by the Carter Administration.

Much of the criticism seems to be influenced by a large dose of nostalgia for the age of US nuclear superiority. There *had to be* a decline in American nuclear power compared to the Soviet Union, if equality was to be established. Another point is that in the early 70's the Republican Administration including Henry Kissinger did not see the military balance as delicate as is now argued from hindsight. SALT opponents cannot have it both ways. They may hold Carter's moderation and the Soviet "great leap forward" in the late 70's responsible for the imbalance they see ahead, but then they cannot say the whole SALT process was a "tranquilizing factor". It is simply not true that the US has been standing still during the last ten years. Between 1970 and 1979 the number of US warheads increased from 4000 to about 9600, with the difference alone bigger than the total of Soviet warheads in 1979. Even a neutral person, let alone an adversary, will have great difficulties to see this as an example of benign restraint in nuclear armaments. The United States deployed 550 Minuteman III missiles, hardened ICBM silos, and is up-grading its ICBM force with new guidance systems and new warheads. The US introduced about 1000 SRAM's on its bombers, keeps modernizing its B-52 bomber force and develops a highly accurate modern air-launched cruise missile. It deployed close to 500 MIRVed SLBMs, developed a quieter and more capable new submarine and the longer-range Trident I missile.

As far as Carter's cutbacks are concerned, the picture again is not quite as impressive as is suggested. Some of the delays have more to do with technical and other problems of acquisition policy than with political decisions. And in the case of the B-1 and the neutron weapon, the two weapon systems Carter stopped, other weapon programs, which were considered at least as or even more cost-effective, were developed and funded instead, such as cruise missiles and conventional precision-guided munitions. The most important point, however, is the fact that SALT II and the whole ratification debate have not served as a tranquilizer but rather as a stimulant to US defense policy and arms programs.

While the Joint Chiefs of Staff supported SALT as a "modest, but useful step", because it helped the US to "restore the military balance", the treaty opponents did not even see SALT II as a beneficial appendix to increased weapons programs. Besides "incapacitating" US minds, SALT II was said to nail down the strategic imbalance and to allow the Soviets to move from equality to superiority. While not all the critics would support Edward Teller's or Eugene Rostow's opinion that SALT II freezes the US into a permanent inferiority,[35] the general direction of the argument was that SALT did not restrain the Soviet Union, while it interfered with important American programs. Administration spokesmen and supporters have said just the opposite: SALT II did restrain the Soviets while protecting every ongoing and planned US program. As for Soviet programs, the difference in 1985 was said to be 2250 (with SALT) versus 3000 (no SALT) strategic nuclear delivery vehicles, 1200 versus 1800 MIRVed SNDVs, 820 versus 1300 MIRVed ICBMs, and 6000 versus 10-15000 hard-target counterforce warheads.[36]

Of course it is very difficult to tell what the Soviets would really do without SALT. But it is very strange for the hawks, who continuously emphasize the Soviet military build-up and who fear Soviet military power most, to argue that the Soviets would not do more without SALT II than they would do with the treaty in force. SALT II opponents want to reject the treaty, increase US defense expenditures, speed up US strategic nuclear programs, and still hold the Soviets to the limits they have agreed to in seven years of very hard bargaining. It seems the Soviets will be charged by US SALT sceptics whatever they do. If they stick to the ceilings, even though SALT remains unratified, critics will argue that the Soviets did not want to do more anyway. If they start say testing the SS-18 with more than 10 warheads, it will be "stop thief!". Inadvertently, Senator Tower ridiculed the position of the opponents, when he presented a list with what the Soviets were allowed to do in SALT II, a list that included 1200 SLBMs with 14 warheads each.[37]

It is probably fair to say that the high estimates for Soviet forces without SALT are unrealistic. At least in one instance, however, we have some evidence that the Soviets did want to go higher than the limit that was negotiated. The Soviets at first rejected any ceiling on MIRVed ICBMs, and then rejected the ceiling of 820 as too low. Intelligence information suggests that they were planning to build over 900 MIRVed ICBMs.[38] As far as fractionation is concerned, it could be, as Nitze has suggested, that 10 RV's are the ideal configuration for the SS-18 at least for the time being.[39] But SALT II forbids *testing* the SS-18 with more than 10 RV's, so any Soviet program to eventually increase the number of RV's on the SS-18 (an intention which is invoked by other SALT critics, who argue that the SS-18 will be a threat even to the MX) is at least slowed down. And the Soviets are in the process of developing their fifth generation of ICBMs, which is bound to be restrained by the limits on ICBM modernization that were negotiated.

SALT is much more tailored around US programs. Everything that the US wanted to protect was in fact protected against Soviet opposition, especially mobile ICBMs with MIRVs and ALCMs and other cruise missiles. Only in two cases does the SALT II Treaty infringe on US programs. The US must reduce their number of MIRVed ICBMs, if they want to go beyond 120 cruise missile carriers. And the multiple-vertical-protective shelter basing mode for the MX is probably not in accord with SALT. Treaty opponents have made much of the point that SALT prevents a timely solution to the problem of Minuteman vulnerability. But it is not just SALT that made the difference between the MVPS system and the MX as now planned. It is true that the question of verifiability played a part in the decision. Any mobile ICBM system will pose verification problems, and it certainly is in the interest of the US to build a system that can be verified by national technical means. Any other system, if copied by the Soviets, would make US planning much more difficult and would destroy the basis for the verification of any future SALT treaty. Most of the difference in expenses between the MVPS and the racetrack scheme can be justified in strategic and military terms, and the time difference for initial deployment is so low that it would not in any major sense contribute to the solution of Minuteman vulnerability.[40]

4. SALT and Verification

Some people have talked about grain elevators loaded with ICBMs or fishing trawlers equipped with SLBMs, or the possibility of launching missiles from warehouses and factories. The Foreign Relations Committee rejected an amendment calling for on-site inspection in connection with SALT, with a 9:6 majority only.[41] No conceivable SALT treaty can calm down all wild phantasies, and some people just do not want any SALT. But verification is a serious problem, which in the 50's and 60's had stalled arms control negotiations for many years. It was clear from the beginning that SALT II would be more comprehensive than SALT I and thus would raise more verification problems. There is a huge and structural asymmetry between the United States and the Soviet Union, and the stubbornness and rigid attitude of the Soviets in all matters that concern the monitoring of their military potential still is one of the major roadblocks to meaningful arms control. The loss of US military installations in Iran, which monitored Soviet missile tests, during the final phase of the negotiations, added to the sensitivity of the issue.

In debating verification the US faces a double dilemma. Too much precision and explanation in the negotiations would compromise sources and methods of US intelligence, and in the domestic debate much information must remain secret or be discussed in executive session for the same reason. Only very few people may claim to know and understand all the details, and the 17 volumes of study that the Senate Select Committee on Intelligence collected indicate the size of the task.

Apart from sweeping generalizations about the non-verifiability of the treaty, SALT II opponents have especially taken issue with limits on launchers instead of missiles. These limits do not take into account excess missiles already in existence and the production of more missiles to be used for reloading launchers. The critics, however, seem to demand more than is either necessary or achievable. While launchers and associated equipment can be verified, missiles and missile production much less. SALT II prohibits the stationing of more than one missile per launcher in the deployment areas and thus helps to reduce the reload problem, but the greatest barrier to the reloading of missiles are technical problems, especially the loss of hardness protection during the process.

The critics also suggested that the US could not verify the restrictions on missile modernization. SALT supporters agreed that it is close to impossible to monitor changes in parameters with a 5 % accurary. But it was the US who wanted the 5 % limitation. It had preferred these tougher limits, which pose difficulties for verification, to more generous limitations, which could be verified more easily. It is true that the US does not have an agreed upon data base of the parameters of Soviet missiles, but it does have a huge body of data from Soviet missile tests, stored in computers, which serve as a basis for comparison. Intelligence experts have stressed that they can more easily verify relative changes than absolute ones.

Telemetry encryption had been one of the most critical issues in the negotiations, with the CIA and the KGB both with their backs up, and SALT opponents were not satisfied with the compromise reached. It is true that the Soviet Union has since 1974 encrypted telemetric information from its missile tests. While the US does not encrypt telemetry, it has in some instances used other methods to deny an outside observer information about the performance of its missiles.[42] The negotiating record shows both sides to agree that each party is free to use various methods of transmitting telemetric information during testing, including its encryption except that in accordance with the provisions of paragraph 3 of article XV of the treaty, neither party shall engage in deliberate denial of telemetric information, such as through the use of telemetric encryption, *whenever such denial empedes verification of compliance* with the provisions of the treaty.[43]

There is no SALT treaty which could be verified with 100 % certainty. A final judgement should rest on expert testimony, on the experience with Soviet compliance, and on the difference which SALT makes. The top intelligence experts say that SALT II is adequately verifiable provided that new monitoring equipment is deployed to compensate for the Iranian stations. The Senate Select Committee on Intelligence concluded that SALT II enhances the ability of the US to monitor Soviet components subject to the limitations of the treaty.[44] There are some areas which can be verified with only low or moderate confidence. But the Soviet Union will not be able to tilt the strategic balance by violating the treaty without the US knowing it early enough to respond. Minor violations might not be detected, but their small military advantage would not make up for the political risks and possible embarrassments involved. The record of compliance and the handling of complaints in the Standing Consultative Commission suggest that the probability of significant violations or of sustained, low-level evasion is indeed very low.

The Soviets have made several concessions to at least mitigate the structural asymmetry in verification: They finally agreed to a mutual data base, to be revised regularly, and with this "reversed four hundred years of Russian history", in the words of one of the leading Soviet negotiators.[45] They accepted clear definitions, although they continuously preferred to be vague. They accepted counting rules for MIRVed launchers, as well as the verification aids of Functionally Related Observable Differences, Externally Observable Differences, and Externally Observable Design Features. And they gave up their mobile SS-16 to avoid the problem of commonality with the SS-20.[46] Without a SALT II treaty the Soviets are entitled to withdraw these concessions, and even the basic provision about non-concealment, which was carried over from SALT I, could be in danger. Since the US cannot force the Soviet Union to become a more open society, these reversals would be a desaster mainly for the United States itself. Uncertainties about Soviet programs and intentions would be much greater without the verification clauses that SALT II provides.

5. SALT and Arms Control

One of the most interesting features of the SALT debate was the new coalition between the two extremes of the controversy. Senator McGovern and Senator Helms both repeatedly called SALT II an arms escalation treaty. The agreement is only superficial, however. While Helms again and again pointed to the Soviet build-up of strategic nuclear forces, a build-up that will not be stopped by SALT II, and while one gets the impression from his indictment that it is only the Soviets who possess nuclear weapons at all,[47] the left has stressed the escalation of the arms race in general, with special emphasis on US nuclear weapons. Thus Senator Hatfield complained that the US arsenal had increased three times since the first talks about strategic arms limitations, US plus Soviet weapons had increased twice since SALT I, the US had deployed more than 2 warheads every day since SALT I and would during SALT II produce almost five new warheads each day.[48] Senator McGovern at one time announced that about half a dozen Senators would not vote for the illusion of arms control. Since 1969 the US had spent about 125 Billion Dollars on strategic nuclear forces, and they still found themselves feeling more threatened, more insecure, and more vulnerable.[49]

There is another difference between the two camps. While the left has no power to veto arms escalation measures, and will always eventually support even the "illusion of arms control", the right has the veto power to block a SALT treaty or to negotiate trade-offs for their support. The concerns of the right about a lack of real arms limitation are mainly genuine, but their amendments to the treaty and their proposals for US weapons programs suggest that this concern is clearly subordinate to their objections against the state of the military balance.

The arguments of the center cannot be easily refuted. They readily agree that SALT is less than one would wish to have, but stress the fact that it is at least a step to reduce the growth rate of strategic nuclear forces. SALT II is no doubt a much better treaty than the Interim Agreement of 1972, and in theory it could be used as a building block for more meaningful arms control. The various ceilings in the treaty and the verification provisions provide at least some arms race stability. Its greatest shortcoming obviously is the failure to solve the problem of (theoretical) ICBM vulnerability and of crisis stability. Good arms control should help to protect the invulnerability of strategic weapons and should prevent even the semblance of pre-emptive advantage. In this, SALT II cannot be defended against its critics. The Soviets were not willing to see the problems of strategic instability in American terms. They consider their ICBM throwweight advantage and counterforce potential an asset which they cannot sacrifice. But although SALT did not prevent ICBM vulnerability, it did not create it either, and it is not only the Soviets, who are responsible for the major strategic instability ahead. SALT opponents must be reminded that the US first introduced MIRVed ICBMs and that the US did not want to give up its MIRV advantage in SALT I, when there might still have been a slight chance to avoid the counterforce race.

With MIRVs a fact of life and no arms control solution to the vulnerability of fixed-site ICBMs, mobile ICBMs have become almost unavoidable. There has been much talk about buy-offs for the military and the conservatives in exchange for their support of the treaty. Certainly, these groups have established a linkage between SALT ratification and increased military expenditures, sometimes implicitly, sometimes explicitly. But one does not have to buy off majorities, and the MX is much more a product of international arms race competition than of internal pressures not related to interaction. Only a minority among US decision-makers thought the US could live with Minuteman vulnerability, which is only theoretical after all, and should stop short of procuring mobile ICBMs, which they regard as an "ingenious absurdity."[50]

Was there an alternative to the final version of the treaty? Serious strategic arms control should at least stop further growth of the arsenals and even strive for reductions. A really "good" SALT II treaty should include a total ban on new ICBMs, deep cuts in MIRVed ICBMs, and a ban on mobile missiles. It would try to establish sanctuaries for strategic nuclear submarines, ban testing of depressed trajectories, and provide for minimum stand-off distance from shore for SLBMs. It should also sharply restrict missile testing in order to reduce confidence in plans for and reduce fears of first-strike and pre-emption. Carter's comprehensive proposal of March 1977 was a big step in that direction.[51] It was not just a public relations exercise for a new administration, disassociating itself from its predecessors, although this was also a consideration. Unfortunately, the comprehensive proposal was handled badly diplomatically. The way it was put forward was bound to increase Soviet misgivings about the new moralism in US foreign policy. And the proposal was blatantly one-sided, too much consideration had been given to wooing the domestic opposition. The Soviets did not live up to the challenge anyway. If they had really wanted disarmament, as they had been insisting year after year, they ought to have sensed their chance

39

and put forth equally radical counterproposals. The Soviet bureaucracy was set on the Vladivostok approach. Soviet arms control policy is like the Soviet political system: rigid, security-minded, conservative, and incrementalistic. Thus, only a few reminders of the comprehensive approach could be negotiated into SALT II.[52]

The SALT II negotiations contain another painful lesson for peace researchers: you need bargaining power, and unilateral restraint does not work, if it is not integrated into the bargaining approach. Arms control negotiations are not seminars on stability, but trading sessions dependent upon evidence of real programs.[53] The B-1 cancellation may be a case in point. Had it been connected to the comprehensive proposal or been used as a bargaining chip until the end of the negotiations, it might have elicited a more favorable Soviet response. The way it was handled probably irritated the Soviets and certainly gave the domestic opposition another issue to be used against SALT.

6. SALT and Linkage

The debate about linkage comprised three major aspects: 1. the role of SALT in US-Soviet relations and its relation to détente, 2. the question if SALT could and should be used as a lever to influence Soviet behavior, and 3. the role of nuclear weapons in US foreign policy in general. Many treaty critics attacked SALT II as a symbol of US military and political decline. The most pathological scenario in the whole debate was discussed by Mrs. Schlafly from the American Conservative Union. She suggested that ratification of SALT II would deliver to the Soviets the power to cut off US oil, to destroy the US Dollar, and to use Cuba as a Soviet base. By 1980, the Kremlin would invite the oil-producers to Moscow, convince them of the new Soviet military superiority, and then ask them for an oil embargo against the West. This would ruin the US, and the Soviets could then demand that America hand over its nuclear and conventional weapons.[54] This is an extreme point of view, to be sure, but there is a widespread feeling among treaty opponents that the United States was "being pushed around in the world by one country after another",[55] and that SALT was just another sign of US weakness. Many Senators see not only a correlation but a causal link between the whole SALT process and increased "Soviet adventurism". A rejection of SALT II could do no harm to détente, because there had never been a relaxation of tension, they said, the Soviets were simply using detente to increase their political and military advantages, with the Carter Administration appeasing the Soviet program of expansion.

The conservative group within the Republican minority in the Senate Foreign Relations Committee reported that it had been a decisive mistake by the administration not to establish a clear linkage between SALT and Soviet behavior all over the world. Thus, SALT had become a signal that the Soviets could do to the United States whatever they wanted to.[56] Henry Kissinger also stressed the political dimension of arms control, and he complained about the Soviet "assault on the international equilibrium". He demanded, US adherence to SALT should in the future be made conditional upon a bi-annual review of Soviet conduct.[57] Kissinger had thus changed his line of argument substantially, because as National Security Advisor and as Secretary of State he had consistently warned against *such* kinds of linkages, and especially against Congressional linkage policies, in arms control as well as in trade.

Most of the assumptions behind the linkage debate are questionable. The first is a misconception of SALT as such. SALT is not a value judgement about Soviet foreign policy, and the ratification of a SALT treaty does not end the political, military, and ideological rivalry between the superpowers. SALT is a means to reduce the risk of war, especially of nuclear war, between the US and the Soviet Union or between NATO and WTO. From that follows that SALT should be in the interest of both the US and the Soviet Union. The concept of "high pressure linkage" assumes that SALT is more important to the Soviets than to the United States, otherwise it would not make sense to condition the signing of a SALT treaty on Soviet concessions in other fields. The Soviets have indicated that they might as well in their turn ask for linkage between SALT and American foreign policy towards China, e.g.[58]

The second is a misunderstanding of detente. While developments in the core area of the East West conflict, i.e. in Central Europe, are proof beyond doubt that a relaxation of tension had in fact taken place, detente has never reached the status of a mechanism to regulate all areas of conflict and confrontation between the United States and the Soviet Union, although such expectations may have been voiced occasionally. For all the rhetoric, there has never been a serious effort to work out a set of standards by which the two would try to manage regional conflict without resort ot violence.[59] The United Staes may certainly list many grievances about Soviet conflict behavior; but Soviet hopes connected with détente have also been disappointed. The Soviets had been promised MFN-status by Kissinger, but Congress failed to deliver, economic cooperation between the US and the Soviet Union has remained low. The US pushed the Soviets out of Middle East diplomacy, pressed them openly on human rights, established political and even military contacts with China, retreated from SALT, and strengthened the "second front" in Western Europe.

As for the Soviet assault on the "geopolitical equilibrium", some qualifying remarks are in order.[60] A comparison of the relative positions of the Western alliance and the Soviet Union at the end of the 1960's with their relative positions today would show a decline of American power, but not to the same degree of the Western alliance and the capitalist system as a whole. The unavoidable enhancement of Soviet military power has not yet been translated into major lasting strategic gains. The Soviet Union is still surrounded by hostile forces on all sides, and its gains in the Third World are only a small part in the overall picture. The Soviets have lost influence in the International Communist

Movement, and they have again been challenged even in their core area of Eastern Europe. They have "lost" Egypt, and have traded Somalia for Ethiopia. Their influence in Guinea has decreased, while it has increased in the Congo and Angola, with Angola and Mozambique openly courting Western investment. If Soviet military prestige is high, its prestige as a model for or partner in national development has never been lower. The "fall" of Nicaragua had much more to do with the Somoza dictatorship than with the Cuban connection, and the fall of the Shah was not related to Soviet activities. The "loss" of Iran was among other factors the result of gross mistakes in US diplomacy, mistakes for which rather the hardliners in the Carter Administration were responsible.[61]

The basic fallacy of SALT criticism is an overestimation of military, especially nuclear power, in the course of world politics. As the period of US nuclear supremacy correlates with its maximum political weight, treaty opponents assume that nuclear weapons must have been the basic cause of US influence. But US nuclear power did not prevent the Berlin Blockade, the Czech Coup, the Korean War, or the intervention in Hungary, nor did it help in Vietnam or the Bay of Pigs. Not even the Cuban missile crisis, which is cited as *the* example, was decided by American nuclear preponderance alone; it is quite likely that US nuclear superiority was one of the reasons for Soviet action in the first place. Soviet nuclear equality coincided with détente in Central Europe and the Berlin Agreement. And Soviet nuclear power did not prevent China's rebellion against its former ally and China's approaches towards Western Europe, Japan and the United States. It could not prevent the reduction of its influence in the Middle East, nor the problems with its allies. The stakes involved and the regional military and political balance of power are much more important factors in the solution of local conflict than the fine-tuning of the strategic balance.

7. SALT and the NATO Allies

Although America's NATO allies were not direct parties to the dialogue between the superpowers, they were involved in the development of the US negotiating position. Naturally, the Europeans were especially concerned about the euro-strategic balance and any influence that SALT II might have on it.[62] They wanted to protect the cohesion of the alliance and its established ways of co-operation in military technology. They urged to keep open any options to counter increasing Soviet nuclear capabilities against Western Europe. Whatever legitimate concerns the Europeans could have had during the negotiations about a neglect of their "Eurasian" view of the strategic balance, they were increasingly recognized and taken into account by the US administration. Soviet efforts to negotiate a non-transfer clause along the lines of the ABM treaty into SALT II failed. In an interpretative statement on noncircumvention the

US reiterated what it had stated in alliance consultations during the negotiations, namely that the noncircumvention provisions would not affect "existing patterns of collaboration and cooperation with its allies", nor "preclude cooperation in modernization".[63] The protocol to the SALT treaty does not restrict ground-launched cruise missiles, and lingering doubts about its precedential effect (after all, the protocol *does* mention Western and only Western eurostrategic systems, although it does not restrict them) were laid to rest by the NATO decision of December 1979.

In the US, supporters and critics of SALT alike predicted as much as the demise of NATO, if the treaty was either rejected or ratified, respectively. Both predictions are rather unlikely to be borne out. There can be no doubt, however, that Western European governments and NATO officials had all come out in favor of ratification, although many politicians and representatives of the military have voiced concerns about the general trend in the military balance. This posed a dilemma for treaty opponents in the US. They wanted to avoid the image of spoiling the concensus in NATO (after all it was the *Russians* who used SALT as an instrument to divide the US from its allies),[64] and they knew that they were a minority even in the United States. Thus, they reinterpreted the position of their allies. The way in which they did that is not very flattering and in some instances even insulting to the Europeans. The SALT critics suggested that while the Europeans were publicly for the treaty, they were against it in private, which in plain English means they are liars. And they said that the Europeans had to support SALT, because they were "under the gun" of the Soviets, self-finlandized, or pressured by the Carter Administration, all of which implies that the Europeans are cowards. Certainly, every SALT critic in the Senate could find *some* politicians or *some* military in Europe who shared his doubts. But various staff missions to Europe, constant negotiations between Vance, Brown, and European officials, and on top of it the mission of Senator Byrd have all established that the European governments representing the majorities of their respective electorates, were genuinely in favor of ratification.[65] Henry Kissinger was honest enough to list the good reasons which Western Europeans had to be against rejection of the treaty: SALT II, which had taken years to negotiate, was an agreement endorsed by the two superpowers. Failure to ratify this agreement would be another sign of the weakening of US executive authority and would badly reflect on the political system of the United States, which would produce another domestic stalemate after an extended and highly complicated negotiation processs.[66] It should be added that in Europe the political balance between defense and arms control is much more delicate than in the United States, as was demonstrated by the enhanced radiation weapon controversy and the linkage of the Pershing II/GLCM decision with a commitment to arms control.

Conclusion

The crisis of SALT II is a symbol of the crisis of the US political system and political culture at least as much as it is a symbol of the crisis in US-Soviet relations. Salt II became the victim of a general, in many respects irrational political mood which had nothing or very little to do with the treaty itself; and of a provision in the US constitution which owes its existence to a chance constellation of different economic interests within a newly founded federation towards the end of the 18th century,[67] an environment totally different from the requirements of 20th century diplomacy. SALT II was complicated and difficult to negotiate. And although it was a much better treaty than the SALT I Interim Agreement, it was used as a grab bag of political and military problems by every Senator (and their staff) who wanted to find fault with it. The treaty opponents raised some serious questions, but they failed to make their case that SALT would hurt US security. SALT II allows all the modernizations and defense increases which the critics deemed necessary, while it contains at least a few constraints on Soviet programs. The treaty provides improvements in the area of verification; and although it is not a very effective arms limitation treaty, the critics are plainly inconsistent, when they demand more arms control, but would not even give such small a step as SALT II a chance. The treaty was supported by the Defense Department and by the Joint Chiefs of Staff. The military and the treaty opponents got as much assurances as they could have hoped for and a broad consensus on a stimulation of US defense efforts. And America's allies definitely wanted SALT. Still, the minority did not deliver their votes even after the bargain, and used their one third veto power to delay ratification instead. First the Soviet intervention in Afghanistan, and then the elections helped them out of their predicament. It was them, who obstructed the domestic consensus and America's capacity to act, and who added to the strains in the alliance. They were not willing to compromise, neither with the Russians, nor with NATO, nor with their government and the majority in Congress, but chose unilateralism instead.

The world has changed, however. The days of unquestioned US military, economic, and political superiority are gone. America's allies in the First World, its enemies in the Second and its subordinates in the Third World have all increased their status and power relative to the United States. It could not have been otherwise. An obsession with calculations of strategic nuclear equivalence, as if they could provide a firm and measureable handle over the uncertainties and complexities of international relations, and an overemphasis of politically very improbable military scenarios[68] demonstrate how narrow the debate in the US about foreign policy has become. No amount of military expenditures can reverse the changes in the structure of the international system, changes, with which SALT has almost nothing to do and which could certainly not be regulated by it.

Depending on which forces in the Reagan camp will finally prevail, the US may turn to a much more fundamental unilateralism than the rejection of SALT II.

If the radical hard-liners, who aim at a full-fledged superior nuclear war-fighting capability, have their way, there will be no arms control at all. This the Europeans, liberals, social democrats, and conservatives alike, couldn't and wouldn't accept. If Reagan moves toward the center of his party and the political spectrum as a whole, then he will strive for a "new" SALT II. His dilemma will be that the Soviets — for understandable reasons — will only be prepared for cosmetic changes, and that he must "sell" these as substantial concessions to his constituency.

Notes

This is the English version of PRIF-Report 1/1981. An earlier version was presented at the PRIF-Conference on "Trends and Perspectives in US Economic and Security Policy Towards Europe", in Bad Homburg, Dec. 7–10, 1980. I am grateful for comments by Richard Lebow, I. M. Destler, Pierre Hassner and Joseph Coffey. I alone am responsible for any errors concerning facts or judgement, of course.

1 Cf. Gert Krell, Rüstungsdynamik und Rüstungskontrolle. Die gesellschaftlichen Auseinandersetzungen um SALT in den USA 1969–1974, Frankfurt (Haag + Herchen) 1978; and the votes in: Congressional Quarterly Almanac 1975, nos. 199, 200, 205, 207, 213, 479, pp. 30–S, 31–S, 32–S, 73–S and in: Congressional Quarterly Almanac 1976, nos. 190 and 444, pp. 20–S, and 62–S.

2 Congressional Quarterly Almanac 1979, vote no. 289, p. 48–S.

3 Congressional Quarterly Almanac 1977, vote no. 41, p. 8–S.

4 Only Senators McGovern and Pell objected; 96/1 US Congress, Senate Committee on Foreign Relations, Report: The SALT II Treaty, Washington (GPO) 1979, pp. 23–24, 55–56 (hereafter cited as SFR, R)

5 SFR, R, p. 26; Ayes: Church, Pell, McGovern, Biden, Sarbanes, Muskie, Zorinsky, Javits, and Percy. Nays: Glenn, Stone, Baker, Helms, Hayakawa, and Lugar. Senator Glenn's special concern was verification. With further improvements in US monitoring capabilities coming along, he would eventually have supported SALT. Senator Zorinsky, on the other hand, had proposed or supported several amendments in the markup that would have made renegotiation necessary, and he asked his colleagues to support some of them on the floor. SFR, R, pp. 458–461 (Glenn), and 472–473 (Zorinsky). Congressional Quarterly Almanac 1979, S. 428; the abstentions in the Armed Services Committee were motivated by considerations outside the SALT discussion. It was doubtful whether the committee was entitled to issue such a report in general.

6 See the Statement of General Wilson, US Marine Corps (retired), in: 96/1 US Congress, Senate Armed Services Committee, Hearings: Military Implications of the Treaty on the Limitation of Strategic Offensive Arms and Protocol Thereto (Salt II Treaty), 4 parts, Washington (GPO) 1979 (hereafter cited as SAS, 1 through 4), part 2, pp. 583–585.

7 Cf. the letter of the Coalition for Peace through Strength, signed by 1678 retired and reserve general and flag officers, in: 96/1 US Congress, Senate Committee on Foreign Relations, Hearing: The SALT II Treaty, Whashington (GPO) 1979, 5 parts (hereafter cited as SFR, 1 through 5), part 4, pp. 61–78.

8 95/1 US Congress, Senate Committee on Armed Services, Hearings: Consideration of Mr. Paul Warnke to be Director of the U.S. Arms Control and Disarmament Agency and Ambassador, Washington (GPO) 1977, and 95/1 US Congress, Senate Committee on

Foreign Relations, Hearings: Warnke Nomination, Washington (GPO) 1977 (hereafter cited as SAS, Warnke, and SFR, Warnke, respectively).

9 SAS 1, pp. 30–33.
10 For an excellent comment on the problems of negotiating equity, see the prepared statement of General David Jones, in: SAS 1, pp. 156–160, pp. 157–158: "I have been struck by the confusion that appears to exist in some quarters regarding the difference between unequal provisions within the Agreement and the issue of equity of the Agreement when taken as a whole. We should bear in mind that one of the objectives of SALT is to regulate, in a balanced fashion, aspects to two fundamentally dissimilar and asymmetrical force structures. Not only are the force structures different in their composition, but different features on each side's forces are viewed as more threatening by the other side. These differing perspectives have produced a negotiating process marked by various compromises and tradeoffs as each side seeks to protect the essential character of its own forces while attempting to minimize the most threatening aspects of the other side's. The result is an Agreement with some provisions clearly favoring one side and some clearly favoring the other. The question of equity, then, cannot adequately be addressed by a narrow and selective critique of portions of the SALT II Agreement. Only a balanced appraisal of the total will yield an adequate evaluation."
11 Strobe Talbott, Endgame: The Inside Story of SALT II, New York (Harper and Row) 1979.
12 SFR 2, p. 190, and Congressional Quarterly Almanac 1978, p. 331.
13 See for example SFR 2, pp. 77–79; SFR 5, pp. 281–282; SAS 1, pp. 73–74; SAS 4, pp. 1448–1449.
14 Sources for the negotiation tradeoffs are Talbott, Endgame, and the Senate Hearings, see for example SFR 1, pp. 243–245.
15 A few Soviet SLBMs are not SALT accountable. The Military Balance 1980/81, London (IISS) 1980, pp. 118–119, counts 60 SS-N-5 and 9 SS-N-4 among the Long- and Medium Range Nuclear Systems for the European Theater. 21 of the SS-N-5 on 7 H-II submarines are SALT accountable, as are the Poseidon RV's.
16 SFR 1, p. 490; SFR 5, p. 156.
17 For a critique of this consensus see Dieter Lutz, Das militärische Kräfteverhältnis im Bereich der ‚Nuklearkräfte in und für Europa', in: Gert Krell/Dieter S. Lutz, Nuklearrüstung im Ost-West-Konflikt. Potentiale, Doktrinen, Rüstungssteuerung, Baden-Baden (Nomos) 1980, pp. 11–89; see also Raymond Garthoff, "The TNF Tangle", in: Foreign Policy No. 41 (Winter 1980–1981), pp. 82–94.
18 See the various Baker amendments, SFR, R, pp. 68–71, and Donald Brennan, SFR 4, p. 377.
19 Talbott, Endgame. p. 180.
20 Prepared Statement of Donal Brennan, in: SFR 4, pp. 369–376, 371.
21 For a complete list of the status of all B-52's see SAS 4, p. 1607.
22 SAS, Warnke, p. 250.
23 Cf. SAS 4, pp. 1543–1544, questions submitted by Senator Stevens, Alaska; for US systems see SAS 1, p. 96.
24 See the exchanges between Senator Warner/Secretary Brown and Senator Culver/Secretary Brown, SAS 1, pp. 47–48, and 72; Senator Stone, Fla., tried to make an issue of Soviet SLBMs on Golf diesel submarines in Cuba, see SFR, R, p. 67 and elsewhere.
25 Cf. Daniel Goure and Gordon H. McCormick, Soviet Strategic Defense: The Neglected Dimension of the U.S.-Soviet Balance, in: Orbis XXIV, 1 (Spring 1980), pp. 103–127.
26 Talbott, Endgame, p. 208.
27 And to the peace research community, which had predicted a large "lethality" advantage for the US well into the 1990's, see Kosta Tsipis, Offensive Missiles, Stockholm Paper 5, Stockholm (SIPRI) 1974, and SIPRI (Hg.), Rüstung und Abrüstung im Atomzeitalter, Reinbek (rororoaktuell) 1977, p. 22. It remains to be seen, whether the left is

willing to learn from these and other false estimates, as far as its arms control philosophy and arms race theory are concerned.

28 SFR 1, pp. 126–127, 391.
29 SAS, Warnke, p. 252.
30 Sources are: Joint Chiefs of Staff, United States Military Posture for Fiscal Year 1981, Washington (GPO) 1980, pp. 7–13, and Gert Krell/Dieter Lutz, Nuklearrüstung im Ost-West Konflikt. Potentiale, Doktrinen, Rüstungssteuerung, Baden-Baden (Nomos) 1980.
31 See Henry Kissinger, Nuclear Weapons and Foreign Policy, dt. Kernwaffen und Auswärtige Politik, München (Odenbourg) 1959, p. 123.
32 SAS 1, p. 170; as to the weaknesses of the "counter-deterrence" scenario see Krell/Lutz, op. cit., pp. 144–150, and Secretary Brown, in an exchange with Senator Tower, SAS 1, pp. 29–30.
33 Cf. Prepared Statement of Fred Charles Iklé, in SFR 5, pp. 155–157.
34 Cf. the comment by Adminral Kidd, a SALT supporter, that the falling behind in military strength was "sort of like being nibbled to death by a flock of ducks . . . . No one bite has been excruciating, but taken in the aggregate, our total stockpile of national military competence has shrunk." SFR 2, p. 221.
35 SFR 1, p. 438 (Paul Nitze); Prepared Statement of Eugene Rostow, SFR 4, pp. 31–38.
36 SFR 5, p. 25, and elsewhere.
37 See Senator Tower's chart in: SAS 1, p. 292, which has more Soviet weapons with SALT than without SALT, and the comments by Senator Hart and General Allen, SAS 1, p. 335.
38 Talbott, Endgame, p. 103, 108.
39 SFR 1, p. 508.
40 See Statement of William Perry, Under Secretary for Research and Engineering, and discussion, SFR 4, pp. 438–480.
41 SFR, R, p. 71.
42 Cf. Talbott, Endgame, pp. 194–202.
43 SAS 4, p. 1571.
44 SFR 5, pp. 270–273.
45 Talbott, Endgame, p. 98.
46 They also agreed to advance notification of tests beyond their national territory, and of tests involving multiple launches. This, however, is not much of a concession, and the basic asymmetry remains. Tests extending beyond national boundaries must be notified in advance anyway. The Soviets usually test within their national territory, while the US usually tests beyond its borders.
47 I have in mind especially this comment: "Today the Soviets have an arsenal of nuclear weapons in their strategic force with the combined explosive power of 626880 Hiroshima bombs. They have enough weapons to destroy the United States completely 2 1/2 times. They have four weapons for each and every county in the United States. One would have thought that any arms limitation treaty the United States would have signed would have required as a minimum a freeze on further increases in these forces. A freeze is necessary since any overkill in strategic forces causes nuclear instability; such excess forces can only be used as a means of 'blunting' any potential enemy's responses to a pre-emptive strike. As the Soviets pile nuclear weapons on top of nuclear weapons, this nuclear instability increases." (SFR, R, p. 514) This is a classical example of autistic perception, because he is not even considering that what he says about the Soviet Union is also true of the United States.
48 SFR 5, pp. 2–3.
49 SFR 1, p. 132.
50 As to the controversy in the administration about the MX see Talbott, Endgame, p. 168.
51 Cf. Gert Krell/Dieter Lutz, Von SALT I zu SALT II, in: Osteuropa 29, 12 (Dec. 1979), pp. 1008–1020; Talbott, Endgame, pp. 46–67.

52 For a comparison of the Comprehensive Proposal and SALT II see SFR 1, pp. 599–600.
53 On this point, Colin Gray is right; the phrase is his, see the quotation in: SAS 1, 295.
54 Prepared Statement of Mrs. Phyllis Schlafly, SFR 4, pp. 219–227.
55 Paul Nitze's phrase, SFR 1, p. 506.
56 Statement by Senator Howard Baker, Senator Jesse Helms, Senator S. I. Hayakawa, Senator Richard Lugar, in: SFR, R, pp. 491–509, pp. 491–492.
57 Statements by Henry Kissinger, in: SFR 3, pp. 160–176, and in: SAS 2, pp. 828–831.
58 Talbott, Endgame, p. 251.
59 For an excellent comment on the crisis of detente see Robert Legvold, "Containment Without Confrontation", in: Foreign Policy No. 40 (Fall 1980), pp. 74–98.
60 SALT critics often assume a steady increase in Soviet power all over the world, connecting all changes, including the revolution in Nicaragua, to the Soviet menace. Even a brief glance at international developments in the last 15 years shows that the picture is much more complicated than that. See Tom J. Farer, "Searching for Defeat", in: Foreign Policy No. 40 (Fall 1980), pp. 155–174.
61 See William H. Sullivan, Dateline Iran: The Road Not Taken, in: Foreign Policy No. 40 (Fall 1980), pp. 175–186 and the series of articles in the International Herald Tribune of October 27, 28, 29, 30, 31 and November 1/2, 1980.
62 For an example, see the statement by Alois Mertes, CDU, on the floor of the Deutsche Bundestag, March 9, 1979, Stenographischer Bericht, Protokoll 8/142, pp. 11257 and 11258.
63 SAS 1, p. 54.
64 Eugene Rostow, SFR 2, p. 406.
65 Senator Robert C. Byrd's Report on Trip to Soviet Union and Western Europe, in: SFR 5, pp. 259–267; Vance, SAS 4, p. 1459 and elsewhere; 96/1 US Congress, Senate Committee on Foreign Relations, Subcommittee on European Affairs, Staff Report: SALT and the NATO Allies, Washington (GPO) 1979; 92/2 US Congress, House Committee on Foreign Affairs, Report of a Staff Study Mission to Seven NATO Countries and Austria: NATO and Western Security in the 1980's. The European Perception, Washington (GPO) 1980; 96/1 House Committee on Foreign Affairs, Subcommittee on International Security and Scientific Affairs, and Subcommittee on Europe and the Middle East, Hearings: Western Security Issues. European Perspectives, Washington (GPO) 1979.
66 SAS 2, p. 832.
67 See Falk Bomsdorf, Zur Senatsdebatte über SALT II in den USA, in: Aus Politik und Zeitgeschichte B 37/79 (Sept. 15, 1979), pp. 19–33, 22–23.
68 This phrase was taken from Stanley Hoffmann's excellent testimony, see Prepared Statement of Stanley Hoffmann, in: SFR 4, pp. 289–297.

Joseph I. Coffey

Issues in West German Security Policy: An American Perspective

1. Introduction

It is no exaggeration to say that the security of the Federal Republic of Germany depends more on the support provided by the United States of America than on any other factor; as the West German White Paper of Defense put it, "It is only in alliance with the North American countries that the security of Europe and the Federal Republic of Germany is assured".[1] It is only a slight exaggeration (if it is one at all) to say that the attainment of American security objectives in Europe depends first and foremost on the support of the FRG, which has the strongest economy of any European member of the alliance and the most powerful ground and air forces. However, despite this situation of mutual dependence, which is widely recognized and generally accepted, the two countries are seemingly far apart with respect to the means of achieving the security that both desire; thus, one gives priority to arms limitations and the other to arms build-ups.

Such divergencies of views among allies are not peculiar to the United States and West Germany; at one stage in the War of the Spanish succession the Duke of Marlborough threatened to abandon his Dutch associates if they did not agree to the British proposal for a new campaign against the French. Nor are differences between the US and the FRG anything new; the two states have disagreed for years over the best way to deter Soviet aggression in Europe. What makes these disputes over security policy significant is not *their* novelty but the novelty of the setting in which they take place, one marked by increasing concerns over the potential Soviet threat to Western Europe and be decreasing confidence in the military capacity, economic strength and political wisdom of the United States of America.[2]

Under these circumstances, there is an understandable tendency on the part of West Europeans to dissociate themselves from the United States on some issues, to oppose it on others and to question its judgement on all. And there is an equally understandable tendency on the part of Americans to insist that the

I would like to express my appreciation to Mr. George Glass and to Mr. Richard K. Herrmann, Instructor in the Department of Political Science, University of Pittsburgh, for a critical and constructive reading of my original text.

West Europeans adopt US policies, partly because European support may be essential to the success of those policies, partly because of a belief that this constitutes "leadership". Unfortunately, as Edward Heath points out, ". . . in the realm of security policy. . . no international rules exist for ironing out such differences of opinion as do occur and for preventing them from repeatedly generating political controversy."[3] And political controversy may not only further exacerbate German-American relations but also weaken the strength and erode the cohesion of the Atlantic Alliance, which already suffers from the partial dissociation of France, from the rift between Greece and Turkey, and from the splits between Belgium, Holland, and Denmark and other members of NATO on such crucial matters as force modernization.

Obviously, it would be impossible, in a necessarily brief paper, to examine every issue dividing West Germany and the United States, so I propose to concentrate on those relating to security policy.[4] In an attempt to further focus the discussion, I will deal only with four issues: varying interpretations of the Soviet threat; contrasting approaches to deterrence of aggression in Europe; differing definitions of detente; and divergent views on the importance of arms limitations. After describing and comparing the policies of the two countries on these issues, I will attempt to identify the structural, situational and procedural factors influencing American positions, as well as the more transitory attitudinal variables. And finally, I will try to differentiate betweeen the more or less fixed influences on American thinking and those which are mutable, with a view to establishing the limits of change — and hence of congruence — in security policies.

2. Current Issues in Security Policy

As indicated earlier, differences between the United States and the Federal Republic of Germany over security policy are not new. In the past, the two allies have held divergent views on strategic doctrine, as they did from roughly 1963 to 1967 with respect to the US-proposed doctrine of flexible response. They have disagreed on political issues, as they did in 1973 with respect to both basic American policy in the Middle East and with respect to the use of German bases by American transport planes carrying supplies to Israel. The two countries have been engaged in a long-standing controversy over burden sharing, manifested at various times by questions of German payment of support costs for American troops, of German participation in the operation of American depots and maintenance facilities and, above all, of the percentage of the Gross National Product of the FRG which should be allocated for defense.[5] The two countries have also had problems in adopting and implementing common policies with respect to weapons procurement (as in the case of the neutron bomb) and with respect to weapons control, as in the case of the late and unlamented MLF

(Multi-lateral Nuclear Force). Each of these has its own history, as has each of the current issues I will discuss; the question is whether there are any common influences underlying these and other differences between the United States and West Germany.

Before attempting to answer that question, I would like to look at the policies of the two allies on current security issues, chosen so as to fit the categories listed in Mr. Steadman's definition: the structure and deployment of military forces, budgets and/or matters of high policy affecting the military. Those specific issues picked for discussion were chosen partly because they are important partly because of the extent of divergencies on these issues, and partly because of the depth and intensity of feeling about them. While I recognize that other – and perhaps better – choices might be made, I hope that these will serve the intended purpose.

Varying Interpretations of the Soviet Threat

The United States and the Federal Republic of Germany, along with the other members of the Atlantic Alliance, generally agree that the Soviet Union is engaged in a long-term, large-scale program for the modernization of its armed forces and that this modernization extends across the board, to include strategic nuclear forces, tactical nuclear forces, ground and air forces and the Soviet Navy. They agree further that these improvements, if not checked or off-set, could pose a number of threats to the security of the West. To be more specific, there are fears that these on-going programs would enable the Soviet Union to smash or overrun NATO defenses in Europe, either by means of a surprise attack with forces already in place or after some degree of mobilization; to determine the course and nature of any conflict in Europe, if not its outcome, by applying superior military capabilities at successive levels of conflict: conventional, tactical nuclear and theater nuclear; to deter the use of the American strategic deterrent by the threat to devastate the United States and/or to launch a highly effective disarming strike against the land-based complements of that deterrent: ICBMs, bombers and missile submarines in port; to interfere with the sea lines of communication of the Western Allies, not only in time of war but perhaps in time of "peace", by mining critical passages, by intercepting vulnerable tankers and cargo vessels or by turning over to proxies weapons with which these could perform the same tasks; perhaps to match – or even to overmatch – Western forces in crucial areas such as the Persian-Arabian Gulf and the Indian Ocean, thereby making their own intervention in adjacent countries less risky and that of the United States more so; and in these areas, as well as in Europe, to reap the benefits accruing to the possessor of superior military power: respect, influence and the modification of political behavior, perhaps even to the extent of "self-Finlandization".[6]

Surprisingly enough, there are few or no differences between the US and the FRG with respect to the size and scope of the Soviet armament program nor even with respect to the potential consequences if it is not halted or offset. There are, however, divergent opinions concerning both Soviet motivations for the arms build-up and the likelihood that it will be self-limiting. Many officials and defense analysts in the United States see the Soviet Union as seeking an exploitable military superiority, a view shared by many in the Christian Democratic Union/Christian Social Union in West Germany. These same individuals deny the validity of the argument that Soviet military measures are a response to American ones (as do some among the Liberal Democrats and Social Democrats), maintain that the USSR will continue its force improvements until convinced that the West will match or overmatch them and assert that the Soviet Union is, therefore, an "irresponsible partner" in arms control negotiations and other political attempts to insure peace and stability in Europe. Conversely, the Liberal Democrats (FDP) and the center group of the Social Democrats (SPD) see the Soviet Union as aiming at the attainment of a military balance, after which its program of force modernization will slow or stop, and consequently deem it a "responsible partner" in arms control negotiations, which should be approached in a business-like fashion of give and take. And the left wing of the SPD goes so far as to say that the Soviet build-up is essentially a defensive one.[7]

To these differences in attributing motivation must be added those over the measures which should be taken by the West. The US response has tended in some sense to be an "across-the-board" one, marked by major increases in the defense budget scheduled to rise from $137 billion in FY 80 to $171 billion in FY 81 (and to $367 billion by 1986); by the creation of a Rapid Deployment Force of approximately 100000 men with appropriate arms, equipment and transport; by the dispatch of additional army brigades and air force squadrons to Europe and by the agreement to finance the deployment of longe-range theater nuclear forces in Central Europe. But the element receiving the most attention, if not the most money, is the strategic deterrent, where efforts are under way not only to reduce the vulnerability of some components but also to give them a war-fighting capability, in both of these ways enhancing their credibility. To these ends, the Carter Administration embarked on a program to re-deploy some 200 ICBMs from single silos to multiple launch sites, to place in these launch sites a new, more powerful and more accurate Minuteman X, to upgrade the 300 Minutemen III Missiles remaining in hardened silos, to deploy some 2400 ALCMs (Air Launched Cruise Missiles), etc. And the Reagan Administration is considering further additions, such as the production of a new strategic bomber. More significantly, the United States has codified a series of shifts in targeting doctrine and in concepts of deterrence by issuing Presidential Directive 59, which provides for selective strikes against crucial target systems in the Soviet Union (centers of political control, military depots and other logistic support facilities, troop cantonments and concentration areas, and so on) and for controlled strikes over time against missile silos, bomber bases, submarine pens, surface-to-air missile systems and other elements of Soviet strategic nuclear forces, as well as for a civil defense program comparable in concept, if not in actuality, to its Soviet conterpart. Thus a major share of US intellectual and financial resources are devoted to refurbishing both US strategic nuclear forces and US concepts for their employment.

Broadly speaking, many political leaders, officials and defense analysts in the FRG share the concerns of their American counterparts with respect to the impact of the Soviet arms build-up on the credibility of the US deterrent. They see SALT II as not only codifying the achievement of strategic parity by the Soviet Union but, as Chancellor Schmidt put it, neutralizing both US and Soviet strategic nuclear capabilities.[8] These West Germans, like other Europeans, judge that the acquisition by the Soviets of significant counterforce capabilities could tilt the strategic balance in their favor, and recognize the need to keep that balance stable — though some would prefer to see this done by a process of "leveling down" through strategic arms limitations rather than by the kinds of force increases described above. Moreover, many West Germans would probably share the concern of Mr. Edward Heath, former Primer Minister of Great Britain, that the "exaggerated fear" in some quarters of the United States of the strategic and political consequences which would flow from the impending vulnerability of America's land-based nuclear system might result in diverting "unnecessarily large resources into reinforcing America's central strategic arsenal to the detriment of the far more serious weaknesses in her capability for conventional defense"[9] — or of other weaknesses in NATO defenses.

The one that political elites in the FRG felt most keenly was the lack of any counter to Soviet long-range nuclear weapons, which could cover Western Europe, and specifically to the new SS-20 IRBM, which was seen as particularly threatening because of its mobility, its accuracy and the fact that it carried not one but three independently targetable warheads. As Hans Rühle, Director of the Social Science Research Institute of the Konrad Adenauer Foundation, put it, "[Soviet] superiority is not, at least for the time being, in the form that it has been, and continues to be, perceived by the United States; it is not taking shape through unilateral expansion of the strategic-nuclear capabilities directed against the United States, but rather through the creation of a nuclear imbalance in Western Europe, the region most important to the security of the United States".[10] Their basic concern was that the Soviet Union had not only gone a long way toward decoupling the US strategic deterrent from the defense of Europe but had created a superior medium-range potential which the West was unable to counterbalance by any comparable force.[11] In the eyes of many West Germans and other Europeans this meant that the Soviet Union could practice escalation dominance, by ensuring that no war in Europe went beyond the tactical nuclear level — and even that was fraught with risk for NATO. By virtue of this, the USSR could also exercise crisis control: the Allies would be very reluctant to take measures which could result in a war that they could not fight, much less win.[12] Under these circumstances, the Soviet Union might be able to practice "nuclear blackmail" or, at the very least, to exert significant influence on political decisions by the European members of NATO.

Whether or not these concerns were valid is perhaps questionable, since they assumed both a rationality in decision-making which is rare and a rashness on the part of Soviet leaders which is perhaps even rarer. Nevertheless, they did — and do — exist. And they have led both Germans and other West Europeans to seek to redress the Euro-strategic balance by a judicious mixture of arms control and force improvements, with priority to the former.

Contrasting Approaches to Deterrence

These differing perceptions of the importance of the several aspects of the military balance reflect and epitomize divergent American and West German views as to how best to rule out the possibility of Soviet aggression in Europe. Both countries agree that such aggression is possible, though they may disagree as to its likelihood or as to the causative factors. Both accept the need to deter potential agression through the development of countervailing military power, which must necessarily be deployed across a number of levels in order to meet a spectrum of threats. However, they differ with respect to the best way to practice deterrence, i.e. "to hinder or to prevent action by fear of consequences, or by difficulty, risk, unpleasantness, etc."[13]

Leaving aside "unpleasantness", which scarcely fits into discussions of war and peace, the United States, which initially emphasized deterrence through punishment, now stresses deterrence through difficulty, i.e., through defense. At the strategic level this has led, as we have already seen, to programs for the development of a strategic nuclear war-fighting capability and to doctrines for the employment of the resultant forces against a broad range of targets in the USSR, if necessary over an extended period of time. At theater level it has meant, first and foremost, an American emphasis on conventional forces sufficiently strong, well-enough prepared and properly deployed to meet and check any Soviet assault, if at all possible without recourse to nuclear weapons. It has also meant that nuclear weapons, if and when they are employed, are to be used to blunt the armored spearheads of Warsaw Pact forces (hence the large numbers of nuclear capable artillery pieces and short-range missiles like Lance) or to break the shaft of the spear by strikes on advancing reinforcements, supporting weapons, supply points, and so forth.

The United States has, of course, agreed to enhance the risk of escalation by employing theater nuclear forces against targets deep in Eastern Europe, or even in the Soviet homeland, as set forth in NATO plans. This is not, however, a desirable response, since escalation by the United States involves the reciprocal risk of escalation by the Soviet Union and hence is very much a two-edged sword. Accordingly, the United States has sought:

1. To minimize the possibility that it might be called on to carry out such strikes by the priority accorded to the development of conventional forces and, to a lesser extent, of short-range tactical nuclear forces;

2. To insure that the means of delivering strikes deep into the territory of the Warsaw Pact countries are either themselves American or under American control — a policy which has been only recently and partially modified by the acknowledgement, at the Ottawa Conference of 1978, that British and French regional nuclear forces did contribute to deterrence in Europe.

For its part, the Federal Republic of Germany approaches deterrence with a keen awareness that defense, whether with conventional weapons or nuclear ones, could mean the destruction of West Germany. As numerous spokesmen have pointed out, two-thirds of the 60 million West Germans live within a 120 mile strip along its borders with the German Democratic Republic and Czechoslovakia and hence are vulnerable to invading armies or attacking air forces. As Josef Joffe puts its, "Any [conventional] war will be fought primarily in and over German territory. Thus, if war comes, West Germany will be its prime battlefield and victim. Any successful defence, even if achieved, will be hardly distinguishable from defeat".[14] And as Helmut Schmidt said almost twenty years ago, "Those who think that Europe can be defended by the mass use of such [tactical nuclear] weapons will not defend Europe, but destroy it."[15]

These opinions, both of which are still current in West German thinking, are reflected in the force posture and force plans of the Federal Republic. Conventional forces have been developed and deployed partly because the FRG is persuaded that these can contribute to deterrence but more largely because they are a way of binding the United States to the Atlantic Alliance. However, anyone looking at the size, the weapon stocks, and the mobilization plans of the *Bundeswehr* will immediately recognize that it is not preparing to fight a large-scale conventional conflict nor indeed to wage *any* protracted war. (In the event of war, the German Air Force plans to close down its training schools and to form pilots and aircraft into operational squadrons. When these are destroyed, there will be no more.) Nor, despite its contribution to NATO short-range tactical nuclear forces, is West Germany prepared to fight a nuclear war, especially one in which the bulk of the weapons are detonated on its own territory or on that of its fellow nationals to the east. As General Johannes Steinhoff stated on German national television in 1977, "I am in favor of retaining nuclear weapons as political tools but not permitting them to become battlefield weapons . . . I am firmly opposed to their tactical use on our soil."[16]

What the West Germans *are* interested in is deterrence through risk — specifically, through the risk that any Soviet military venture would lead quickly and directly to a strategic nuclear exchange whose effects would far outweigh any possible gains from even a successful war in Europe. In attempting to enhance this risk, however, the West Germans run up against a polylemma. One horn is that they themselves are barred, both by treaty obligations and by the political consequences of violating that treaty, from themselves acquiring nuclear weapons and thus threatening escalation on their own. A second is that they have found no way to engage British and French regional nuclear forces in this role: the best-laid plans for an Allied Nuclear Force or an Anglo-French Nuclear Force with a German financier on the Board of Directors have, like those of the mice in Robert Burns' poem, "gang aft agley". The third horn is that the FRG cannot, as already noted, depend on the US to wage all-out nuclear war on its behalf by initiating direct attacks with strategic nuclear forces on the Soviet homeland. Nor can it count in advance on the United States launching those long-range theater nuclear weapons stationed in or near Western Europe. As Theo Sommer has pointed out, it would be "naive to assume that an American president reluctant to push the big button would lightly launch American nuclear weapons stationed in Germany, Italy, United Kingdom, The Netherlands or Belgium against the Soviet Union. For how could an American president ever be sure that Russian retaliation for the destruction of Minsk would be limited to Munich and not extend to Minneapolis?"[17] Hence West Germany is reduced to trying to redress the theater balance (thereby improving its military position) without any assurance that this will more closely involve the United States in its defense and thus enhance the credibility of the deterrent on which it must necessarily rely.

Divergent Views on Arms Limitations

Here, moreover, the FRG runs up against another problem: the United States has both differing opinions on how to redress the theater balance and different priorities with respect to the conclusion of arms control agreements. Basically, the United States has sought to bolster long-range theater nuclear forces in NATO Europe rather than to reduce those in the hands of the Soviet Union. To this end it conceived and promoted the idea of deploying such weapons — in part, it must be admitted, as a response to expressions of concern over theater imbalances by Helmut Schmidt and other German leaders. It developed the weapons to be deployed: the Pershing II short-range ballistic missile, which can strike at targets one thousand miles away, and the ground-launched cruise missile, which in its current configuration has a range of fifteen hundred miles, readily extensible to twenty-five hundred. It has offered to finance the estimated $5 billion it will cost to develop and procure the 572 launch vehicles scheduled for installation in Europe, if the Allies will provide the necessary basing facilities. Perhaps most significantly, the United States took a fairly stiff stand in the NATO ministerial meeting of December 1979 against suggestions to defer the decision on deployment of these weapons pending negotiations on arms control with the Soviet Union, or to set conditional ceilings on their deployment, contingent on a slow-down or stoppage of Soviet construction of SS-20s. This stand has become even stiffer under the Reagan Administration, with Secretary of State Haig suggesting not only that these negotiations should not start until the

Allies took "the corrective actions [in the form of TNF deployment] that are called for in our own defense . . ." but that "the concept of linkage would be applied to assure that we have corrected the difficulties we are experiencing with respect to Soviet global interventionism."[18] And though Mr. Haig has agreed, under pressure from Italy, West Germany and other allies, to initiate negotiations on SALT III in 1981 he has extracted from them a pledge concerning "linkage" which does not bode well for the success of those negotiations.

Conversely, the Federal Republic of Germany, though it also urged that NATO agree to deploy long-range TNFs, has been actively seeking to redress theater imbalances through arms control rather than (or, at most, along with) force build-ups. Thus Chancellor Schmidt, in the 1977 Alastair Buchan Memorial Lecture, expressed a preference for arms control as a means of creating parity within the European theater, a preference which he pressed within NATO and in bilateral discussions with United States officials; in fact, as late as mid-October of 1979, two months before the NATO decision, Mr. Schmidt was quoted as saying that if East-West negotiations on theater nuclear forces were successful, it might not be necessary "to develop all of them, perhaps only many fewer [than 572], and in ideal cases absolutely none.[19] And it was he who, on his trip to Moscow in June of 1980, persuaded Mr. Brezhnev to reverse his earlier stance of no negotiations without cancellation of the NATO decision on deployment and to agree to the preliminary discussion on limiting theater nuclear weapons which are now under way in Geneva. Thus it can be fairly argued that Mr. Schmidt, and perhaps a majority of the SPD, are seemingly less anxious to acquire a deep-strike capability against the Soviet Union than they are to use the threat of obtaining such a capability to wrest concessions from Moscow on the SS-20 and other theater nuclear weapons.[20]

One problem with the approach favored by the SPD is that Moscow, by attaching to its acceptance of negotiations conditions such as the inclusion of US forward-based systems, could render any agreement on theater nuclear weapons unlikely, if not impossible. Another is that Washington, in other forums or for other purposes, might be willing to slow down, reduce or even reverse the program for the deployment of long-range theater nuclear forces in Western Europe. Since the Soviets regard these forces as extensions of US strategic nuclear forces, placed in Europe to circumvent the restrictions imposed by SALT II, they are likely to bargain for constraints on these weapons as part of any new agreement for the limitation of strategic armaments. To the extent that the United States is interested in an agreement providing for meaningful reductions in central strategic systems — especially in those which contribute to the vulnerability of American ICBMs — it might be tempted to trade away European-based systems. The end result would be to deprive the FRG (and other allies) of the possibility of offering these weapons as bargaining chips in any Soviet-American negotiations or of deploying them as off-sets to the constantly increasing Soviet theater nuclear forces.

To an American, such an outcome to future negotiations is not very likely, and perhaps even less likely following Mr. Reagan's election than before it, but to some Europeans it undoubtedly seems plausible. Certainly, similar fears were widespread during the negotiations on SALT II, both with respect to the non-circumvention clause (which seemingly limited the transfer of weapons and nuclear technology to the European allies) and with respect to Article II of the Protocol, which forbids until the end of 1981 the deployment of land and sea-based cruise missiles with ranges in excess of 600 kilometers. Even more distressing, especially to West Germans, was the fact that the United States seemingly ignored Soviet weapons systems targeted against Western Europe, such as the SS-20 IRBM and the Backfire medium bomber, the former not being discussed at all and the latter being considered only in the context of its intercontinental delivery capabilites. Thus there are, in German eyes, precedents for concern lest SALT III (or even the modified SALT II which President Reagan announced he intends to negotiate) advance American interests at the expense of European ones.

To some extent, the position of the Federal Republic smacks of eating one's cake and having it too. On the one hand, the FRG seeks freedom to deploy long-range theater nuclear forces as a means of increasing coupling, and for this reason opposes constraints on these weapons, whether these originate with the United States or arise out of any arms control agreements. On the other hand, the West German themselves are prepared to bargain away these weapons for changes in theater balances and for improvements in their relations with the Soviet Union. Perhaps one clue to these ambivalent, if not contradictory, approaches lies in the fact that the Federal Republic of Germany is pushing both deterrence and detente, and that it sees the latter as deriving not only from the maintenance of allied strength and cohesion but also from "military détente", i.e. from agreements on the limitation of armaments. To quote Joffe again, "These two commitments — to deterrence as well as to detente — do not necessarily clash, but they do pose painful dilemmas for German foreign policy. A strong deterrence posture should be taken, by all means, but not at the risk of endangering SALT and alienating the Soviet Union. A flexible detente and SALT posture are also viable but not at the cost of bargaining away Western ability to retain 'escalation control' ".[21]

Differing Definitions of Détente

The dilemmas noted by Mr. Joffe derive to some extent, as he has stated, from efforts by the FRG to reconcile deterrence and arms control and to use both to promote détente. (As with the old shell game, however, the pea of peace and stability may not be found under any of these three headings.) But West German dilemmas derive also, as Pierre Hassner has stated, from "conflicts of priorities and resource allocation in defense budgets, arms control proposals, and technological transfers to the east — all implying different attitudes toward the Soviet Union".[22] Perhaps most significantly, they derive from the fact that West Germany cannot afford to abandon détente, which helps to secure West Berlin, makes the partition of the German nation more tolerable in human terms and, above all, contributes to stability in Europe. Any falling back from détente would mean not only the loss or the jeopardy of these interests but, as Chancellor Schmidt said earlier "a return to the Cold War from which nothing is to be gained".[23]

A West German emphasis on detente reflects the desire not only to retain the gains of the past but also to make additional ones in the future: expansion of its trade with the East, extension of people-to-people contacts, perhaps even the liberalization of East European societies and the loosening of ties between these and the Soviet Union. Whatever the realism of these hopes, they add to the incentives to promote détente, despite the chill cast by the Soviet incursion into Afghanistan. Furthermore, they encourage a policy which not only largely dissociates détente in Europe from events elsewhere but which displays marked resistance to sweeping proposals to sacrifice détente in Europe to those same events by breaking off political contacts, reducing cultural exchanges, freezing on-going arms control efforts, and so on. As Theo Sommer suggests, "If the Europeans should want to put pressure on the Kremlin, then it will not be so much a reprisal for the Afghan adventure as to gain some leverage against a Soviet leadership that refuses to talk arms control with the West".[24]

Conversely, many Americans have become dissatisfied with the paltry rewards of détente, which they expected to result in a codification of superpower rules of behavior along the lines of the draft written by the United States but which seemed instead only to give the USSR greater freedom of action. They have become increasingly suspicious of Soviet motives in building up their armed forces and of Soviet intentions with regard to the use of those forces — as many Soviets are of American motivations and intentions. Above all — and unlike the Europeans — these Americans did not believe that conflict in one area could be separated from stability in another; they saw détente as indivisible. And when conflicts did arise (as, most recently, they have in and over Afghanistan) the United States tended to alter its behavior in Europe as well as its behavior in the Middle East, i.e., to practice linkage.

Even more importantly, it tended to emphasize military responses to what it regarded as military pressures by the USSR, the Rapid Deployment Force being a case in point. This response pattern also spilled over into Europe, as illustrated by the strengthening of American ground and air forces in that theater and by the preference for arms build-ups over arms control described above.

This response pattern put Washington, to some extent, in conflict with Bonn, since the FRG, while prepared to follow the US lead on some political measures (such as the boycott of the Olympic Games in Moscow) was not prepared to reduce interactions with the Soviet Union to the extent that the United States was. (In fact, even while Chancellor Schmidt was in Moscow last June condemning the Soviet incursion into Afghanistan his ministers in Bonn were signing a long-term trade agreement with the USSR.) Most significantly the FRG was not, as discussed previously, prepared to change the relative priority given arms control and other measures to promote détente in Europe over those designed to further strengthen defense. One analyst summed up these differences neatly by saying that, ". . . whereas Bonn wants détente *cum* defense, Washington wants defense *cum* detente, punctuated by periodic oaths of allegiance from Bonn. This role reversal, when compared to to the days of the Adenauer government, is a source of doubt and suspicion between Washinton and Bonn whose depths are far from plumbed".[25]

Security Issues and Geman-American Relations

In sum, the US and FRG differ over détente, as they do over the interpretation of the Soviet threat, over concepts of deterrence and over arms limitations. In some instances these differences are sharp and exchanges between the two governments are correspondingly acerbic, as were those in advance of Chancellor Schmidt's visit to Moscow in June of 1980. (Exchanges might have been more acerbic if French President Giscard d' Estaing had not met with Mr. Brezhnev prior to the time that Mr. Schmidt did so, and thus become an earlier target for criticism.) In other instances, differences between the two states have either been left unresolved (as in the case of approaches to deterrence) or worked out pragmatically, as have prodedures for negotiations on long-range theater nuclear forces.

I do, however, think that there are a number of respects in which German-American relations (and with them, cohesion of the Atlantic Alliance) may be in jeopardy. One of these is over detente, where differences are likely to grow to the extent that the United States continues to stress linkage policy and the Federal Republic of Germany does not, or the United States emphasizes military responses to Soviet moves to the extent that it currently seems inclined to do.[26] Another may be over the substantive aspects of arms control negotiations, since the FRG is at one and the same time anxious to push further and faster than the US on M(B)FR and on reductions in present and programmed long-range tactical nuclear forces and is concerned about future US policies on SALT II/$\frac{1}{2}$. A third area of potential difference is over future measures for the defense of West Europe, where the increasing American preference for the development of warfighting capabilities may clash with West German insistence on maintaining a deterrent posture and where interallied disputes as to whether the FRG is allocating sufficient resources to defense may intensify under the Reagan Administration.

Obviously, these fissures need not open; in fact, one purpose of this paper is to gauge the likelihood that they will do so. Although this could be affected by a number of developments, the current inquiry is limited to those arising from prospective changes in US security policy — and, even further, from changes related to American perceptions of the international environment and from domestic influences on foreign and defense policy. Hence, before looking specifically at prospective American accomodations to, or divergencies from, West German views on key security issues it is necessary to examine the kinds of variables that impact on American security policy in Europe.

3. Influences on American Positions

In the Introduction to their book, *Structure and Process in International Politics*, Hopkins and Mansbach say "The task of simple survival is bound up with the ability to think accurately about the unknown and sometimes even the unknowable".[27] This sentence both defines the nature and indicates the difficulty of my task, even though that task is limited to security policy rather than to policy as a whole and even though it deals only with selected issues in German security policy rather than with all those that could be of concern. Moreover, even if I agreed with everything that Hopkins and Mansbach say on this subject (which I do not), I could not replicate their book here. What I propose by way of substitution is to discuss some of the influences on US security policy deriving from the structure of the international system, from domestic factors and from the process whereby these interact.

Structure from an American Perspective

Most American defense analysts and government officials would agree with Snyder and Diesing that military power and potential are *the* determinants of structure in the international system.[28] In their view, this makes for a bipolar world; no third country can match the US or the USSR militarily and none is likely to do so for at least a generation — unless, of course, the two superpowers destroy each other!

Whether those individuals agree also with the theory that in a bipolar world rivalry between the two superpowers is structurally ordained is immaterial: that rivalry exists. The Soviet Union is seen as ideologically hostile and as politically opposed to the United States, as trying to sap US strength, erode US influence and undermine the American position in the world at large.[29] In consequence, it is widely held that the United States must, in its own interests as well as those of its allies, meet this challenge, whatever form it takes.

There are, of course, differences of opinion as to the form of the challenge, with some arguing that the constraints imposed by the international system inhibit the USSR from the untrammelled use of force (as they do the United States) and others insisting that the only constraint that matters is countervailing force. Nevertheless, even those who deem the Soviet Union cautious and restrained in its competition for power and influence, or who believe that domestic considerations and internal developments in the USSR may mute that competition, recognize the danger that growing Soviet military capabilities may change Soviet behavior for the worse[30] — as, some say, has been true in the case of Afghanistan.

This judgement about the bipolarity of the international system and the nature of the competition with the USSR has, it seems to me, a number of implications for US security policy. One is that it may strengthen the feeling that the United States has both the mission and the responsibility of containing Soviet "expansionism", inasmuch as no other country can (or shows signs of wanting to) undertake this task. Another is that it may incline the United States to be impatient with those who hold different views of Soviet motivations and intentions, who question the necessity for and the viability of the American mission, or who cavil at the way it is carried out. A third is that it may induce the United States to judge its allies in terms of their support for the American "mission". And a fourth is that it may cause the United States to discount the situational variables which make some among the allies hesitant to extend that support. (In fact, one West German academician expresses perfectly the American position when he wrote that ". . . the states of Western Europe cannot in the long run expect the United States to maintain combat troops and the necessary transport capabilities, or carry the necessary financial and political costs of military bases singlehandedly only in order to secure the West Europeans against threats to their flanks".[31]) And in this attitude are buried, not too deeply, the seeds of trouble.

Nuclear Weapons and Alliance Relations

For over twenty years the United States has sought to insure the security of its allies and to safeguard its vital interests by the threat to utilize nuclear weapons in their defense, should this prove necessary. This threat was backed up by, and made credible by, the development of nuclear forces, strategic and tactical, which could inflict on any adversary enormous damage, one classic formulation being that the United States could "bomb'em back to the Stone Age". For most of these twenty years American policy-makers were well aware that the USSR, against whom this threat was mainly directed, also possessed nuclear forces which could wreak enormous damage in the United States, should they ever be directed against it. Thus the object of the game was to deter the use of force, or meaningful threats to use force, without ever having to undergo a nuclear exchange — or even to run a high risk of such a "happening".

As applied to NATO this meant that the United States pursued two contradictory policies. On the one hand it sought, by pledges, by the deployment of nuclear-capable weapons, and by the adoption of doctrines implying that nuclear weapons would be, could be or might be used in the event of Warsaw Pact aggression to make the deterrent credible to allies and adversaries alike.[32] On the other hand it endeavored, by building up conventional defenses and by maintaining ambiguities in NATO doctrine, to avoid having to use nuclear weapons if it could and it tried to retain in its own hands the decision whether, when and how to employ these weapons, should they prove necessary.[33]

Whatever West Europeans may think of this approach, it makes perfect sense from an American perspective — and perhaps even in terms of deterrence theory. It enables the United States to put the full weight of its nuclear capabilities behind the NATO allies without having to fear that this will inevitably mean strategic nuclear war. It enables it to avoid pledging responses which would not be believed (such as that of an all-out strategic strike in the event of Soviet aggression in Europe) while at the same time creating uncertainties as to whether this might not happen if the Soviets *did* attack. And perhaps most importantly, it enables American decision-makers to deal with threats to stability and risks to peace with some assurance, which they might not possess if the deterrent were set on a hair-trigger.

The approach does, however, have undersirable aspects. For one thing, the vagueness and inconsistencies of US policy may puzzle and anger West European leaders, cause them to lose confidence in the United States or otherwise adversely affect alliance relations. For a second, it may require the allies to increase and upgrade their armed forces, at heavy financial and political cost; if the conventional component of deterrent forces is to be meaningful it must be effective — and in today's world, effectiveness is expensive. For a third, it necessarily leaves the allies uncertain about the willingness of the United States to employ nuclear weapons in their defense and hence about the credibility of the deterrent. This in turn may aggravate their feelings of dependence, limit their freedom of of action vis-á-vis the United States and enhance their doubts about "decoupling". As one analyst summarized the issue, "It lay obviously in the European interest to insist on anchoring deterrence to the notion that any Soviet aggression, no matter how limited, would risk escalation to a strategic strike on the Soviet homeland. It remained in the American interest to hedge against that very risk."[34] And these divergencies remain, even though blurred by doctrines and programs intended to reassure both sides as to the outcome of any situation in which the threat to employ the US deterrent might be invoked.

Trends in American Opinion

It does not take a specialist in opinon polls or elite surveys to recognize that American attitudes on security are changing. The tone of articles in professional journals, the tenor of speeches in Congress, the claims or denunciations of rival candidates for office all indicate an increasing belief that the USSR is threatening US interests and a growing concern over the ability of the United States to cope militarily with these threats. Perhaps more importantly, these attitudes have been reflected in the approval of weapons systems, in proposals to accelerate the new procurement of equipment and the rebuilding of stocks of munitions and in hikes in the defense budget.

These manifestations of concern are, moreover, borne out by more structured assessments of attitudes. According to one (not unique) survey both the public at large and "national leaders"[35] perceived a growing military threat from the Soviet Union and many among them (72 % of the "attentive public", i.e. those who regularly seek out information on public affairs) believe that the US is falling behind the USSR militarily. In consequence, 52 % of the attentive public polled in 1978 favored an increase in the defense budget, as did 19 % of the non-attentive public and 31 % of the national leaders.[36]

Perhaps more significantly, between 1974 and 1978 the percentage of the public at large who deemed defense spending too low jumped from 13 % to 32 % and the percentage viewing it as too high dropped from 32 % to 16 %.[37] And along with these changes went an increase in the percentage of respondents willing to use force to protect key US interests; for example, 92 % of the national leaders and 54 % of the public favored sending troops if the Soviets invaded Western Europe, compared to 77 % and 39 % respectively in 1974.[38]

In general, these trends both reflect and reinforce the sense of mission mentioned previously, indicating broad support for measures to contain the Soviet Union. As far as NATO is concerned they are not, however, unambiguous, either in their nature or in their potential implications. To give just two illustrations:

1. Although the percentage of those willing to increase the US commitment to NATO rose from 5 % in 1974 to 13 % for the public and 21 % for leaders in 1978, this apparently reflected existing relationships rather than perceptions of threat; from 8 to 20 times as many respondents deemed the Middle East "the biggest foreign policy problem."[39]
2. The three major foreign policy goals for the United States were listed as keeping up the value of the dollar, securing adequate supplies of energy and protecting the jobs of American workers, "defending our allies' security" ranked seventh, just behind "combating world hunger."[40]

Drawing the conclusions about the policy outcomes from elite and public opinions is both difficult and risky: we simply do not know enough about the process. If, however, one is willing to plunge in where angels fear to tread it is possible to infer that there will be continued improvements in the capabilities of American forces in, or destined for, Europe, an outcome which should gladden the hearts of many. At the same time, both the priority given to economic issues and the heightened sense of threat are likely to lead to intensified demands for contributions from all parties, i.e. for more burden-sharing by the European allies. (This is particularly true in that the speedy dispatch of sizeable US forces to the Middle East can, in the short run, only be achieved by drawing on American units in Western Europe; for this reason, the allies have been asked to fill any resultant gaps from their own resources.) Hence, increases in US defense expenditures for some purposes may generate pressures for corresponding increases in West European expenditures for other purposes, in an American version of "the division of labor".

Presidential "Style" and Security Policy

As Sarkesian points out, "the President is at the center of the national security policy process" — and hence plays a dominant role in the formulation of that policy.[41] This means that the personality and character of the President, his views on the role and use of force, his ability to formulate and implement a coherent security policy and the ways in which he arrives at that policy, in short, his "style", are extraordinarily important.

In theoretical sense, personality is important because it embodies a "system of predispositions of psychological and social behavior" which shape the perceptions and world view of political actors.[42] In the case of Mr. Carter, he brought to the White House views supportive of human rights and favorable to arms control which grew to some extent out of his religious convictions. Moreover, he tended, according to some analysts, to view the national interests of the United States in "moral" terms and to believe that morality is self-enforcing, i.e., that political leaders can be brought to share this sense of what is right and hence, automatically, to act on that basis. Combined with this was a sense of self-confidence, which may in part have stemmed from the predilections mentioned above. To quote Sarkesian, what emerged was a man "absolutely convinced of his own strength of character, integrity and moral "good", who attempts to apply these individual characteristics to solving the problems of American national security".[43]

Mr. Carter's emphasis on the importance of moral and ethical values, and his belief that these would provide a new and more effective thrust to American foreign policy, obviously would lead him to downgrade force as an instrument of policy, as indeed he did. He entered office proclaiming that his goal was the abolition of all nuclear weapons and his first major act was the development of a proposal for strategic arms limitations more far-reaching (if also less equitable) than those flowing out of the Vladivostok Agreement of 1974.[44] He campaigned on a pledge to cut the defense budget by 5 % and although this promise was not literally carried out, he did revise downward President Ford's proposed budget; in fact, some of Mr. Carter's critics have charged him with reducing the defense budget in real terms and as a percentage of the GNP and with deferring or cancelling weapons systems programs[45] — at least until the need to swing Senatorial votes on SALT II and the Soviet incursion into Afghanistan prompted a change of heart. And he has prided himself on maintaining the peace.[46]

These are neither ignoble goals nor mean accomplishments and their mention should not be taken as suggesting that they are. What they do suggest is that

Mr. Carter's security policy has been marked by some inherent contradictions, between personal preferences and political necessities, between his vision of the future and his inheritance of the past, and between his own sense of what should be done and that of some of his senior officials. Furthermore, it has been marked not only by wide-spread criticism (as noted above) but by marked differences with the Congress. Without ascribing causation to any of these factors, it is fair to say that the Administration's defense policy has been marked by simultaneous advances and retreats (as in the case of limitations on arms sales), by reversals of position on politically important issues (such as the Soviet "brigade" in Cuba) and by unilateral decisions, unilaterally arrived at, as with the decision on the "neutron bomb".

To some extent, these and other examples which came to mind may have stemmed from Mr. Carter's tendency to deal with specific issues, such as the "neutron bomb", in isolation, rather than in an overall context. They may have reflected his predilection, perhaps based on his prior political experience, to take individual initiatives on particular issues rather than to turn his un- doubted talents to the establishment of such a context, perhaps by the formu- lation of more comprehensive policies. Moreover, they may have been aggra- vated by the nature of his staff appointees, with none of his close and loyal associates really qualified to assist him on national security policy and with the individual who did have that responsibility himself more given to suggesting individual initiatives than to supervising the preparation of comprehensive policy options. In any event, some among the allies, allegedly including both Chancellor Schmidt and President Giscard d' Estaing, reportedly concluded that even after two years in office Mr. Carter was "to inexperienced and indici- sive" and that "The signals from the White House were confused and incon- sistent".[47] And this judgement can only have been confirmed by Mr. Carter's own conclusion, communicated on television later that same year, that his administration was floundering and that he himself needed to change his style!

It is too early to say what differences a President Reagan will make, but on the basis of observations to date one can say that Mr. Reagan, though also a "born-again Christian", has very different views concerning arms control, human rights and other "liberal" approaches to international politics than does Mr. Carter. In consequence, his approaches are likely to be less moralistic – though perhaps not less simplistic – than those of Mr. Carter. One can also say that Mr. Reagan, no less than Mr. Carter, seems to be convinced of the "rightness" of his views, which reflect deeply held values and long-standing attitudes. He has, however, shown some willingness to modify the ways in which his principles are put into practice and gives some evidence of pragmatism; in fact, one observer has commented that there are two Reagans, one "the rhetorical right-winger" and the other "the pragmatic practitioner of power".[48]

This pragmatism may be less evident with respect to security policy than in other areas. Mr. Reagan is seemingly convinced that the Soviet Union is im- placably hostile, that it respects force above all else, that the United States lacks the military capacity needed to constrain Soviet adventurism and that only "military superiority" will suffice to induce changes in Soviet behavior and in Soviet positions, as on strategic arms limitations.[49] In accordance with these convictions, he will probably adopt a military-oriented security policy, marked by increases in defense budgets (and pressures for similar increases by the allies), by less emphasis on arms control, by a greater willingness to confront the Soviet Union, in and out of Europe, and so on — a policy which will please some of the allies (or some elements within some countries of the alliance) but not all. He may also seek to develop a more consistent and more comprehensive security policy, designed to give the United States a war-fighting capability at both strategic and operational levels and in all parts of the world; this could, of course, mean greater emphasis on conventional capabilities than many Europeans would like and perhaps greater attention to areas such as the Middle East at the expense of Europe. In short, Mr. Reagan's security policies may not be as appealing to the current government of the FRG as those which Mr. Carter sponsored — at least prior to December 1979.

Whether Mr. Reagan's "style" will be any more highly regarded than that of Mr. Carter is as yet an unanswerable question. On the one hand, Mr. Reagan is taking a very different tack to the process of organizing the Presidency by attempting to decentralize decision-making in the national government, as he did in California; by appointing a Counselor to coordinate the work of the half-dozen Cabinet-level officials on whom he will seemingly rely for advice; and by looking beyond his personal associates for members of his staff, as well as for high-level officials. On the other hand, the squabbles over "turf" among these same officials and the disputes over security policy between Secretary of State Haig and Secretary of Defense Weinberger indicate that the machinery of government is not yet running smoothly. Furthermore, Mr. Reagan himself has been prone to make statements (as on the importance of human rights or the status of Taiwan) which have subsequently had to be modified or withdrawn. Thus, even if one does not accept I. M. Destler's conclusion that American institutions encourage presidents to "become sources of uncertainty, discontinuity and idiosyncrasy",[50] there may be some doubt as to whether President Reagan can provide that firm and constant leadership which he (and others) seem essential to the success of American policy and to the re-establishment of American primacy in the Western Alliance.

The Policy Process and Security Policy in the United States

Although the President is the most important figure in the development of US security policy, he is not the only influence in that policy. Also involved are various agencies of the Executive Branch, such as State, Defense, Treasury, the Arms Control and Disarmament Agency and the National Security Council, with its staff; the Congress, which must appropriate monies for defense, approve major security programs (such as the construction of a new bomber) and ratify treaties or agreements; interest groups such as the Americans for SALT, the American Security Council and the Navy League; and individuals who either hold positions of power (as does Senator Charles Percy, Chairman of the Committee on Foreign Relations), aspire to them or simply seek to steer the country in directions which they think it should go. All this does not make for a coherent security policy; to quote Desmond Ball, "the American national security establishment is so large and consists of so many disparate groups, each with its own interests, perspectives, and quasi-autonomous power-political bases, and with varying responsibilities for each of these aspects of policy, that it would be most surprising if a single, coherent, comprehensive policy did emerge."[51]

The first of these "disparate groups" may be found within the Executive Branch itself. Quite understandably, the various agencies concerned have different perspectives on both issues and outcomes. For example, the officers of the armed services are professionally concerned with the possibility that they might have to fight a war and hence inclined to develop weapons and forces for that purpose, without attaching much importance to their implications for arms control or for detente. Where it is necessary to justify defense programs politically rather than militarily, they may do so in terms of deterrence through defense, rather than in terms of deterrence through risk, as does the goverment of the Federal Republic of Germany. And they may also be inclined to downgrade military requirements that stem from political directives but which are difficult to carry out operationally, as is true of the concept of "forward defense". (The Emperor Napoleon once asked one of his marshals who proposed to deploy troops in a cordon along the eastern frontiers of France whether he was attempting to stop an invasion or to catch smugglers.)

Morover, each of these agencies or offices seeks to maximize its influence on policy while minimizing the influence of others (including the President) on its own policies and programs. In this endeavor some have been more successful than others; according to one study, the Department of Defense has largely insulated its decisions on weapons, programs and forces from inputs by the Department of State, the Arms Control and disarmament Agency and the NSC Staff.[52] Without suggesting that the latter agencies are the sole repositories of wisdom, one can say that largely unilateral decisions by the Department of Defense may result in policies which are different from, or at least not maximally supportive of, those pushed by the White House. More significantly, a process which permits such decisions suggests that the Presidency, despite thirty-five years of experimentation, has not yet been able to achieve the "comprehensive integration" of national security policy which was the aim of the National Security Act of 1947.[53]

Even if a new President could effectively achieve this aim, his success would not insure that American security policy would be comprehensive and integrated; in many areas the Congress is an "equal partner" — and not necessarily either a unitary or cooperative one. For one thing, Congress is ill-suited to the task of developing overall policy and tends to function more as a collection of special interests than as a cohesive body. (As an example, the SALT II agreements were endorsed by the Senate Committee on Foreign Relations but disapproved of by the Senate Committee on the Armed Forces.) For another, the party system in the United States does not provide a unifying mechanism, either within the Congress or between the Legislative and Executive Branches. For a third, Congress is jealous of its constitutional prerogatives, which lead it to question not only the process but the substance of Presidential decisions, with the Congressional rebuff to Mr. Nixon's attempt to supply arms to the rebels in Angola illustrative of both.

The difficulties of obtaining approval from a particularistic Congress for a cohesive and consistent policy are aggravated by the fact that the Congress is a "sounding board" for special interest groups, in and out of government. Although overall American participation in political life is low, such groups are numerous, active and influential. They exercise that influence not only through participation in elections but through fund-raising, the use of the media and lobbying. In all four ways, these groups impact on individual Congressmen and Senators, while through lobbying (i.e., the provision of information, testimony before committees, arguments on the merits of proposals, etc.) they affect directly the making of Congressional policy. In this latter role, external interest groups are joined by bureaucratic ones, which can frequently achieve their aims by "end-running" the President and appealing to the Congress — in fact, the Joint Chiefs of Staff are charged by law with giving the Congress their "professional opinions" even when these differ from those of their civilian superiors. And, in the aftermath of Vietnam, the power of the Congress to act on those opinions has increased relative to that of the President.

Furthermore, the attitudes, the opinions and the policy preferences of both President and Congress are affected by influential individuals outside of government. Although the United States government has never gone so far as to institutionalize a council of advisers (as Imperial Japan did with the Genro), Presidents since McKinley have had their "kitchen cabinets" of political cronies, their trusted advisers or their confidential emissaries, such as Colonel House. Moreover, in recent years Presidential advisers in foreign policy, as well as a number of key appointees within the Executive Branch, have tended to come from a fairly small number of academicians, bankers, businessmen and lawyers known colloquially as "the establishment". Although the "establishment" was never a formal one, and "members" differed among themselves on may issues, they tended to endorse an activist and generally "liberal" foreign policy and to support that policy both through public statements and in their extensive govermental service.[54] When, therefore, prominent members of this group approved a particular policy, its chances of being adopted improved; when they opposed it or were silent, its prospects diminished. This means that any analysis of security policy must take into account the predilections and personalities of leaders other than the President, whether these be members of the "establishment" such as Dr. Harold Brown and Mr. Paul Nitze,[55] political figures such as Senator Strom Thurmond of South Carolina and Senator Henry Jackson of the State of Washington or the Reverend Jerry Falwell, spokesman for the "Moral Majority".

Trying to translate process in the American system into judgements about security policy is, as the preceding discussion suggests, extraordinarily difficult. By and large, however, all of the elements mentioned seem to be moving in the same direction as Mr. Reagan (and the public at large): toward a more confrontationist foreign policy, accompanied and supported by expanded defense programs. To give just a few illustations of this movement, in the 1980 elections six "liberal" Senators and ten "moderate" ones lost their seats, to be replaced by twelve "conservatives" and four "moderates"; even if Mr. Reagan had not withdrawn the SALT II treaty from consideration, the current Senate would never have ratified it. As for the House of Representatives, it recently defeated overwhelmingly a proposal to cut the defense budget in order to safeguard social programs and seems likely to give Mr. Reagan all that (or more than) he wants in the way of vastly increased appropriations for the armed services. The senior officers in those services (whose role in decision-making has been upgraded by Secretary of Defense Weinberger) have, quite understandably, supported the Administration's plans for the expansion and up-grading of military capabilities, some of which (like the 600 ships projected for the Navy) have long been advocated. Many of the "establishment" figures have been replaced by men and women with different backgrounds, others by fellow-members with less liberal views, for example, twelve members of the very conservative Committee on the Present Danger have received high posts in the Reagan Administration — among them, Eugene V. Rostow, a strong opponent of SALT II, as Director of the Arms Control and Disarmament Agency — a classic illustration of the old adage about setting the fox to guard the geese. Thus in contrast to former times (when liberals like Fulbright and Mansfield led opposition in the Senate to a more conservative President Nixon) all the major elements influencing national policy seem to be more or less aligned; in fact the problem is not one of lightning from the left but of thunder from the right, with Secretary of Defense Weinberger taking tougher stances than Secretary of State Haig and Senator Jesse Helms of North Carolina holding up the confirmation of some of Mr. Reagan's appointees on the ground they are too liberal!

All this suggests that the policy-making "system" will endorse (and may promote) alliance policies very different from those prevalent in recent years. For one thing, there will be little or no support for the improvement of relations with the Soviet Union; not only do Americans tend to view politics as essentially bipolar, as noted earlier, but they were disenchanted with detente even before former President Ford expunged that word from his political lexicon. For another, there will be intense opposition to arms control, which is seen as contributing to the decline in American military power and as incompatible with (or at least secondary to) the measures which have to be taken to restore that power. For a third, there will be strong pressures for increases in European defense expenditures, both as a means of meeting the "threat" and as a way of freeing up American resources for other purposes such as the upgrading of strategic nuclear forces or the creation of the so-called Rapid Deployment Force. Finally, there may well be calls for increases in specific types of weapons or kinds of forces on the basis of their consonance with US doctrine or their utility to American force planners, rather than on the basis of their relevance and importance to the situation in Europe. And while this may spring as much from a propensity to overlook or to downplay the importance of the situational variable in Europe as from process *per se*, the system permits this, if it does not encourage it.

4. American Approaches to Security Policy

If these judgements are correct (which they may not be) and if all else stays the same (which it will not) one could draw the following conclusions concerning the policy differences between the US and the FRG discussed in Section II:

1. *The two countries will continue to interpret differently the Soviet "threat".* The United States, partly because it is engaged in a military competition with the USSR, will continue to see the threat primarily in military terms. Moreover, because it is conscious that it is the only country able to match the USSR militarily, and because it feels that it must do so on a global basis, the United States will probably define both threat and response in its own way, without much regard for the inputs of its allies. This propensity is likely to be reinforced by:

a) The relative freedom of the Department of Defense to determine forces, programs and contingency plans on its own;
b) The growth of conservative sentiment reflected in recent opinion polls, demonstrated in the 1980 elections and strongly felt in the Congress and within the Executive Branch.

Furthermore, the fact that the most direct and most dangerous threat to the security of the United States is that of a Soviet nuclear strike suggests that American decision-makers will give high priority to countering that particular threat. This does not necessarily mean an end to the deployment of long range tactical nuclear forces in Europe; in fact, these may assume greater importance because they can add to the weight of an American strike against the Soviet Union. It does, however, suggest that these weapons will be chosen, deployed and programmed more on the basis of their employment as auxiliaries to American central strategic systems than on the basis of their effects in Europe.

71

2. This is especially true since *the United States and West Germany will maintain their contrasting approaches to deterrence*, the one emphasizing war-fighting and the other the multiplication of risks. On the part of the United States this may well reflect two influences: the belief of the military (and of many defense analysts) that deterrence is best insured through the ability to beat an adversary on his own terms and the apparent readiness of the Reagan Administration to provide the resources required for this task. It may also take two forms: a build-up of conventional components, land, sea and air, and a further modernization of tactical nuclear forces, short-range as well as long-range, since this would not only maximize "deterrence through defense" but also hedge against the possibility of an unwanted strategic nuclear exchange,[56] while simultaneously expressing the will and determination on which Mr. Reagan and most of his associates set such great store.

If this is the case, the FRG may find itself in a difficult position. On the one hand, it will get all it asked for in the way of improvements in US strategic nuclear forces and deployments of LRTNFs — and perhaps more. On the other hand, these may well be accompanied by targeting doctrine and firing procedures aimed at "fighting" a nuclear war in and on Europe, a consummation that the West Germans devoutly do not desire. And they will certainly be accompanied by pressures for the upgrading of the *Bundeswehr* and for increases in the FRG's defense budget, both to facilitate the upgrading and to substitute for US resources diverted elsewhere.

3. *Furthermore, the United States will certainly be less supportive of arms control in the future than in the past.* There are a number of reasons for this, one being that a sense of threat and a belief in continuing competition militate against arms control — for both superpowers. Another is that the new administration (as well as many members of the present Congress) believe that past arms control agreements have contributed to the decline of US military power, that reconstituting and perhaps enlarging that power is a first priority and that it is also a *sine qua non* for Soviet agreement to "equitable" agrrangements. A third is that the improvement in war-fighting capabilities which the United States may seek is also incompatible with arms control; even if the Soviets were prepared to limit or to reduce *their* conventional and/or theater nuclear forces in order to head off an American arms build-up, they would scarcely be willing to do so while that build-up went untrammelled.[57]

4. Finally, *their differing definitions of detente will become an item of dispute between the United States and the Federal Republic of Germany.* It is almost impossible for the United States to reconcile a global approach to containment with one that seeks exceptions on a regional basis, or to abandon "linkage politics", which have become part and parcel of American thinking about relations with the Soviet Union. Furthermore, the Reagan Administration is likely to reinforce that mind set; in fact, Mr. Reagan has already announced

that progress in arms control negotiations and other discussions with the USSR will depend on Soviet behavior in the Third World. Moreover, even if it wanted to modify its views of, and policies on, detente, the new administration would find it hard to do so in the face of Congressional sentiment and the probable opposition of extreme elements among its already dubious and restless supporters. Thus here again, a number of influences combine to push US security policy in a direction contrary to that of the FRG.

I do not mean by these finding to suggest that Mr. Reagan and his supporters are the cause of all the difficulties I have listed though they may reinforce trends in US opinion. Those trends already existed — as indicated by Mr. Carter's inability to induce the United States Senate to ratify SALT II. Nor do I mean to imply that popular feelings are the main sources of US public policy, with Mr. Reagan, in the role of Robespierre, rushing out to head up his "followers"; shifts in power from President to Congress, the difficulty of guiding and controlling the Federal bureaucracy, and the diffuse nature of the American policy process all facilitated the growth of "counter policies" during the Carter Administration. Most significant of all is the fact that the structure of the international system and the differing situations of the United States and of West Germany almost inevitably meant the adoption of US policies out of phase with, if not opposed to, those of the FRG.

This latter observation suggests that on some issues, such as the nature of the Soviet threat and doctrine for the defense of Western Europe, differences may well be sharp. On other issues, such as the practice of detente, the FRG may again play successfully the role of intermediary which it has filled so well in the past and help bring the US and the USSR together. And on some issues, such as arms control, Mr. Reagan may prove more flexible and adaptable than he seems at this stage; if only because such adaptability may be necessary to achieve others of his objectives, such as a balanced budget. If, however, differences are to be ameliorated, greater emphasis will have to be placed on the maintenance and development of German-American relations since, as Uwe Nerlich points out, present circumstances "prove the need for mutual responsibility . . ."[58] If both sides do live up that responsibility, then their differences over security issues may be less than I have forecast and German-American relations may improve, rather than worsen. For the sakes of both countries, as well as that of security and stability in Europe, let us hope that this occurs.

Notes

1 West German White Paper on Defence, September 1979, excerpted in Survival Vol. XXI, No. 6 (November/December 1979), p. 273.
2 For an excellent discussion of the nature and sources of European concerns see Edward A. Kolodiej, Rethinking US Security Policy for the 1980's, a paper presented at the Seventh Annual National Security Affairs Conference, Fort Lesley J. McNair, Washing-

ton, D.C., 21–23 July 1980, pp. 5–15. Those wishing a review of the factors under-lying "West European Relations with the United States" are referred to Uwe Nehrlich's article of the same name in Daedalus, Vol. 108, No. 1 (Winter 1979), pp. 87–111.

3 The Rt. Hon. Edward Heath, The 1980 Alastair Buchan Memorial Lecture, 16 June, 1980, printed in Survival, Vol. XXII, No. 5 (September/October 1980), p. 201.

4 To borrow from Richard Steadman, security policy encompasses "the full spectrum of matters relating to the military aspects of security [i.e., to the ability to protect the nation from the use of or the threat of force]; for the structure of the [armed] forces and their deployment, to the budgets that support them, to individual matters of high policy [affecting the military] . . ." Quoted in Final Report, The Role of the Military in National Security Policy Formulation in the 1980's (West Point, NY: 1979), p. 25.

5 The most recent manifestation of this is the tentative decision by Bonn to trim the increases in its defense budget below the 3 % agreed upon among the members of NATO in 1977, even as Washington is planning increases of 7 % or more in real terms.

6 Herbert Kremp, Finnlandisierung der Budesrepublik hat schon begonnen, Die Welt, 14 October 1979, p. 4.

7 Herber Wehner, Wehner erschwert uns das Geschaft, Der Spiegel, No. 14 (31 March 1980), pp. 19–21. (Though Mr. Wehner has subsequently retracted his statement, other proponents of this view remain active – and vocal). For a summary of the CDU/CSU arguments see Hans Ruhle, A European Perspective on the U.S.-Soviet Strategic Military Relationship, in: U.S. Strategic-Nuclear Policy and Ballistic Missile Defense: the 1980's and Beyond, Special Report, Institute for Foreign Policy Analysis, Inc., Cambridge, Mass., April 1980, pp. 57–61. A good exposition of the "centrist" view will be found in Helmut Kohl, "Reply to Government Statement in the Bundestag". 11 May 1978, FBIS-WEU-78-93, 12 May, 1978, pp. J1–J12 and in Friedrich Zimmerman, "Speech in Bundestag", March 9, 1979, pp. J–10–J17.

8 The 1977 Alastair Buchan Memorial Lecture, op. cit., p. 3.

9 The Rt. Hon. Edward Heath, The 1980 Alastair Buchan Memorial Lecture, Survival, Vol. 22, No. 5 (September/October 1980), p. 196.

10 "A European Perspective on the U.S.-Soviet Strategic Military Relationship", in: U.S. Strategic-Nuclear Policy and Ballistic Missile Defense: The 1980's and Beyond, p. 50. Cf. Helmut Schmidt's earlier statement to the effect that SALT "magnifies the dispa-raties between East and West in nuclear tactical and conventional weapons" and that our security will be impaired "if we do not succeed in removing the disparities of mi-litary power in Europe . . .", "The 1977 Alastair Buchan Memorial Lecture, op. cit., pp. 3–4.

11 West German White Paper on Defense, op. cit., p. 276. This statement is not quite accurate, as the White Paper, while counting MR/IRBMS, medium bombers and European SLBMs on both sides, leaves out the 400 warheads (out of 800) on five US missile submarines which are allocated to SACEUR. If these are added in, the West can muster approximately 220 launch vehicles, as against some 900 for the USSR, and about 740 warheads compared to the 1300 or so available to the USSR. The Military Balance, 1979-1980.

12 According to one study, the percentage of West Germans willing to defend their country against attack drops from 50.8 % in the event of a conventional war on German terri-tory to 14.6 % if nuclear weapons have to be used on the soil of the FRG. Ralf Zoll, "Public Opinion on Security Policy and Armed Forces in the USA and the FRG – A Comparative Study", paper presented at the 20th Anniversary Conference of the Inter-University Seminar on Armed Forces and Society, October 23–25, 1980, Table 15.

13 Webster's New International Dictionary of the English Language, Second Edition, Un-abridged (Springfield, Mass.: The G.C. Miriam Company 1969), p. 711.

14 Joseph Joffe, "Why Germans Support SALT", Survival, Vol. XXI, Number 5 (Sep-tcmber/October 1979), p. 209.

15 Helmut Schmidt, Defense or Retaliation: A German View, Translated by Edward Thomas (New York: Frederick A. Praeger, 1962), p. 101, quoted in Alex A. Vardamis, Geman-American Military Fissures, Foreign Policy, No. 34 (Spring 1979), p. 93.
16 Quoted in Vardamis, German-American Military Fissures, op. cit., pp. 94–95.
17 Europe and the American Connection, Foreign Affairs, Vol. 58, No. 3 (Winter 1980), p. 629.
18 "Interview Given by the Honorable Alexander M. Haig, Jr., Secretary of State, to French Television, Antennae 2, at Department of State, Washington D.C., February 23, 1981", Press Release No. 15, February 24, 1981, p. 9.
19 The New York Times, 15 October 1979.
20 Conversely, some members of the CDU/CSU coalition have taken positions much closer to those of the United States; thus Manfred Woerner, CDU Chairman of the Bundestag Defense Committee, argued that NATO should "exploit . . . cruise missiles", for the "Soviet Union cannot be allowed . . . to become a sanctuary in the nuclear phase of conflict in Europe". Quoted in Vardamis, German-American Military Fissures, op. cit., p. 98.
21 "Why Germans Support SALT", op. cit., p. 209.
22 Pierre Hassner, Western European Perceptions of the USSR, Daedalus, Vol. 108, No. 1 (Winter 1979), p. 148.
23 The Economist, October 6–12, 1979, p. 54, quoted in Sommer, "Europe and the American Connection", op. cit., p. 632.
24 Op. cit., p. 634.
25 Edward A. Kolodziej, Europe: The Partial Partner, International Security, No. 5, No. 3 (Winter 1980/81), p. 114.
26 According to US Senator Howard Baker, the Majority Leader of the new Senate, the Alliance is torn by "a substantially different interpretation of detente in Europe from that of the most prudent observers in the United States" and by "fundamental disagreement" over the appropriate policies for dealing with the Soviet Union. The New York Times, November 16, 1980, Section IV, p. 1–E.
27 Raymond F. Hopkins and Richard W. Mansbach, Structure and Process in International Politics (New York: Harper & Row, 1973), p. vii.
28 Glen H. Snyder and Paul Diesing, Conflict Among Nations (Princeton, NJ. Princeton University Press, 1977), p. 419.
29 According to a poll conducted by the Roper Institute in February, 1980, 73 % of the American public perceived the Soviet Union as seeking "global domination" – an increase of 18 points from the pre-Afghanistan period. Department of State Briefing Memorandum from PA Hodding Carter, Sizeable Majority of Americans (73 %) Believes Soviet Union Seeks "Global Domination" . . . April 11, 1980.
30 Another group, though one poorly represented in the defense community, maintains that Soviet military programs are by and large responses to US programs which appear to threaten the vital interests, if not the existence of the USSR.
31 Hans-Peter Schwarz, "Atlantic Security Policy in an Era Without Great Alternatives", in Karl Kaiser and Hans-Peter Schwarz, (eds.), America and Western Europe (Lexington, Mass.: D.C. Heath and Co., 1978), p. 219.
32 One such doctrine is that of "flexible response" embodied in MC 14/3. Another was the so-called "Schlesinger Doctrine" on the limited first use of strategic nuclear delivery vehicles against targets in the Soviet Union, recently resurrected from its political grave and re-born as Presidential Directive 59.
33 Perhaps the most open statement of these intentions by (former) American officials is that by Alain C. Enthoven and C. Wayne Smith, in How Much Is Enough? (New York: Harper & Row, 1971), pp. 117–164.
34 Walter F. Hahn, "The U.S.-European Strategic Linkage" in Walter F. Hahn and Robert L. Pfaltzgraff, Jr., Editors, Atlantic Community in Crisis (New York: Pergamon Press, 1978), p. 76.

35 In this context, "national leaders" refers to "Americans in senior positions [in govern-ment, industry, education, the media, etc.] with knowledge and influence upon international affairs and foreign policy." John E. Rielly, Editor, American Public Opinion and U.S. Foreign Policy 1979 (Chicago, Illinois: The Chicago Council on Foreign Policy March 1979), p. 3. Much (though not all) of the assessment made here is based on this study, a condensed version of which appeared in Foreign Policy, No. 34 (Spring 1979) under the title: The American Mood: A Foreign Policy of Self-Interest.

36 This sentiment was particularly strong among key elements such as foreign policy elites and members of Congress, with 87 % of those polled among the former group and 79 % of those from the latter willing to pay more taxes in order to improve defenses. Ibid., p. 26.

37 Ibid., Table V-I, p. 25. By 1979—80, the number of Americans deeming the defense budget too low had risen to 41%, according to one poll conducted by the Roper Institute and to over 60 % according to two (less structured) polls carried out by the National Broadcasting Corporation. Department of State Briefing Memorandum, Attitudes Toward Defense Spending and U.S. vs. Soviet Military Strength, February 11, 198. pp. 2 and 3.

38 Rielly, op. cit., pp. 26—27. By July 1980 the percentage of the public willing to "come to the defense of its major European allies if any of them are attacked by the Soviet Union" had risen to 74 % with only 19 % opposed. Department of State Briefing Paper, How Americans Perceive NATO and the NATO Countries, November 25, 1980, p. 1.

39 Rielly, op. cit., Table II-3, p. 13.

40 Ibid., Table II-1, p. 12. Other assessments give this objective fourth or fifth place, but none I have seen ranks it first. cf. New Directions in US Foreign Policy, A Survey of Members and Associates of the International Management and Development Institue, the Council on Foreign Relations and its Corporation Service Program (New York: 1981), Table No. 2, p. 2.

41 Sam C. Sarkesian, National Security Policy and the Presidency, a paper presented at the Wingspread Conference on "U.S. Defense Policy: Trends and Prospects", 16 May 1980, p. 29. A am indebted to Professor Sarkesian for many of the insights in this section.

42 James Barber, The Presidential Character, Second Edition, (Englewood Cliffs, N.J., Prentice-Hall, 1977), pp. 607, quoted in Sarkesian, op. cit., p. 7.

43 Sarkesian, op. cit., p. 14a.

44 J. I. Coffey, SALT Under the Carter Administration, Naval War College Review, Vol. XXXI, No. 3 (Winter, 1978).

45 Lawrence Korb, The FY 1979-1983 Defense Program: Issues and Trends (Washington: The American Enterprise Institute for Public Policy Research 1978), Vol. Two, No. 2, pp. 4—5, 21, 22—23.

46 President Jimmy Carter, State of the Union Address, 1978, Vital Speeches of the Day, Vol. XLIV, No. 8 (1 February 1978), p. 226.

47 Jack Anderson, "If Carter Could see Himself As European Leaders See Him", Chicago Sun-Times, June 19, 1978, p. 38, quoted in Sarkesian, op. cit., p. 35a.

48 Hedrick Smith, "Reagan's World", in Reagan the Man, The President, Hedrick Smith et. al., (New York: MacMillan Publishing Co., Inc., 1981), pp. 98—99.

49 Ibid., pp. 118—124.

50 I. M. Destler, "National Security Management: What Presidents Have Wrought", Political Science Quarterly, Vol. 95, No. 4 (Winter 1980/81), p. 574.

51 Desmond Ball, "Developments in U.S. Strategic Nuclear Policy Under the Carter Admi-nistration", ACIS Working Paper No. 21, University of California, Los Angeles, Center for International and Strategic Affairs, February 1980, p. 15.

52 Philip A. Odeen, "Organizing for National Security", International Security, Vol. 5, No. 1 (Summer 1980), pp. 123—127.

53 Destler, "National Security Management: What Presidents Have Wrought". op. cit. p. 535.
54 For example, Dr. Harold Brown served, inter alia, as Secretary of the Air Force and Director of Defense Reasearch and Engineering under President Johnson, as a member of the SALT delegation under Mr. Ford and, most recently, as Secretary of Defense under Mr. Carter. Mr. Paul Nitze was Director of the Policy Planning Staff, Department of State, under Mr. Truman, Assistant Secretary of Defense under Mr. Kennedy, Secretary of the Navy and Deputy Secretary of Defense under Mr. Johnson and a member of the SALT delegation under Mr. Nixon.
55 In the case of Mr. Nitze, for example, an extensive analysis of his positions over time suggests that these have been marked by a consistent emphasis on the military factor in security, a tendency to overstate the nature of the Soviet threat, a strong belief that the Soviet Union is "a compulsively hostile power", and a conviction that any Soviet gain is an American loss. Obviously, if this analysis is correct, and if Mr. Nitze's influence prevails, US security policy will keep well to the right. See Alan Tanelson, Nitze's World, Foreign Policy, No. 35 (Summer 1979).
56 This second purpose, it seems to me, may be less important to the new administration than the first, as many of Mr. Reagan's advisers on security believe strongly in the feasibility of limited nuclear war, strategic as well as tactical.
57 Paradoxically, implementation of the West German approach may depend on the validity of the hypothesis that strength induces conciliatory behavior. We may soon have fresh empirical evidence with which to test this.
58 Uwe Nehrlich, "Washington and Bonn", in Kaiser and Schwarz, op. cit., p. 368.

Harald Müller

United States Energy Policy – Foreign Policy Goals Versus Domestic Interests[1]

1. Unilateralism or Multilateralism? The Framework of Analysis

International energy policy is seen by everybody as an area of interdependence: Each actor's decisions influence welfare, security and freedom of action of all the other actors. The United States are the world's leading energy producer, consumer, and importer.[2] This paper focusses on questions related to oil policy, still the most important energy resource of the world. There are three aspects of American energy-related behavior that shape the political environment in which, among others, West European countries and governments have to act.

— The development of American energy consumption and oil imports is the most important factor that affects the development of the world oil market besides OPEC's decisions. This is true for normal market conditions as well as for emergencies.
— The American foreign policy towards the oil exporting countries and towards the whole Near and Middle East area is a decisive parameter of world oil supply.
— The willingness of the American government to share information about the multinational oil companies is necessary to allow Europeans some control over their own 'energy destiny'.

From the European viewpoint it is a critical question whether American energy policy has been developed in an unilateral or multilateral way, whether it solves the energy problem by exacerbating conflicts or by stimulating cooperation. Unilateralism would develop demand and import policy exclusively with respect to interests of the American society, conduct policy towards the OPEC countries in order to pursue goals of U.S. power politics and protect economic advantages originating from the dominance of American oil companies. Multilateralism would accept European demands and compromize them with American interests.

According to David Easton[3], there are two ways by which foreign interests may influence the decisions of a political system. They can be accepted by a societal 'gatekeeper', e.g. an interest group, which mixes them with own wants, and puts them into the political system as part of its demands. In the age of interdependence, activities of interest groups don't stop at the borders of the nation-state. Economic, political and cultural relations have created contacts to foreign actors, at least in the Euro-American context. It is therefore essential to prove empirically whether in the energy area American interest groups act as "transnational linkage groups"[4], i.e. take up 'European demands'.

If foreign interests are not considered by societal gatekeepers the formal roles within the political system, most likely the foreign policy branches, may work out a compromise between their own strategic aspirations and the interests of foreign actors.

2. European Demands

It seems difficult to discover 'European demands'. So far, the EEC has been unable to develop a coherent energy policy for Europe.[5] But the European states succeeded in reaching unity or at least compromises about common demands towards the United States. If we neglect societal actors in Europe and take into account only official statements of the EEC Commission and the Ministerial Council,[6] we can discern the following demand pattern:

— The United States should renounce attempts to confront OPEC in order to lower the European risk of severe supply interruptions.
— The United States should be willing to share the rich American energy resources in the case of an emergency.
— The United States should accept a special responsibility to reduce imports because of their profligate energy consumption.
— The United States should assist the European governments to get more information about the operations of oil companies.

3. The Energy Policy Demands of American Interest Groups

3.1. Energy Policy as Antagonism: The Overall Pattern

In the energy policy debate, there is a limited range of measures, energy policy goals and general domestic and foreign policy goals which the 'gatekeepers' use to legitimate their different positions. Measures are connected with sectoral goals, sectoral goals with general goals. These connections form the characteristic demand pattern of an interest group. In a content analysis of statements before Congress, of organizational resolutions, and of public speeches of Executives between 1973 and 1978, we developed five criteria to differenciate between a 'liberal' and a 'conservative' energy policy position ('liberal' is used in the American sense, to circumscribe a welfare state, interventionist position, comparable to but not identical with the European social democratic parties):

I.   Liberals use social/regional equity more often as general reference for their energy demands than 'preserving of the free market place' (conservatives vice versa).

II. Liberals value consumer protection higher as a means to preserve the free market than incentives for the energy industry (conservatives: vice versa).

III. Liberals value price controls more often positive than negative (conservatives: vice versa).

VI. Liberals value oil and gas deregulation more often negative than positive (convervatives: vise versa).

V.   Liberals value reform of the energy industry more often positive than negative (conservatives: vice versa).

By these criteria, we can marshal interest groups into two coalitions:

Table 1: 'Liberal' and 'Conservation' Coalition by Five Criteria

Liberal Coalition	Conservative Coalition
Labor Unions	Energy Producing Industry
Consumer Associations	Investor Owned Utilities
Environmentalists	Energy Consuming Industry
Communites/Cities/	General Business Ass.
Consumer Owned Public	Motor Vehicle Industry/
Utilities	Appliances Industry/Tourism
Farmer/Minorities	Industry
Independent Refiners	Petrochemical Industry
and Retailers	
Transport Industry	

3.2 Pleading for the Welfare-state: The Liberal Coalition

The liberal groups represent constituencies of the lower levels of the social and economic stratum: working people, small business (except some large independent refiners and the airlines), farmers, minorities etc. It is the soaring price of energy, not the availability of ever-growing supplies that constitutes the energy crisis for them. The majority of these people use a relatively small percentage of national petroleum consumption to fulfill essential needs.[7] The price is of primary concern for the independent oil refiners and retailers, too. Rising oil prices enable the integrated oil companies to cross-subsidy their downstream operations. When consumption goes down, dumping prices pose a serious threat to the independent's competitiveness.[8]

The liberal coalition therefore wants to be protected by an interventionist welfare state. Allocation, even rationing by a state bureaucracy may be somewhat inefficient, but still more likely to guarantee the essential energy supply to the economically weak than rationing by market forces. In the liberal view, conservation may be necessary, but higher prices are not an equitable way to achieve it. Instead government should set up energy efficiency standards for buildings, products, machines, and instustrial operations; these standards shift the burden of conservation away from the consuming public and put it onto industry. The well-off would not be any more in the position to escape conservation by only allocating a slightly larger part of his wealth to energy consumption.

This does not mean that a majority of the liberal coalition does not believe in the free market place. But they deem it disturbed by an oligopolistic structure. The transfer of control capacity from industry to the government, coupled with enhanced public participation, is necessary if the market place shall become competitive again. Among the numerous proposals for the reform of the energy industry are very modest approaches (e.g. protection of franchised dealers, enforcement of antitrust legislation) yet some concepts are very far reaching and comprehensive (horizontal and vertical divestiture of integrated petroleum companies).

The majority of the liberal coalition opposes conservation by energy taxes, if the tax is likely to fall onto the individual consumer, and if the tax receipts will be used to subsidy the energy industry. But they support industrial user taxers. Likewise, they plead for grants and tax credits as incentives for the consumer to invest in energy measures, e.g. building weatherization, but oppose such favors if granted to industry.

There is a division within the liberal coalition about environmental standards. The environmentalists, the National Farmers' Union, and the United Automobile Workers are not willing to sacrifice these standards in order to enhance energy production. However, the small business section of the coalition, the public utilities and AFL-CIO perfer more energy production to environmental quality if necessary to promote economic growth and employment.

3.3. Pleading for the Market Place: The Conservative Coalition

The conservative coalition represents the higher ranks of the social and economic stratum. Some groups, as energy producers, gain immediately from higher oil and gas prices. The other groups are the less and least affected, compared with the liberal coalition. For the energy consuming industries, energy ranged about 2.5% of total costs in the average (mid 70s).[9] Higher prices do not cause losses due to comparative advantages of foreign competitioners and can be passed through to the consumers. On the other hand, the growth of energy supply is seen as an essential pre-condition for the further growth of the whole industry. So it is the supply, not the price, that, in the eyes of conservative groups, is the focus of the crisis. And there is some basic unity among business associations to get rid of government intervention into the market place, if not necessary to assist specific industries.

The situation of upper-middle class constituencies, represented by the American Automobile Association or the Tax Reform Groups is very similar. Energy costs have a low impact on the higher income household (in 1976 4.2% for the richest 10% compared to 29.8% for the poorest 10%).[10] Moreover, these people possess some flexibility to pay even higher energy prices in order to fulfill their rising living standard aspirations. Government intervention will seriously restrict their freedom of choice.

The conservative coalition is not totally opposed to state intervention into the energy economy. The groups accept a role for government in research and development, especially of synthetic fuels. But they restrict this role vigorously: The state shall only set a general framework in which industry can operate free from any further intrusion into its internal decision-making. Market forces are the panacea to solve the energy crisis. The conservative coalition fought for decontrol of oil prices and deregulation of natural gas from the beginning of the energy debate. Freely floating prices, they argued, render allocation, rationing and efficiency standards unnecessary.

Because the conservative coalition is primarily supply oriented it is very interested in weakening the environmental standards. For industry these standards mean costly investments. Thus reduction of the standards widen the managements' freedom of decision.

They oppose proposals for industry reform for two reasons. In their eyes, it would cause a loss of efficiency in the energy industry. Moreover, it could be used as test case to attack the oligopolistic structure of other industrial branches, as conceptualized in the 'Industrial Reform Act' of 1973.

The conservatives share the aversion of most liberal groups against energy taxes.

3.4. America First: Foreign Energy Policy Demands

In domestic policy, there is a sharp division between the liberal and the conservative positions. Thus the conformity in respect to foreign energy policy matters seems astonishing. First of all, both coalitions don't really care about foreign energy policy. Their demands focus almost totally on domestic problems. They were seldom represented during the international energy hearings of Congress and don't express much interest in international cooperation.

This applies even to traditionally transnationalist groups. The Chamber of Commerce used its discussions within the Euro-American Businessmens' Council just as another forum to push its domestic demands. And the AFL-CIO only introduced OPEC as another enemy into its foreign propaganda. On the domestic scene, COC and AFL-CIO did not differ from the main stream of their respective coalitions.[11]

The foreign energy policy demands of both coalitions contain three common elements:

1. They tried to isolate the domestic scene from foreign commitments that could be detrimental to the American public. Therefore those groups, incidentially in accord with European interests, opposed Kissinger's ill-fated floor price concept; the liberals feared higher domestic prices, the conservatives disliked the state intervention involved.

2. They dismissed any responsibility for the world energy situation. There was a common faith in the basic right of Americans to consume oil at their pleasure: a conservative tax reform group declared that Americans are entitled to drive the car of their choice, even a gas guzzling one.[12] Therefore, both sides were inclined to search for scapegoats. They share a militant criticism against OPEC. Reducing the world oil price by knocking out the cartel was the perferred combination of foreign energy policy goals: AFL-CIO demanded that the United States should not admit oppression by "blackmailers and neandertals".[13] On the conservative side, there is no sympathy for the producing countries, too: Their actions are held incompatible with the world economic order and detrimental to American power.

   Notwithstanding the common negative position to *world oil cooperation*, business associations were not willing to abandon trade and investment opportunities created by the new oil wealth. During the Arab boycott debate they pleaded not to risk these options by offending the Arab partners through strict legislation.[14]

   Among the liberals, the oil companies were also a favorite scapegoat. Industry reform should not only restore the free market in the United States, but, at the same time, blow up the symbiosis between the companies and OPEC. Divestiture is thus believed to provide for a lower world oil price. In liberal statements, there was not a single mention of possible consequences for the European supply system, no single proposal to consult with foreign partner about this problem.

3. Both sides projected their domestic interests and positions into the international scene without any reference to the interests of foreign actors. At the liberal side, there was a deep distrust and even opposition against the IEA and any consumer country cooperation, because they suspected the political legitimization of the companies' oligopolistic behavior. Liberal groups were also opposed to sharing American resources with foreign partners; instead they called for energy export controls.

   For the conservatives the IEA was not very problematic, as long as it didn't intervene into the activities of the oil industry. But they wanted the American delegates to IEA to be promoters of further U.S. penetration of the European market.[15]

This pattern reflects a common attitude of both coalitions to foreign policy goals. They mentioned in their statements goals with immediate relation to American interests ("national security" and "economic advantage") far more frequent than goals that refer to global commitments of the United States within an interdependent structure ("world order", "world economy", "leadership").

Besides foreign policy elite groups like the Committee on Economic Development or the Trilateral Commission[16] only the multinational oil companies and banks deviated from this pattern. Both are heavily interested in appeasing international oil tensions. They, therefore, prefer a climate of world energy cooperation, among consumer states as well as between consumers and producers to any risk of confrontation. Of course, their support for cooperation diminishes when intrusion into their own decision-making could be involved. Thus they opposed any logistic capacity for the new international organization and asked for stiff restrictions on the flow of information from companies to IEA. The responsibility for emergency decisions should rest with an international body, but *not* the capability to carry out these decisions. On the domestic scene, the oil companies sided with the conservative coalition, but they were far more able to compromize than, for example, the independent oil producers.

In summary, interest groups did not act as gatekeepers for European demands. There was virtually no reference to European interests in their demand pattern. Obviously, interest groups are expected to represent their interests. But in an age of interdependence and on a interdependent issue area one could hypothesize that at least a significant part of gatekeepers shall pay attention to demands of foreign actors just because their own interests are interconnected with those of foreign actors. The broad "America First" – conformity among the interest groups is, therefore, not trivial. They mostly run counter to European demands and seldom comply with them.

4. International Leadership and Domestic Compromises: The Energy Policy of the Executive

The political system has to mediate between the domestic demands, the interests of foreign actors and its own long-term goals. U.S. foreign energy policy since the 1973 embargo has been shaped by Henry Kissinger's strategic conceptions. For Kissinger, the actions of the oil producers were just another factor that endangered the world political and economic order, particularly the rules for stable change acceptable to the United States, and that undermined the

American position in the balance of power system.[17] Economic interests and the delicate task of Middle-East policy forbid massive U.S. power politics in the bilateral relations with oil producers. It thus was the prevailing short term goal to unite the consumer countries. A common Western commitment to reduce drastically oil imports was the only remaining opportunity to shift the market power and thus the political leverage away from OPEC. Moreover, only an united Western front allowed the United States to reimpose oversight, if not control over the orderly development of consumer-producer relations after a growing bilateralism had taken place in the aftermath of the embargo. The reluctance of the State Department to stress the oil price question in bilateral negotiations with Saudi-Arabia and Iran is therefore not a proper proof that the United States' government encouraged OPEC to rise prices.[18] Kissinger intended to confront OPEC as *producer organization* by a *consumer organization* while maintaining and improving *bilateral relations* with *individual producer governments*. Therefore, the State Department fought energetically for short-term import reductions at home and within the IEA from 1973 to 1976. The foreign policy strategists, then, believed in the possibility to change the market power immediately and to push OPEC to the negotiation table. A set of rules according to American interests could be worked out. This concept contained the famous floor price as a reference point for the consuming countries, comparable to OPEC's posted price.[19]

As the agreement about an International Energy Program (IEP) of 1974 and the long-term program of IEA of 1976 show, the American energy diplomacy was successful in principle. Although the European did not want any new organization, the IEA and the Financial Support Fund, too, were established formally within OECD, but outside of the former OECD Oil Policy Committee and with a decision-making rule of its own. This rule gives the United States an influential position which is neither justified by its GNP percentage of total IEA-GNP nor by its oil imports nor by its contributions to the budget of IEA. It was energy consumption that provided the measure for the voting weights in IEA. The procedure makes it necessary for the United States only to persuade one or two other member governments to reach a veto position in the two important issues: a) blocking a motion to waive the invocation of the emergency allocation scheme, b) changes in the procedure of the scheme. The cost burden of the emergency system is borne by the most import-dependent countries during normal conditions and during emergencies: The most expensive obligation of members in absence of a shortage, petroleum storage, is not calculated on the basis of consumption (this would be costly for the United States) but on the basis of imports. The allocation rights, however, are not calculated on the basis on imports (that would be costly to the United States) but on the basis of consumption. Moreover, American security in selective embargos is enhanced by the 'regional clause', that invokes the emergency system when an import shortfall of 7% is met only by a *certain part* of a member country; this clause is only applicable to the American East coast.

The State Department even succeeded in pushing through its unloved floor price against the majority of partner governments. The most important achievement of the Europeans, the inclusion of cooperation with OPEC as a mandatory goal in the IEA charta was neutralized a) by the well-timed staccato of militant anti-OPEC speeches and remarks by top American leaders at the end of 1974/beginning of 1975; b) by the demonstrative lack of interest in the Conference on International Economic Cooperation (CIEC) and the American insistance to restrict the agenda to the energy (price) question; the State Department dropped this position in mid-1975 after IEA countried reached an agreement about their long-term program including the floor-price; c) by the passive U.S. resistance against the activation of the Standing Group on Cooperation in IEA.[20]

Last not least, American diplomacy defended the residual posture of the oil companies: all physical allocation activities under the emergency scheme are to be carried out by the corporations. Information is gathered only in aggregate form — except in very extraordinary circumstances — so that European governments still lack precise information about the operations of individual companies.[21]

American foreign energy policy institutionalized preponderance and preserved at the same time narrow economic advantages. This success resulted from a sophisticated application of the maxime 'divide et impera'. The United States persuaded in every conflict issue one or a few partner governments to follow its line (the United Kingdom in the floor price issue; the United Kingdom and the Netherlands during the data debate; the FRG in the resistance against too much government intervention). Although the main thrust of American policy was clearly to assert American goals, eventually a few European demands were met: more security in severe supply disruptions, and a minimum flow of information.

By and large, the Carter administration followed this path. But it started from a far weaker posture. The hope of breaking up OPEC had vanished, and the United States increasingly had to take the blame for indecisive domestic action. So, in contrast to Carter's campaign rhetoric, his administration started with a far more conciliatory attitude towards OPEC, but did not succeed in turning the course of CIEC to a workable result. On the other hand, the Carter government promoted by no means cooperation between IEA and OPEC. Instead, it stressed even more than the republican administrations did, the bilateral U.S.-Saudi Arabian connection. Particularly, arms sales were used as a means to keep Saudi-Arabia willing to moderate OPEC's price policy.[22] In the IEA, the United States avoided new initiatives until the beginning of 1979. They just tried to use the diplomatic pressure of this organization as support for their domestic energy battles. To appease the criticism in IEA and on the economic summits, Carter and Schlesinger committed themselves to not very far reaching promises. The 1977 and 1978 predictions of reduced U.S. imports were met not because of political success but because Alaskan oil started flowing through the pipeline constructed since 1973.[23]

Besides this low profile policy, the democratic government began a new chapter of international oil policy. In the Energy Department and the Pentagon, there was the strong view that energy policy has to be secured not only by an international oil safety net. Long before the Iranian crisis and Afghanistan, Schlesinger called for a military posture of the United States near to the oil fields. The DOD developed the conception of a special force able to overcome the impediments to a successful attack onto the oil fields that former studies had discovered. (RDF) This was a qualitative step over the Kissinger strategy. Kissinger talked about intervention as a very unthinkable option and tried to assert American goals by diplomatic and economic pressures. To be sure, military intervention is still a least preferred action in American energy policy. But it emerges now as a 'solid' and 'realistic' yet dangerous option for the ultimate case. This development took place again, without consulting the Europeans governments. They are now under heavy pressure to participate themselves in military cooperation around the Persian Gulf.

The military option bears gloomy prospects for European oil security. Although it seems at least highly uncertain, whether the enormously vulnerable oil installations can be 'secured' successfully, American operational thinking has been developed quite independently from this basic consideration. The very broad and elusive definition of trigger contingencies for the deployment of the RDF, the main components of the deployment doctrine — first use (prevention) and maximum speed — and its legitimization within the context of global superpower rivalry all suggest crisis instability, precipitous use of force and lack of appropriate consultation.[24] This risky development is at least partially a consequence of the failure of domestic energy policy.

For the State Department in 1975, the overall political success of its international policy depended on a vigorous domestic energy policy. Kissinger wished to instrumentalize domestic decisions for its ambitious goals of world order and American leadership. He was flexible and ready to compromise on the domestic scene. His approach can be defined as follows: "Which decisions are needed to implement our foreign energy commitments?".[25] But this view was not shared by the most important domestic energy policy actors in the government, Treasury, FEA, and the President. For them, the basic approach was: "Given our principles of economic and social policy and given the necessity to demonstrate the resolve of the President without loosing too much popularity what decisions are still possible?" Thus, a lot of effective measures (gasoline tax, rationing, efficiency standards) were dismissed at the outset.[26] The Treasury in addition killed the floor price by a sophisticated public campaign, so that there was no opportunity that Congress would endorse it. And the President refused to impose the only decisive quantitative measure at his discretion: import quotas. His import fees of 1975 fell disproportionally onto the lower levels of society and they aroused such an uproar among the electorate, interest groups, and the Congress, that he stopped this measure and dropped it at the end of 1975.

Carter's energy task force discovered much earlier than the Republicans that the domestic redistributive conflict would stifle any executive proposal and that the government had to moderate the deep antagonism. Therefore, the Carter program stressed the principles of equality and equal sacrifice. But it was far from being consequent. It was not only weak in supply, especially in renewable energy, but also in conservation. It lacked almost totally mandatory restrictions on energy use.[27] Instead, it stressed − actually overstressed − the tax instrument in order to avoid clear redistributional and regulatory decisions. The tax rebate as a redistributional corrective was not progressive enough to neutralize the overall degressive effects of higher taxes and prices. And the program did say nothing about reform of the energy industry. This policy followed the conservative demand to keep the freedom of consumer choice, even with higher prices − a choice not available to the poor − because this option is unaffected by taxes. But the program was worked out when the middle and upper-middle class became furious about the slightest new increase of taxation. Obviously it provoked overwhelming opposition and proved rather an intellectual exercise than well-drafted policy. Moreover, during the course of the energy debate in 1977−78 Carter avoided decisive actions. From time to time he threatened rhetorically to employ quotas or a sensational 5-Dollar-fee on imports or retaliative actions against oil profiteering but never realized any threat. For his administration, too, the priority was the domestic feasability of policies according to a minimum loss of popularity although Carter proved not very successful in this respect. Implementation of foreign policy goals and commitments was thought legitimate only within these constraints.

In contrast to public rhetoric and common sense, it was not the cleavage between the Executives and Congress that frustrated the foreign domestic energy policy ambitions of government.[28] The weakening of energy legislation began just with the drafting of domestic programs by the Executive.

5. The Art of the Least Common Denominator: Congressional Decisions

Congress did not agree with an internationalist interpretation of energy policy. Instead, it adopted the line of the gatekeeping interest groups. Even the specialists for foreign policy and energy policy did not accept the principle that the new international situation and especially the American commitment to Western cooperation created unavoidable imperatives for domestic decisions. The initiatives derived from the wisdom of these congressional specialists remained negligible. In 1973, there was an amendment of Senator Javits to the Energy Emergency Bill advising the Executive to commit itself to consumer countries' cooperation. This amendment was dropped by the conference and remained the single initiative aiming at Western cooperation during the whole period 1973 to 1978. The other remarkable approach promoted by an important foreign policy parlamentarian was the bill of Senator Church to monopolize import rights in the hands of government so that the United States would be able to confront OPEC more effectively.[29]

In the committees responsible for domestic energy legislation, reference to foreign actors was non-existent during the hearings and the drafting of legislation. Of course, nobody can critisize U.S. law makers for considering American interests an important factor in their decisions. But in an evidently interdependent field of action, it seems astonishing to discover the total lack of questions like "How does this policy affect U.S. international positions?", "What impact have U.S. imports on our Western allies?", "What kind of policy do the IEA allies expect from the United States?". Instead in these hearings Congressmen asked not to commit American energy resources to an international sharing, not to commit the money of American taxpayers to "bail out" the oil deficits of sick western economies, but to protect the American consumer by export controls on energy products.[30] Accordingly, the drafting of domestic energy legislation developed independently from foreign policy considerations. Of the four most important committees, the Senate Interior (later Energy) Committee and the House Interstate and Foreign Commerce Committee tried to protect the consumer from rising energy costs by controlling oil and gas prices. They were reluctant to impose more than very modest mandatory measures. Efficiency standards for automobiles were kept within the range Detroit could accept. The committees voted for some standards for certain consumer products (1975 and 1977) and industrial processess (1977) and a set of discretionary power for the executive to convert oil and gas burning boilers to coal (1975 and 1977).

On the contrary, the Senate Finance Committee sided with the conservative energy demands. It abolished the rest of the interventionist Ullman plan in 1975 and most of Carter's energy taxes in 1977. Instead the Senators tried to stimulate supply by higher profits. They constantly refused to tax oil and gas at the well-head be it in form of a windfall profit tax or an equalization tax without refunneling most of the receipts back to oil producers. On the consumption side, Senate Finance minimized the burdens for the industry and the consumer (industrial taxes and the gas guzzler tax) and drafted a lot of tax favors to stimulate investment in energy saving equipment.

The House Ways and Means Committee undertook in 1975 the only remarkable congressional attempt to succeed with a balanced, partly interventionist, partly market-orientated program of its own. But even in 1975 and to a smaller degree in 1977 it weakened the draft during the mark-up sessions. Even this body could not avoid severe reductions in its ambitious energy policy goals in order to mitigate the sacrifices of the public.[31]

Therefore, the common pattern of legislative work in all four committees was the weakening of bills, if measured by their likely consequences for American imports. This weakening occurred in order to protect the interests of one or both coalitions or to reach a minimum acceptable compromise by excluding effective yet unpleasant energy policy instruments.

The same pattern is true for the debates and floor decisions of both Houses and for the work of the conference. From the foreign policy viewpoint, the most important events were the debates about the Energy Policy and Conservation Act in 1975, containing the provisions for American participation in the IEA. Congress refused to let American energy decisions automatically be bound by the IEA agreement. The act contains the frank declaration that Congress was not willing to ratify or otherwise accept the agreement or protocols and amendments hereto. By this statement, Congress legitimated its deviation from the automatic IEA decision process concerning the emergency system and banned any possibility that the United States could be coerced to accept specific import savings.

In detail, Congress preserved its right to deny the President the most important emergency measure, gasoline rationing. Moreover, it opened the opportunity for the Federal Trade Commission and the Attorney General to withdraw the antitrust exemptions for the oil companies and therewith destroy the IEA allocation system. It made American strategic oil storage dependent on cost and economic considerations, not on the obligations under the International Energy Program.

Besides this most important law, one can observe from 1973 to 1978 a continuity of laws forbidding the export of crude oil and other energy products. The Transalaska Oil Pipeline Act of 1973, the Energy Policy and Conservation Act of 1975 and the Export Administration Act of 1977 in this respect contradict the intention of the International Energy Program. To be sure, the EPCA contained a provision that banned export controls under the IEP. But floor manager Senator Jackson, making legislative history, explained before the Senate that in case of a serious goal conflict between the IEA commitment and the EPCA goal to preserve regional and social justice in the United States, the latter goal would prevail as the "prime goal of this legislation, even in case of such such an emergency".[32] Likewise, tax reform acts of 1975 and 1976 denied incentives for oil exploration and production to foreign operations in order to concentrate the search for oil onto the American territory. But they not only deleted incentives for the risky OPEC area, but for Western Europe, too.[33]

In summary, the congressional decisions tended to isolate the American energy scene from foreign interference as far as possible without directly destroying international agreements; only the Financial Support Fund was given up because of congressional inactivity.

On the domestic side, Congress worked out compromises without any detectible reference to foreign policy. The main pattern in both Houses was a further weakening of import reducing measures that could have any detrimental effects to specific constituencies or the public as a whole. The most convincing example occurred in 1977 when even the fuel tax for private motorboats and airplanes was deleted.

Table 2:   Amendments affecting American oil imports during the debates about the Energy Emergency Bill (1973), the Energy Policy and Conservation Act (1975) and the National Energy Act (1977)

Type of measure	Direction of amendment							
	enhances import reduction				diminishes import reduction			
	adopted		rejected		adopted		rejected	
	HR	USS	HR	USS	HR	USS	HR	USS
positive incentive (e.g. tax credit)	10	38	9	2	–	2	3	5
negative incentive (e.g. gasoline tax)	7	9	22	19	15	22	14	13

Congress phased out oil and gas price-controls over a period of some years (until 1979 respective 1985). These decisions lead to world market prices for American oil and gas in the long run, thus giving high profits to the industry over the years. The consumer was protected in the short term by a slight roll-back in oil prices in 1975 and the temporary extension of regulation into the intrastate gas market in 1978. Congress wrote only very weak redistributive provisions into law – a small weatherization program for the poor, insufficiently funded and neglected by FEA and DOE[34] and the non-mandatory possibility to consider lifeline rates during state power commission considerations.

A liberal republican energy stamp proposal for the poor was rejected by the conference even in the very modest form of a five community pilot program (1978). Not using price as a strong conservation yardstick, the laws did not provide for any effective alternatives. Gasoline consumption is restricted by average fleet, but not minimum efficiency standards, a watered-down gas guzzler tax, and, most admirably from the German point of view, a 55 mph speed limit. The use of home-heating oil will be influenced only by the weatherization program and tax credits for energy saving investments by home-owners. The new public utility advisory program, aimed at helping home-owners to identify conservation opportunities has not the power of mandatory law. Federal building standards, passed in 1976, still in development and applicable only to new buildings at the end of the Carter presidency, are now renounced by DOE. Industrial consumption will be affected by conversion orders that mandatorily phase out oil biolers until 1990. By setting an effective date Congress drew consequences from the complacency of the Federal Energy Administration; this body only reluctantly used its discretionary power granted in 1974 and renewed in 1975. But even in the National Energy Act Congress opened, by a lot of exemption clauses, loopholes for industry to escape the seemingly strict conversion imperative. The new Administration, moreover, is considering the repeal of this law.

Congress followed neither a genuine liberal-interventionist nor a genuine conservative market oriented approach. It did not combine the most effective aspects of both. Congress instead simply dropped the most characteristic and — from an import reduction strategy point of view — most efficient elements of both. This seems to be the only way to reduce step by step the number of constituencies sharply opposing the bills and thus building a majority for a comprehensive yet weak energy bill.

However, in the long-run, the conservative approach will prevail. After the implementation of all provisions of EPCA and the National Energy Act, there will be less governmental intervention into the energy market than during the last 30 years. Natural gas regulation at the well-head, in effect since the Philips case of 1954, will be gone as will oil price controls. Import controls were abolished on the eve of the embargo of 1973. To be sure, government now is better informed about the companies' operations, although most of the important data is classified as proprietary information. But the government's instruments to use this information are fairly modest except in case of emergency. Governmental exploration on federal lands is still a pure option; the separation of the exploration and production stages is not demanded by legislation concerning licence procedures. The only measures containing some consequences for industry structure are the protection of franchised dealers against an aprupt cancellation of contracts (1978) and the prohibition of joint ventures of major oil companies on the outer continental shelf (1975).[35]

6. The United States — A Reliable Partner for Energy Policy? Unilateralism and its Consequences

6.1. Why Unilateralism? American Society and the Energy Question

Kissinger's energy strategy was obviously unilateral, although he employed a formally multilateral organization, IEA, to reach his goals. The State Department derived a set of foreign and domestic energy measures from American policy interests. It then attempted to impose this strategy on the international environment. This kind of unilateralism is somewhat annoying for allies, but still calculable, and it offers the chance to negotiate at least some modest compromises.

But the domestic energy decision-making process reinforced the unilateral effects of the foreign policy strategy. The actors there do not aim primarily at changing the international environment. They are acting on behalf of the interests within the domestic scene. Their main attitude towards international relations is to isolate the domestic energy policy from negative effects of a changing international environment. In searching for a viable domestic compromise they undermine the compromises of foreign energy policy, render United States' behavior in an emergency totally uncalculable for the allies and impede the necessary reductions of oil imports. In effect, this pattern of action is even worse for international cooperation than the strategic unilateralism of American energy diplomacy.

But why is this the case? In other issue areas, the American political system is able to reach compromises with its allies and to impose these compromises on its own society, as Reinhard Rode showed for the area of foreign trade. It is not convincing to state that the crowd of differing interests in energy policy prevents a coherent political decision: Rode discovered many different interests in foreign trade, too. It is also not satisfying to seek the causes in the interests of multinational business; the business community presented a very united front in energy matters yet they did not realize their demands without serious set-backs.

Trade and energy are different "political arenas" as Lowi labels it.[36] Trade is basicly a distributive arena in the United States. The overwhelming majority of society, consumers as well as industry, is likely to gain by the prevailing liberal trade policy, while disaffected groups can be appeased by compensating allocations. Energy policy in contrast is a redistributive arena in which internationally induced change of the most important variables, price and supply, shattered a very precarious balance, a hard disputed consensus within society. The change causes an income transfer from the consumers and from the oil consuming states, notably the east coast, to producers and the producing states, particularly in the South-West, the mountain region and Alaska. Moreover, the fulfillment of the basic needs of the poor and the nearly poor are at stake. Exceptionally low energy prices contributed significantly to the modest living standard this part of the population enjoyed in the past. The opportunity to consume at pleasure is apruptly redistributed to societal actors owning enough capital resources to allocate a higher amount to energy consumption. This redistributional conflict splits society into the two big coalitions mentioned earlier, and it determined the decisions of Congress to a great extent. I analyzed roll call votes in the 93rd, 94th and 96th Congress by rank order correlation on three issue areas: distribution of economic advantage (oil, gas and coal prices; taxes on energy industry profits), distribution of consumption opportunities (rationing, specific allocations to the poor, i.e. energy stamps, efficiency standards) and distribution of decision-making power (i.e. government intervention in company decision-making, divestiture, federal exploration, reporting requirements). The rank order of the oil interests of the states was measured by the difference of per capita income from oil production and the per capita expenditure for oil products.[37] The rank order of the voting behavior was measured by the average voting index of the state delegation. Oil interests correlated significantly with "economic advantage" and "decision-making power" in all three Congresses and the average of them for both Houses.

Even more significant was the correlation of all three voting areas with "ideological position", measured by average "conservative support and opposition" indexes of the Congressional Quarterly for state delegations. This fits well into the above interpretation, because the "conservatives" consist mainly of free market believers resisting redistributive remedies of the welfare state, while the "liberals" generally plead for state intervention for this purpose. Energy decisions, therefore, are determined by the position of the law maker to redistributive politics in general and are fairly modified by the regional distribution of oil interests.

Table 3: Rank-Order Correlation (Spearman's rho), Energy Policy Voting of State Delegations, 93rd to 95th Congress

	Oil Interests		Ideological Position	
Issue Area	H.R.	US.S.	H.R.	US.S.
Economic Advantage	0.55^X	0.57^X	0.85^X	0.90^X
Consumption Opportunity	-0.39	-0.41	-0.91^X	-0.92^X
Decision-Making power	-0.49^X	-0.56^X	-0.90^X	-0.93^X
Ideological Position	0.35	0.42		

^{X}Significant on the 0.1% Level

The unilateral isolation against foreign commitments seems to be the modus of adaptation to solve the redistributional conflict. For it is the common interest of the liberal as well as the conservative groups in society at least to preserve the position achieved so far. By changing the previous balance only slightly, the domestic energy decisions provided for a minimum consensus and, thereby, defended the traditional incremental decision-making approach against an international constellation that demands a far more rapid adaptation. The unilateralism of the State Department then can be reinterpreted. Although Kissinger intended to instrumentalize domestic policy for foreign policy goals, he helped to shelter the domestic adaptation modus against the most severe threats. Energy diplomacy lessened the danger that the United States could find itself isolated in the case of a significant shortfall of supply and that disunity and disorder within the western alliance could push international relations out of United States' control. It thus gave society and its political system the opportunity to pursue their own way independently of outside pressures and needs.

6.2. Energy Crisis, Second Round: The Consequences of Unilateralism and Maladaptation

The Iranian crisis of 1979 offered an unique 'opportunity' to 'test' the Western readiness and ability in using the developed political instruments to cope with a relatively small shortfall – about 4% of supply. But it was quickly revealed that the measures at hand could not stand the test.

Western solidarity fell apart: Just one week after an IEA ministerial meeting, the Department on Energy introduced without previous announcement a five

94

Dollar/barrel entitlement for fuel oil; on the other side, European countries didn't care about their IEA commitments to reduce consumption; instead, the stronger countries, like the FRG, Japan and the United States bid for maximum priced oil at the spot market in Rotterdam; they could afford it even at high prices; Japanese companies were impeded to buy Iranian oil embargoed by the United States only after a sharp and outspoken diplomatic intervention by the State Department. It turned out that the framework of western cooperation was unable to prevent a very small supply shortfall to transform into a doubling of world oil prices. Storage was too small and demand restrictions too weak to ease the fears of spot market buyers of getting dry during the crisis. Instead of restraining spot market activities, companies and governments built up stocks rapidly because they feared larger disruptions and lasting shortfalls.

Again, the price hike endangered the precarious political balance in the United States, leading to violent upheavals at gasoline stations and to soaring profits of oil companies. Even the residual control capacity of multinational oil companies, the old American goal, cannot be regarded as secure as producing countries accelerate their bilateral deals with consumer state companies and their direct selling to the spot market.

This is not to pretend that the Iranian crisis did not induce some progress in the IEA. For the first time member states showed willingness to accept specific – if not binding – long-range import ceilings. OPEC's price hikes triggered what Western governments were not able to reach: a significant reduction in oil imports in 1980, caused by recession and real conservation. And this demand restraint, combined with very high stocks built up in 1979 and the first half of 1980 enabled the IEA countries to weather the Persian Gulf war up to date quite comfortably; IEA coordination of stock policies in December 1980 proved very helpful. But it would be a terrible mistake to be led into complacency again: the favorable market conditions are as temporary a phenomenon as those in 1977 and 1978.

Stabilizing oil supply by keeping conservative producer regimes in power has proven an ambiguous instrument. The Carter doctrine and the organization of the rapid deployment force seem to signal a growing willingness to risk even a violent conflict for the sake of energy supply. This implies a destabilization of the international energy system that the United States diplomacy after the embargo strived to avoid.[38]

After the Iranian oil crisis, President Carter's energy policy seemed much more successful.[39]

The antitrust exemptions for the participation of oil companies in the IEP were extended until 1981. The Senate tried to add as a 'rider' a congressional veto on oil import quotas. But this time the House rejected the amendment for constitutional reasons, because, as a tax related measure, it has to originate with the House of Representatives.

Congress refused restrictions on outdoor lightening advertising and weekend closing of gasoline stations as emergency conservation measures. It only accepted ceilings on temperature in public buildings. The administration's gasoline rationing plan was rejected twice. Congress then changed the law so that the rationing plan now is "on the shelves". It can only be applied if gasoline supply is cut by 20% for 30 days or for obligations under the IEP. But the International Energy Agency cannot invoke specific measures in member countries. Thus the letter clause will inevitably provoke juridical disputes about whether rationing is really needed to fulfill international obligations. In any case, either House of Congress can prevent rationing by a simple majority.

Congress changed the emergency conservation plan provisions of the EPCA. These plans now are to be developed and applied by the states. The federal government may step in only if a state fails to develop a plan or if the plan is applied in an emergency, and falls short of its conservation goals by as much as 8%. Finally, for the first time Congress has the opportunity to reject by a resolution of disapproval an import quota set up by the President. The only positive step of Congress was to mandate a filling up of the strategic petroleum reserve by 100000 barrels/day. The storage system consisted in 1980 only of 96 million barrels, far from the 1 billion barrels legislated in 1975. Therefore, the implementation of IEA obligations in case of an emergency is even more in doubt than before.

It is no accident that the focus of attention in the Carter administration shifted even during the dramatic 1979 energy events from the foreign policy implications back to the domestic game of re-asserting the presidential posture on the eve of the election race.[40]

In spring 1979, President Carter decided to decontrol oil prices. In early 1980, Congress passed a windfall profit tax to mitigate the redistributive effects of decontrol. The oil industry was expected to make 1 trillion Dollars extra profits before taxes and slightly over 500 billion after taxes through 1990. The windfall profit tax takes another 227.3 billion Dollars of this money with a bias in favor of independent oil producers. Of this money, about a quarter is earmarked for social assistance (about 55 billion Dollars); by passing the Energy Security Act, Congress followed the 'hard energy path', allocating 84 billion Dollars to synthetic fuel commercialization and only 4 billion Dollars for solar energy, bio-mass and conservation. Because the number of government owned plants is restricted to 3 at maximum, most of these 84 billion Dollars will flow as subsidy to the energy industry. Because the windfall profit tax is deductible as business expense, decontrol will result, in spite of the assistance to the poor, in a remarkable allocation in favor of the oil industry.

Besides Carter's failure to get emergency preparedness in order, his attempt to shelter the windfall profit tax receipts from yearly budget deliberations by putting it into a separate Energy Trust Fund proved abortive as did the Energy Mobilization Board proposal, designed to bypass bureaucratic inertia in approving energy projects.

The half-success story of Carter's energy policy must be put in perspective: the new administration seems to be committed to cut down the residual 'New

Deal' parts of energy law and regulation. Renewable energy and conservation budgets are reduced drastically. While smaller Synfuel subsidies will be kept, the overall receipts from the windfall profit tax will be used to finance tax cuts which favor large taxpayers. In contrast, energy assistance to the poor will be minimized. The precarious Carter compromises, therefore, are broken to pieces. While the redistributional conflict is buried for the moment, it very likely will face a revival. Because the Reagan team is considering leaving contingency management totally to the market, the U.S. will be as unpredictable an energy partner as in the past.[41]

7. Conclusion

The effects of American energy policy disqualify unilateralism as a successfull mode of political adaptation to a changing international environment. The relative strength and the position of the United States in almost any issue area of international relations may create the illusion that the American society can be isolated effectively from outside events and that foreign demands, therefore, are negligible for the United States decision-making process. For example, the American posture in the currency sector helped very well to finance oil imports, because, as the German Federal Bank remarked critically, national reserve boards of partner countries bailed out the Dollar and thereby subsidized United States Petroleum imports.[42] But the interdependent structure of the energy area leads inevitable to severe yet delayed repercussions for the American society.

The construction of the American political system conscientiously minimizes the opportunity for foreign influence. When domestic support is needed to implement foreign strategies, the control capacity of the political system is very low.[43] It is then bound to implement domestic demands, not vice versa. In an economic political issue area like energy, its control capacity is even more diminished by the independent decision-making of companies that influence heavily important variables. The only way not to destroy, but to check this private control capacity is in cooperation with other governments. But here, the American government is constrained a) by its own goals to assure leadership/predominance in connection with the more narrow interests of economic advantage, b) by its inability to overcome domestic pressures to abstain from intervention in private control capacity, c) by the total incalculability of domestic political outcomes as long as basic redistributional questions remain unresolved. On the other hand, it seems that the central decision-makers are not willing or able to pacify the domestic redistributional conflict, to transform it into a purely distributive one and so to enhance the freedom of action for foreign policy commitments. For this would mean compromising their basic value orientations or, perhaps, their chances for reelection. It is this complex dilemma that makes it unlikely that the United States political system is able to change its adaptation mode of unilateralism in issue areas like energy in a quick, cooperative and self-regulated way.

Notes

1 This paper summarizes the results of a larger study funded by the Volkswagen Foundation. The conclusions are drawn from an extensive analysis of governmental and private sources. The positions of interest groups are derived from statements during congressional hearings, mainly before the Committee on Interior and Insular Affairs (later Co. on Energy and Natural Resources), and the Co. on Finance in the Senate, the Subc. on Energy and Power of the Co. on Commerce and the Co. of Ways and Means in the House of Representatives. Additionally, hearings of the two Foreign Relations Committees and the Energy Subcommittee of the Joint Economic Committee were studied. Some hearings of the Subc. on Antitrust and Monopoly of the Senate Co. on the Judiciary, the Co. on Government Operations in both Houses, the Senate Commerce Co. and the House Co. on Science and Technology were of some interest. Interest groups assisted kindly by submitting special studies, resolutions, speeches and giving interviews during a research visit to Washington in April 1978. Reports and Studies from the Executive Departments (Interior, Energy, Treasury, and State), the Monthly Energy Review, The State Department Bulletin, the Wireless Bulletin and the Weekly Compilation of Presidential Papers were, besides statements during the Congressional Hearings, the main sources for the Executive, also complemented by personal interviews. Of particular assistance were the numerous studies about energy policy questions of the General Accounting Office, the Congressional Budget Office and the Congressional Research Services. Political developments were checked by analyzing the Congressional Record, the Congressional Quarterly and the National Journal. As regular sources about energy events served the Petroleum Economist, the Oil and Gas Journal and World Oil.

   The author owes debt to Louis Turner, Guy de Carmoy, Bob Lieber and Leon Lindberg for their critical comments during the Conference, which very much helped revise and, hopefully, improve the paper. With respect to the last developments, discussions with Mrs. Despres from Sen. Bradley's staff, Robert Keohane and Joseph Yeager were highly enlightening.

2 The paper of Prof. de Carmoy contains detailed information about U.S. impact on the world energy market.

3 David Easton, A Systems Analysis of Political Life, New York/London/Sydney [2] 1967; see Ernst-Otto Czempiel, Amerikanische Außenpolitik, Stuttgart 1979, p. 13–19

4 Karl W. Deutsch, External Influences on the International Behavior of States, in: R. Barry Farrell (ed.), Approaches to Comparative and International Politics, Evanston [2] 1969

5 See Guy de Carmoy, Energy for Europe. Economic and Political Implications, Washington D.C. 1977; Robert J. Lieber, Oil and the Middle East War. Europe and the Energy Crisis, Harvard 1976

6 As documented by the Europa Archiv, D 1973–1979

7 Distributive Impacts on Proposed Changes in National Energy Policy. Hearings, Committee on the Budget, Task Force on Distributive Impacts of Budget and Economic Policies, U.S. Congress, 95/1, House, 1977, p. 165; Jill A. King, The Impact of the Energy Crisis on Low Income Families, FEA, Washington, D.C. 1975, pp, 1/2

8 Bonner and Moore Ass., Analysis of Integrated Refinery Operations, Washington 1976; Petroleum Marketing Practices Act, Report, Committee on Interstate and Foreign Commerce, U.S. Congress, 95/1, House, 1977

9 U.S. Department of Commerce/Federal Energy Administration: Voluntary Industrial Energy Conservation. Progress, Report 5, July 1976

10 Distributive Impacts . . . (see note 7), p. 124

11 Freigewerkschaftliche Nachrichten 11/1975, pp. 7/8; 12/1976, p. 6; U.S. Section, European Community – U.S. Businessmen's Council, Energy Task Force: Energy Supply and Vulnerability, 1975

12 National Taxpayers Union in Energy Tax Act, Hearings, Comm. on Finance, U.S. Congress, 95/1, 1977, pt. 3, Senate, p. 1056

13 Andrew Biemiller of AFL/CIO in Energy Independence Authority Act of 1975, Hearings, Comm. on Banking, Housing, and Urban Affairs, U.S. Congress, 94/2, Senate, 1976, p. 153

14 Statements of John S. Withers, Jack Carlson and Lawrence H. Fox in: Arab Boycott, Hearings, Subc. on International Finance, Comm. on Banking, Housing and Urban Affairs, U.S. Congress, 95/1, 1977, Senate

15 International Diffusion of Energy Technology, Report on a Workshop of Massachusetts Institute of Technology, July 1976, pp. 1–5

16 Committee on Economic Development, Economic Consequences of High-Priced Energy, New York 1975; Trilateral Commission, Task Force Reports 1–7, New York 1977, Triangle Papers 5, 6, 7

17 For Henry Kissinger's position, see his testimony in: United States International Energy Policy, Hearings, Subc. on Energy, Joint Economic Committee, United States Congress, 95/1, 1976; also Wireless Bulletin 3/4.1.1974, pp. 3–8; 7/11.1.1974, p. 4

18 This was the thesis of V. H. Oppenheim, The Past: We Pushed them, in: Foreign Policy 25/ Winter 1975/76

19 Wireless Bulletin 188/ 15.11.1974, p. 11; see Richard Mancke, Squeaking By. U.S. Energy Policy since the Embargo, Columbia University Press 1976, pp. 84–86

20 Melvin A. Conant/Fern R. Gold, United States Foreign Policy Impact of the Energy Situation, pp. 690–713, in: Congressional Research Service: Project Interdependence. U.S. and World Energy Outlook through 1990, Washington, D.C. 1977, p. 702; James A. Akins, The Arabs and the United States in an Election Year, pp. 187–197, in: Ragaei El Mallakh/Carl McGuire (eds.), United States and World Energy Resources. Prospects and Priorities, Boulder, Calif. 1977, pp. 193/194; New York Times Index 1976, 14.12., p. 1203

21 The section about the IEA relies heavily on Peter Roggen, Die Internationale Energie-Agentur. Energiepolitik und wirtschaftliche Sicherheit, Bonn 1979

22 Congressional Quarterly Weekly Report, Vol. 38, No. 2, pp. 59–62; see also Louis Turner/James Bedore, Saudi-Arabien: eine Geldmacht, pp. 397–418, in: Europa Archiv. Vol. 33/1978

23 Wireless Bulletin 192/1977, pp. 17–19; Wireless Bulletin 146/1978, pp. 7/8; Der SPIEGEL, 27/1979, pp. 19–21

24 James A. Schlesinger, A Testing Time for America, p. 5, in: Fortune, February 1976; Wireless Bulletin 13.2.1979, pp. 4–6; former doubts about the feasibility of military intervention are summarized by John Collins/Clyde Mark, Military Solutions to U.S. Petroleum, pp. 726–751, in: Project Interdependence . . . (note 20); for the doctrine see U.S. Military Posture for Fiscal Year 1981 (Joint Chiefs of Staff), pp. 28; DOD Annual Report, Fiscal Year 1981, Chapter I, Sects. VI and VII; Wireless Bulletin, March 3, 1981, pp. 16/17; Wireless Bulletin, May 6, 1981, pp. 18/19

25 See testimony in: U.S. International Energy Policy (note 17), pp. 61, 63, 67

26 National Journal, 14.12.1974, p. 1865; Business Week, 13.1.1975, p. 44

27 For early criticism of shortcomings of President Carter's energy policy see Congressional Research Service: An Initial Analysis of the President's National Energy Plan, June

1977; Congressional Budget Office: President Carter's Energy Proposals: A Perspective. Staff Working Paper, June 1977

28 The specific role of relations between the Executive and the Legislative for energy policy has been analyzed by Walter Goldstein, The Politics of U.S. Energy Policy, pp. 181–185, in: Energy Policy, Sept. 1978

29 Congressional Record, 19.11.1973, S 37564; National Journal, 8.3.1975, p. 363

30 Kissinger-Simon Proposals to Finance Oil Imports, Hearings, Subc. on Energy, Joint Economic Committee, U.S. Congress, 93/2, 1974, pp. 44–46; Congressional Record, 18.11.1973, H 37551; 19.11.1973; S 37583; Windfall or Excess Profit Tax, Hearings, Co. on Ways and Means, U.S. Congress, 93/2, House, 1974, pp. 169/170, 192; Economic Impacts of President Carter's Energy Plan, Hearings, Co. on Energy and Natural Resources, U.S. Congress, 95/1, September 1977, p. 148; Proposed National Energy Plan, Hearings, Subc. on Oversight and Investigations, Co. on Interstate and Foreign Commerce, U.S. Congress, 95/1, House, 1977, pp. 32/33; The Relationship Between the Department on Energy and Energy Industries, Hearings, Co. on Energy and Natural Resources, U.S. Congress, 95/2, Senate, 1978, pp. 34/35

31 As sources for the work of the committees served the Congressional Quarterly Weekly Report and the Reports of the Committees.

32 Congressional Record, 8.4.1975, S 9376

33 In 1979, the Senate refused an amendment of Sen. Javits to authorize $1 billion for energy development in non-OPEC regions. Congressional Quarterly Almanac, 1979, p. 601

34 Congressional Research Service: Project Interdependence – U.S. and World Energy Outlook Through 1990 (note 20), p. 595

35 A precise overview over the remaining freedom of decision-making of the oil companies is given in Louis Turner, Oil Companies in the International System, London 1978, last chapter.

36 Theodore S. Lowi, Distribution, Regulation, Redistribution: The Functions of Government, pp. 245–256, in: A. Wolfinger (ed.), Readings in American Political Behavior, Englewood Cliffs 1970

37 Data from Independent Oil Association of America, The Oil Industry in Your State, 1974 and 1975

38 The 'second energy crisis' is discussed in detail by Robert J. Lieber, Europe and America in the World Energy Crisis, pp. 531–545, in: International Affairs, London, Oct. 1979; Harald Müller, Erdöl und Sicherheit. Zur westlichen Energiepolitik nach der 'zweiten Energiekrise', pp. 21–45, in: 'aus politik und zeitgeschichte', B 6/1980; Alvin A. Alm, E. William Colglazier, Barbara Kates-Garnick, Coping with Interruptions, pp. 303–346, in: David A. Deese/Joseph S. Nye (eds.), Energy and Security, Cambridge, Mass. 1981; Petroleum Economist, Feb. 1981, pp. 46–48 and 69/70

39 For the domestic developments in 1979 and 1980 see Joseph A. Yeager, The Energy Battles of 1979, pp. 601–636, in: Craufurd D. Goodwin (ed.), Energy Policy in Perspective. Today's Problems, Yesterday's Solutions, Washington, D.C., 1981; Congressional Quarterly Almanac, 1979, pp. 601, 649–657; Congressional Quarterly Weekly Report, 4/1980, pp. 183–186; 10/1980, pp. 668/669; 16/1980, p. 1035; 23/1980, p. 1584; 24/1980, p. 1668; 25/1980, p. 1691; 26/1980, pp. 1790/1791

40 Yeager (note 39), pp. 611, 622/623

41 Amerika-Dienst, March 4, 1981; National Journal, March 14, 1981, pp. 463–465; 430/431

42 Öl – Zeitschrift für Mineralölwirtschaft, May 1978, p. 141

43 Stephen D. Krasner, Defending the National Interest, Raw Material Investments and U.S. Foreign Policy, Princeton, New Jersey 1978, p. 271; as to the considerations of the 'fathers of the constitution' to ban foreign influence see The Federalist Papers, New York and Scarborough, 1961, pp. 148/149, 150, 275. 344, 406, 412/413, 451, 42, 53, 65, 256/259, 366, 376

Leon N. Lindberg, Comparing Energy Policies. Political Constraints and the Energy Syndrome, pp. 325–356, in: Lindberg (ed.), The Energy Syndrome. Comparing National Responses to the Energy Crisis, Lexington/Toronto 1977, enumerates as factors impeding energy-political change: bureaucratic conservatism, tecnocratic ideology, interest of dominant classes. His interpretation is very similar to the thrust of this paper. The main difference is probably the stronger point this paper makes concerning the basic unity of American interest groups with respect to foreign energy policy matters.

Guy de Carmoy

Economic and Political Consequences of US Energy Policy on Europe

1. The Issues

Energy is a basic factor of production and an essential element of well being in industrial societies. At the zenith of the oil age, energy in its various forms was considered wrongly as an almost illimited resource. Since the political control over the most abundant reserves of oil has changed hands, oil policy has become what it should always have been: the search for the optimum management of limited resources.

In view of the geographical location of industry on the one hand and of fossil deposits on the other, international trade in primary energy involves three main actors or group of actors: (1) the United States, (2) Western Europe and Japan, (3) OPEC and especially the Middle Eastern oil producing countries. The United States is at the same time the world's largest producer of primary energy, the world's largest consumer (27.7% of total in 1979) and a major importer of crude oil (24.0% of world trade). Western Europe as a group is second to the U.S. as a large consumer (23.3% of total) but is a very small producer and the largest importer of crude oil (36.9% of world trade). Japan's position is even more precarious than that of Western Europe. The Middle East owns 55.7% of the world's proved crude oil reserves and supplies 57.6% of world exports mostly to Western Europe and to Japan and to a lesser extent to the United States.[1] The Soviet Union is presently a net exporter of small amounts of oil to the OECD countries and therefore not a significant trading partner.

Oil trade is taking place since 1973 in a different pattern of economic power relations. The OPEC group of countries has been able to impose two sharp though not uniform increases in the price of crude in 1973—74 and in 1979—80 respectively, and to stabilise the previously pent up supply of exports. The importance of the second oil shock indicates that the adjustment of demand to supply in the consumer countries has been lacking vigor.

In between the political situation in the Middle East has been deteriorating to the detriment of the United States (in spite of its contribution to a peace settlement between Israel and Egypt) and to the benefit of the Soviet Union which is pursuing a forward policy in the area.

Thus the global position of the OECD countries is seriously weakened: its terms of trade have deteriorated, the volume of oil deliveries has probably reached a ceiling and the security of supplies is threatened. The relative position of the OECD countries has changed in the meantime. Japan has engaged in a vigorous energy policy on all fronts. The European response has not been so strong on average. In spite of considerable potential resources the energy policy of the United States has been deceptive. The lack of a strong reaction from all major consumers had a bearing on the oil market and through the oil prices on world inflation, on global demand and on the balance of payments of producer and consumer countries as well. It had also a bearing on security in the Middle East, as oil, security and local conflicts are closely interrelated in the area.

Europe is more exposed than the United States to the economic consequences of higher energy prices and to the political consequences of a change in the power relationship in the Middle East.

It is proposed, after studying the American domestic energy balance, to analyze the energy position of the United States and of Europe in a world economic setting and the geopolitical position of the United States and Europe in the Middle East strategic setting. Suggestions will be made in conclusion for a comprehensive approach by the industrialized countries to the serious risks involved in relation with energy.

2. The United States domestic energy situation and policy

The United States has vast resources and fast growing needs in a very complex energy market. An overview of the supply and demand situation and of the market structure will shed some light on the past policies on a branch basis and will help explain why the attempts towards the setting up of an overall energy policy after 1973 met with considerable obstacles.

The United States is an enormous energy consumer. On a per capita basis its primary energy consumption is 2.5 greater than in the European Community. The United States is well endowed with energy resources which do not fit with its present pattern of consumption. Its share in world reserves of oil (5%) is small compared to its share in world oil production (15.0%) and consumption (27.7%). The ratio of reserves to production has fallen in 1978 to less than 9 years. Its share in world natural gas reserves (7.6%) compares with 38.5% of world gas consumption and a ratio of reserves to production of some 11 years.[2] By contrast, its share in world coal reserves (27.8%) could last several centuries at the current rate of production.[3] The United States also owns 27% of the uranium reserves in the world outside the communist area.[4]

From these figures it would seem that the United States was in a position to substitute coal and nuclear energy for oil and gas in electricity generation and to a certain extent in the industrial sector. As a matter of fact the substitution was not significant. On the contrary net oil imports rose from 83.3 m t.o.e. in

Table 1: UNITED STATES Key Energy Indicators and Data (Mtoe)

	1960	1973	1973	1985	1990
GENERAL					
Energy Demand (A) Energy	1014.2	1744.1	1857.32	22.9	2370.5
Production (B)	956.0	1463.2	1451.7	1722.9	1994.6
BIA 95.1	83.9	78.2	81.2	84.1	
Net Oil Imports	83.3	300.0	414.8	408.6	414.6
Total Oil					
Consumption	452.8	787.3	888.4	919.6	956.6
CONSUMPTION					
TPE/GDP Ratio	1.51	1.55	1.46	1.30	1.25
TPE/GDP Elasticity	1.07	0.50	0.51	0.73	
Per Capita TPE	5.61	8.27	8.44	9.15	9.76
Total Final Consumption	810.2	1306.6	1353.4	1473.8	1628.9
Industry	309.8	467.5	435.2	577.4	677.9
Transport	234.3	406.5	464.1	464.2	487.0
Residential					
/Commercial	266.1	432.6	454.1	432.2	464.0
PRODUCTION					
Solids	251.9	346.2	372.4	529.6	728.6
Oil	382.8	511.2	492.0	534.8	566.1
Gas	293.8	518.7	445.4	420.3	402.1
Nuclear	0.1	20.9	70.9	162.3	217.4
Hydro Geothermal	36.3	65.6	70.1	75.9	80.4
Electricity (TWh)	891.6	2086.9	2401.0	3216.3	3673.0
TRADE					
Coal Exports	22.8	32.8	24.0	17.2	49.7
Imports	0.2	0.7	5.2	–	–
Oil Exports	6.6	10.8	15.6	408.6	414.6
Imports	89.6	310.7	430.4		
Bunkers	16.7	17.5	21.3	23.8	24.1
Gas Exports	0.3	2.0	1.4	32.4	35.1
Imports	3.7	23.6	22.4		
References:					
GDP (1970 US $ billion)	672.1	1125.5	1271.0	1637.0	1901.0
Population (million)	180.8	211.0	220.0	232.0	243.0

Growth Rates of Key Indicators (percent per year)

	1960-73	1973-78	1973-85	1985-80
TPE	4.3	1.2	1.9	2.2
GDP	4.0	1.7	3.7	3.0
TFC	3.7	0.7	1.2	2.0
Net Oil Imports	10.4	4.7	0.2	0.3
Oil Consumption	4.3	2.4	0.5	0.8

Source: Energy Policies and Programmes of IEA Countries, 1979 Review, OECD 1980.

1960 to 300.0 m t.o.e. in 1973 and to 414.8 m t.o.e. in 1978, the share of imports to total oil consumption rising from 18.4% to 38.1% and to 47.6% respectively.[5] This laissez-faire attitude increased the degree of the country's external dependence vis a vis OPEC and the pressures on global oil demand, where Western Europe and Japan were competing for supplies with the United States.

The market structure of the United States explains to a certain extent the drift in the energy balance sheet. It is essentially a vast continental market with, apart from oil imports, a marginal external trade in the form of coal exports and natural gas imports. The large oil companies constitute the main link with the outside world. By contrast, the surface pattern of fossil fuel rights of ownership has multiplied the number of small business enterprises engaged in oil and gas drilling and in coal mining. Furthermore the distance between the major producing and consuming areas of the various fuels has required pipeline networks for oil and for gas, the railroads assuring the transportation of coal. The diverging interests between energy producing and energy consuming states required interstate i.e. federal regulations while state regulations often prevailed for intrastate activities. A complex and cumbersome bureaucratic machine handled the maze of federal and of state regulations on a branch basis. Interest groups were strongly organized along the usual patterns of producers, transporters, distributors and consumers, not to mention the public utilities. With the 1970 Clean Air Act a new factor was inserted in this pattern: the protection of the environment. It created a dichotomy between the price-conscious consumer and the ecology-minded citizen, further complicating the legislation. In this system mainly structured on a branch basis, the need for an overall energy policy could emerge only from repeated external shocks.

Oil production in the United States decreased after a peak in 1970 and despite the contribution of Alaska. Meanwhile oil consumption increased at the rate of 4.3% per annum during the 1960—1973 period and net oil imports at the rate of 10.4%. The policy goal was to protect the individual property owner against cheap imported oil through a mandatory quota system. After 1970 foreign crude prices rose to the level of domestic crude. In 1973 import quotas were abolished and replaced by a tariff.

Natural gas production peaked in 1973. Two thirds of the gas produced was subject to federal price control in the so-called interstate market and was transported by pipeline companies. The last third was sold in the state where it was produced, at a price generally higher than in the interstate market. In the late 1960s prices moved upwards, but intrastate prices rose faster than the inter-prices which were intended to favor the consumer in the residential sector.

The United States has been dubbed "The Persian Gulf of Coal". Coal lost in the 1960s to oil and gas a large part of the industrial market, but expanded in utility consumption. Production gradually shifted from the deep coal mines with high sulphur content in the Appalachian to the surface mines West of Missisipi. The latter mines are far from the consuming areas and the bulk of coal is shipped by rail. Transportation facilities in the West were inadequate and regulated railway tariffs hampered the coal trade. Safety and environment regulations restrained production. So did a 1971 moratorium on mining leases on federal land. As a reult the share of coal declined slightly in the overall energy production.

The nuclear industry developed fast in the 1960s. Two giant American multinationals were attacking successfully the domestic and the overseas markets for Light Water Reactors and were in a position of world leadership. The industry had the mastery of the fuel cycle and developed its research on the breeder reactor. But a reversal in the trend took place in 1975. Orders for new reactors almost stopped. Cancellations and deferrals multiplied. The shortfall was due to the reduction in the growth of electricity demand, to the rise in direct and indirect construction costs and principally to the action of the environmentalists in promoting restrictive legislation and in challenging licensing decisions in the courts. Thus "The Carter administration inherited a stalemate on nuclear power when it entered office in 1977".[6]

In spite of the shortcomings of its domestic energy policy, the overall energy picture of the United States has changed since 1973. During the 1960 −1973 period, total primary energy consumption (TPE) increased at a somewhat faster pace than the gross domestic product: 4.3% per annum vs. 4.0%. During the 1973−1978 period, the relationship was reversed, TPE growing at 1.2% only whilst GDP grew at 1.7% (cf Table 1). The link of energy use with output seems to be breaking. It is reasonable to expect that energy use will grow at a relatively slow pace in the future.

The trends in oil consumption and imports are on the decline. Net oil consumption annual growth fell from 4.3% in the first period to 2.4% in the second period and net oil imports from 10.4% to 4.7%.

Though the trends are moving in the right direction, the results up to 1978 were far from satisfactory. The share of oil in total primary energy consumption *increased* from 45.1% in 1973 to 47.8% in 1978. The volume of oil imports increased from 300.0 m t.o.e. to 414.8 m t.o.e. during the same period and accounted in 1978 for 22.3% of TPE. External dependence, i.e. the ratio of total imports to energy demand also increased from 16.1% to 21.8% in the period (cf Table 1).

The lack of a strong energy policy on the part of the United States had serious macro-economic consequences at the world and at the European levels.

3. The American and European responses to the OPEC challenge

When the oil power shifted from the major Western oil companies to the OPEC member states, the world oil market, previously dependent upon the demands of the industrialized countries, became supply oriented. The new oligopolists were able in a short time to capture the rent, to fix the price and to limit the volume of output.

We shall consider the effects of and the reactions to the two rises in oil prices, the problems ahead in the field of oil and in that of the substitutes to oil so as to assess the policies of the United States and of the European countries and their interaction.

The first oil shock

The rise in prices in 1973–74 reached 350%. During the lull that followed, real oil prices fell by about 10%. The OPEC decision to stabilize production prevented a more substantial fall in prices. Oil output in the world outside the communist area was practically at the same level in 1978 (2397 m t.o.e) as in 1973.

Table 2: US and Western Europe Oil Indicators in m.t.o.e. and in percentage

	United States			Western Europe		
	1973	1978	1979	1973	1978	1979
Total oil consumption (A)	787.3	888.4	826.9	748.9	715.7	726.5
Net oil imports (B)	300.0	414.8	394.0	726.3	626.1	621.3
Share of (A) in TPE	45.1	47.8	45.5	60.3	55.9	54.8
Share of (B) in TPE	17.2	22.3	20.8	58.5	48.5	46.9
1978/73% change						
in (A)		+12.8			− 4.4	
in (B)		+38.3			− 13.8	

Sources: OECD Energy Statistics
Energy Policies and Programmes of IEA Countries, OECD, 1979 Review, Paris 1980
BP Statistical Review of the World Oil Industry 1979

Europe and the United States were buying respectively 46% and 15% of OPEC exports in 1973. Their reactions to the OPEC challenge differed markedly. Western Europe reduced its oil imports thanks in part to its savings in oil consumption and mainly to the development of the North Sea oil fields. The United States increased its oil imports so as to face both a small decline in production and a sharp increase in consumption. If the European dependence on OPEC oil was still much greater than that of the United States, the European record was more satisfactory. Japan's consumption did not increase between 1973 and 1978. The demand in developing countries rose in conjunction with population growth and industrialization. The world oil consumption outside the communist area grew from 2 338.8 m t.o.e in 1973 to 2 480.4 m t.o.e in 1978. The difference i.e. 141.6 m t.o.e was not much greater than the growth of US oil imports, i.e. 114.8 m t.o.e. Thus the rise in American demand was the significant factor in the rise of global demand between the two oil shocks.

The continued strength of world — and especially American — demand for oil comforted the oil producers in their oligopolistic potential to fix high prices, signalling an increase in the relative value of oil as compared to the manufactured goods imported by the oil producers. "This increase raised both the upper and lower limits of the range within which oil exporters exercise discretion over the price".[7] The bulk of the increase in the oil bill accrued to those OPEC countries which has a small absorptive capacity for manufactures. Their surplus funds were mostly invested in dollar denominated instruments. If and when the growing volume of oil imports affected the confidence in the US currency, the dollar holdings tended to decrease. The surplus OPEC countries had no incentive to export more oil and opted for a rise in price which boosted the value of the oil in the ground.[8]

The 1973—74 price increase had a deflationary effect of 2% on the GNP of the OECD area. The current balance of the area moved from a $10.1 billion surplus to a deficit which lasted until the end of 1977. By that time the transfer of income from the industrialized countries to the oil producing countries had taken place through a variety of national adjustment policies.

At the American initiative the International Energy Agency was created in 1974 under the aegis of the OECD with French dissent. The IEA has contributed to collect information to improve technology, to set up a standby emergency sharing programme and to analyze the policies goals and performances of the individual countries in its annual reviews. It is not a decision making body. The European Community also fulfills advisory functions, but its member states have most adopted a common energy policy. In short, no global energy strategy was adopted by the industrialized countries in the interlude between 1974—1979.

The second oil shock

Just as the Kippur war had been the detonator of the first price rise, the Iranian revolution was the signal of a succession of upward movements. The global price rise as of July 1980 was estimated at 130% increasing the oil bill of the OECD countries by 2% of GDP. The consumer price had been moving upward in the meantime by several percentage points and the bulk of the rise can be attributed to oil because of the prevalence of restrictive monetary and fiscal policies in the consumer countries. Current balances of the OECD area moved from a surplus of $9.1 bn in 1978 to a deficit of $37.4 bn in 1979 and to a projected deficit of $81 bn in 1980. As the US current balance was almost in equilibrium, high deficits fell on OECD Europe and to a lesser extent on Japan.[9]

Table 3: World Current Account

	1973	1974	1975	1976	1977	1978	1979	1980
OECD	10 1/2	−26	1/2	−19	−24 1/2	10 1/2	−37 1/2	−81
OPEC	7 1/2	59 1/2	27	36 1/2	29	4 1/2	67	114
Non-Oil developing countries	−7 1/2	−26	−31	−19	−12 1/2	−25 1/2	−34 1/2	−49 1/2
Other non-OECD countries	7	−2	−21 1/2	−15	−16 1/2	−20	−13	−28

Source: OECD Economic Outlook, n° 27, July 1980, table 28, p. 65

The second oil shock brought the consumer countries to a better appraisal of the risks of the situation both at the national and at the international levels. In 1979, for the first time total oil consumption and net oil imports decreased in the United States. In the same year the OECD countries were fighting against domestic inflation with more determination. The leaders of the seven major OECD countries met in Tokyo in June 1979 and decided to limit the imports of their respective countries in 1985 to the level of 1978. In June 1980 at Venice, the same leaders decided to increase substantially their production of substitutes of oil, especially coal and nuclear power, and thereby to reduce the share of oil from 53% to 40% of their energy consumption in 1990. They also committed themselves to decouple economic growth from energy consumption, with the objective of reducing the income/consumption ratio to 0.6.

The ripples of the last price rise have not only inflated the OECD deficit and the OPEC surplus. They have increased the deficits of the non OPEC developing countries, accelerating the rate of their formidable indebtedness. The volume of this debt and its nature are such that individual countries may face bankruptcy and that the world banking and monetary systems are becoming ever more fragile.

Oil prospects in the middle term

In spite of the temporary oil glut caused by the recession in the industrialized countries, the oil prices are not on the decline in the medium term. Short of a drastic reduction in demand, the upper limit of oil prices is dependent upon the selling prices and availability of substitutes. The spread between the price of oil and that of synthetic fuels derived from coal or oil sands is still high and the lead time to bring these products to the market is still long. On the supply side, the OPEC availability for exports which amounted to 28.0 mbd (1400 m t.o.e) in 1978 would be reduced to 26.5 mbd in 1985 and to 25.7 mbd in 1990, these quantities being smaller than the latest submissions of net oil import requirements by the OECD countries. A notional gap would appear as early as 1985.[10] The United States and other importers "are caught in an acute and lasting energy emergency".[11] The 1980 war between Iraq and Iran has interrupted the supplies from both countries which amounted to some 3.5 mbd i.e. about 10% of the crude oil exports to the industrialized countries. Thus the temporary glut mentioned above might change suddenly into a severe shortage followed by a third price hike.

The OECD and OPEC countries have both a primary interest in avoiding the risks of a world durable recession or of a breakdown of the international payment mechanism. OPEC is currently discussing a proposal for a long term strategy to move up oil prices at a predictable rate on the basis of a formula reflecting inflation, currency fluctuation and world economic growth. The OECD countries at some point in time will have to respond by formulating an overall policy taking into account their potential supplies in all primary sources of energy. They will have by all means to devote a sizeable amount of their GDP in expensive investments in all primary sources of energy.

Issues in natural gas, coal and nuclear energy

The United States is potentially a large importer of natural gas. The bulk of its supplies are shipped from Canada and the two governments have agreed on the pipeline network. Imports from Mexico will be rising and the building of a pipeline is under consideration. Thus a North American natural gas supply network may be developed. Disagreements over price have led to the cancellation of a contract for Algerian gas. Algeria is the only gas market where the United States would be competing with Western Europe which imports mainly from the Soviet Union.

The United States has regularly exported limited quantities of coal to Europe. It was suggested that these exports be increased by a factor of 6 until 2000 in the framework of a strong pro-coal policy to be pursed in the OECD area.[12] Considering the above mentioned obstacles to coal development in the United States, it seems likely that the bulk of the increase in exports will take place only in the 1990s once the investments in the coal chain transport have been realised. Thus European countries will have to increase their imports from Australia and South Africa in the 1980s.

The stalemate of the American nuclear industry has already been stressed. The United States is losing to the European countries — essentially to France, Germany and Sweden — and also to Japan its position of leadership in spite of the fact that these two areas had either a weak or a non existent uranium resource base. German appears as the strongest potential exporter of LWRs and France the potential leader in enrichment, reprocessing and the breeder reactor. "Significant deployment of a US breeder development remains perhaps two decades away even if a positive decision is made soon and all goes well with technology".[13] The European countries are diversifying their supplies of natural uranium between the United States, Canada, Australia and several African countries.

A curtailment of American exports of natural and/or of enriched uranium to Europe was feared a few years ago in relation with the United States concern for the prevention of nuclear proliferation. The government adopted the concept of "full scope safeguards" after the explosion of the Indian bomb in 1974 and convened in 1977 all supplier and buyer states to participate in a thorough investigation of the industry entitled International Nuclear Fuel Cycle Evaluation. Contrary to American expectations, the 1980 INFCE report backs the view that the breeder reactor and the reprocessing plant will be needed to meet the future energy requirements of the industrialized countries. Only few European countries and Japan will have such facilities by 2000. It is

111

hoped that the United States will come to the view that "the problem is not sensitive materials and technologies as much as sensitive countries"[14] attempting to achieve "clandestine" proliferation. After the Venice summit meeting's formal encouragement to nuclear energy production, the American non proliferation policy is evolving in a direction acceptable to the European suppliers of nuclear reactors and services.

The policy issues concerning natural gas, coal and nuclear energy involve mainly the member states of OECD. Most of them can be solved within this group. The United States' future policy regarding coal and nuclear energy will have a great influence on European developments in these fields.

Appraisal

The Europeans and the Americans share the blame for their present predicament. The Europeans on a thin resource base switched in the 1960s from coal in their ground to offshore oil without seriously launching a nuclear alternative. The Americans on a huge resource base were improvident oil consumers and importers and almost managed to kill their nuclear industry in the late 1970s. The Euro-American energy system, based on the ability of the major oil companies to supply the growing needs of the industrial countries broke down in 1973.

The United States, the dominant power in terms of consumption and imports of primary energy sources, did not respond adequately to the OPEC challenge. Its laxist behavior on the domestic market affected the European energy market in several ways: (a) the OPEC pricing policy was more aggressive because no restraint was exerted on American domestic consumption so that imports continued to rise after the first oil shock; (b) the depreciation of the dollar, if it reduced temporarily oil bill in real terms for the Europeans, was an inducement for the OPEC producers to seek a compensation in terms of higher nominal prices; (c) the depreciation of the dollar on the one hand and the low domestic prices of energy on the other hand were giving a competitive advantage to the American exporters of manufactures over their European counterparts. This competitive advantage declined when the American administration decided in 1978—79 to defend the dollar parity and to decontrol the prices of oil and gas.

Energy policies in the West were basically national. A modicum of cooperation took place within OECD/IEA and within the EEC. In 1979 and in 1980, the summit meetings of the seven larger OECD countries took joint resolutions on energy conservation and substitution at the request of the Europeans and on the basis of their proposals. They do not amount to a long term global strategy and therefore do not constitute a platform for a future discussion with OPEC.

From a macro-economy viewpoint "no anti-inflation effort, no sustained policy, of growth, and no plan to organise the world's monetary system could survive if the present energy situation were to continue".[15] The economic constraints deriving from the dependence on outside sources of energy are all the more serious since the Middle East is the seat of a major power struggle with far reaching political consequences both for Western Europe and for the United States.

Well-educated Palestinians are filling positions of responsibility in the Gulf states and are the advocates of their brothers living under Israeli rule. The Palestinian people recognize as their spokesman the PLO which has the official backing of all the Arab states. The Arab Israeli conflict is a permanent feature of the Middle East since the creation of the state of Israel. It was exacerbated after the 1967 war when the Israeli refused to comply with UN Resolution 242 recommending the evacuation of the occupied territories. It led the oil producing Arab states associated in OAPEC to use the oil weapon after the 1973 war in the form of an embargo directed primarily against the United States whilst France and Britain were not subject to restrictive measures. In Saudi Arabia society and the regime are almost inseparable. The royal family is the guardian of Mecca, the spiritual centre of Islam. The Wahabist Islamic sect is most influential and advocates the resumption of the pure Islamic doctrine. The historical mission of the state is the revival of Islam. Saudi Arabia is contributing military and economic aid to other Arab states, especially those confronting Israel. As such it is a regional power, supporting the moderate wing of the PLO and disagreeing with the Camp David accords because it considered insufficient the provisions on Palestinian autonomy. Saudi Arabia is also playing a role in the international system as the major OPEC producer and exporter. In this dual capacity it had close economic relations with the United States and was able to exert between 1974 and 1978 a moderating influence within OPEC on the fixation of oil prices. The society was also exposed to the cultural shock of the new wealth. The attack on the Mecca Mosque was viewed by some observers as the limited action of a group of fundamentalist students, by others as a threat to the regime and, therefore, as, in retrospect, "the most important development relevant to energy in 1979".[17] Under the Shah, Iran, a non-Arab country of the Chiite religious faith, enjoyed an apparent stability but social unrest developed under forced industrialisation and the too rapid transformation of the society. An Islamic Republic was proclaimed in 1979 which was unable to maintain order between warring political and regional factions and took a definite anti-American stand. Its oil production which amounted in 1978 to one sixth of OPEC production was cut down by half. Iraq took advantage of the societal and military disintegration in Iran to launch in 1980 an attack on the oil fields near Abadan, seeking dominance in the upper tier of the Gulf. The current fighting is a threat to the safe circulation of the tankers supplying the OECD countries.

The Soviet Union has pursued with a mixture of success and failure its historical goal of influence over and access to the Middle East. It was obliged under American pressure to withdraw from Iran after World War II. It signed a treaty of alliance with Egypt after the 1956 Suez expedition and entered into close association with Syria and Iraq. It gave continuous support to the PLO. Its relationship with Egypt ended when Sadat cancelled the Soviet-Egyptian Treaty and turned towards the United States. Iraq was the only channel for influence in the Gulf region until the Soviet Union acceded to Aden through its ties with South Yemen, an Arab country controlled by a marxist one party regime. The Soviet Union gained control of Ethiopia with the help of Cuban troops. Afghanistan was a friendly country since 1971 and became a satellite under the Taraki regime. Subversion and local resistance led to the invasion of the country at the end of 1979, but the local guerillas turned against the Russians. The effect of the three moves in South Yemen, in Ethiopia and in Afghanistan, coupled with the development of Soviet naval power in the Indian Ocean was to encircle Saudi Arabia and to threaten the Strait of Hormuz. In Iran, the Soviet Union gained a military advantage through American losses, especially after the collapse of the Iranian army. On the one hand Iran's oil resources would conveniently make up for the decline in net oil exports of the Comecon countries. On the other hand its fundamentalist regime could act as a magnet for Soviet muslim populations. Its forward policy has promoted the Soviet Union to the position of a "co-equal global power"[18] in the Gulf area. It is nonetheless embarrassed by the Iraq-Iranian conflict. It could easily kindle the Kurd rebellion. It might support the bid for power of the Iranian leftist groups monitored by the communist Tudeh party. It cannot side with Iran because of the hostility of the Islamic rulers towards Moscow. Therefore it continues to covertly supply Iraq with military equipment, while strengthening its ties with Syria.

The major difficulty encountered by the United States in the Middle East was the contradiction between its military strategy of containment of the Soviet Union and its diplomatic action for the resolution of Israel's conflict with its neighbors. The fullfillment of the first goal required the support of the Arab states and the pursuit of the second was causing dissent among many of the same states.

The containment policy in the Persian Gulf rested on the supply to Iran and Saudi Arabia of a considerable amount of western weapons and of a host of military advisers. The Iranian revolution seriously undermined the American defense planning as the country shifted from alignment to neutralism and ceased to be a regional military power. It also affected the delivery of oil to the OECD member states. The key role of Saudi Arabia was enhanced. This country contributed in 1979 to 25% of OPEC and 44% of Middle East oil exports. 85% of Saudi Arabia's accumulated financial surpluses were held in dollars, of which $35 billion were held in American government securities. Within OPEC, it had at the request of the United States, supported the oil price freeze in 1977–78. At the end of 1978, it accepted with Iraq to offset the cutback in Iranian output.[19] The invasion of Afghanistan in December 1979 reinforced American concern for Persian Gulf security. So did the Iraq-Iranian war in September 1980.

The United States now considers the Middle East as another "theater" in the military sense. A rapid intervention force is being built up so as to protect the "third strategic zone" of American interests in the world after Europe and the Far-East. In between the United States acquired ground facilities in Oman, Kenya and Somalia. It supplied Saudi Arabia with four AWACS planes, thus improving its relations with this key oil producing state. Informal consultations have taken place with France, Britain and Australia to assemble some sixty warships in the Indian Ocean and to undertake contingency planning. The Western diplomats have made clear that interference with traffic through the Strait of Hormuz would not be tolerated. Iraq and Iran have been warned not to extend the war in the Gulf proper, so as to reassure the other Gulf states on their safety. These precautions are certainly welcome but the situation remains explosive.

But the political stability of Saudi Arabia is closely linked to the solution of the Arab Israeli conflict. The Camp David accords and the subsequent arrangements are "not regarded by the majority of Arab states, including those most directly concerned, such as Syria, Jordan and Saudi Arabia, as an adequate basis for peace negotiations with Israel or for the settlement of the Palestine question".[20] The Camp David accords have a positive aspect, in the form of Israel's withdrawal from Sinai. This withdrawal and peace with Israel were a precondition for Egypt to become a special partner for the United States. The negative aspect derives from the stalemate of the negotiation on Palestinian self-determination. The Begin government is expanding settlements on the West Bank in contradiction with the spirit of the accords and with the view of one of Israel's respected political figures: "The avoidance of Israeli rule over the million Palestinians in the West Bank and Gaza is not only a concession by Israel to her adversaries, but also a service that Israel would render to her own interest and destiny".[21] The United States' pressure on Begin is hampered by the presidential campaign. "The United States, having involved itself to the hilt in the Camp David formula, should be prepared to face the Palestinian question frankly and courageously".[22] Such an attitude would help "restoring the United States to an influential role in the Arab Middle East".[23]

The American policy from 1973 on left little room for Euopean diplomacy in the Middle East. Constrained by the need for oil the European countries engaged in bilateral deals, some of which were backed by arms sales. They launched the so-called Euro-Arab dialogue which was hampered both by Arab demand for PLO recognition and by American mistrust. The French initiative for a larger North-South dialogue failed in 1976. The Palestinian stalemate and the American setbacks in the Gulf were the main arguments put forward in June 1980 by President Giscard d'Estaing to convince his EEC partners to adopt a statement supporting self-determination for Palestinians. The Venice declaration was couched in such terms that it did not conflict with the U.S. arranged Israeli-Egyptian talks on the subject. It favored the association of the PLO to a global Middle-East settlement. The EEC countries were prepared to send military contingents on the field for the guaranty of Israel borders. They favored the simultaneous recognition by the Palestinians of the right of Israel to existence within sure and accepted borders and the recognition by Israel of the right to self-determination of the Palestinians.[24] The EEC statement was received with at best skepticism in the United States. Political observers stressed that the initiative satisfied neither the PLO nor the other Arabs and that it was not backed by a proper organization base. President elect Reagan approved during his campaign of the new Israeli settlements in the occupied territories and of the claim for a full sovereignity on Jerusalem. The disagreement between the Europeans and the Americans risks aggravation.

This rapid survey of the Middle East problems shows that the United States and Western Europe have followed so far diverging policies. Their interests in the continuity of oil supply, in the containment of the Soviet Union and in the solution of the Arab-Israeli and Iraq-Iran conflicts are convergent. They differ on the priorities and on the means of action. Europe is primarily interested in the continuing oil flow, the United States in the regional and global power balance.

The interruption or sharp reduction in supplies may be caused by socio-economic pressures accompanying modernization, by direct military action on the oil fields in a local war or by an open threat of the Soviet Union against an oil producing country in order to bring about a shift of direction in its oil deliveries.

The maintenance of the peace in the Middle East has lied exclusively on the United States military capacility and diplomatic leverage. American decisions regarding the area have been unilateral before and after the 1973 war. The Camp David accords have stemmed from an American initiative. The stalemate in the Palestinian issue was attributed by the Europeans to Washington's softness. The decision to build-up an intervention force was the direct response to Soviet enchroachments at the superpower balance in the Gulf.

Europe and Japan as well are uncertain about the goals and the capacity of deployment of the intervention force. The resort to the force would transform the oil fields into battlefields. Would deployment stem from an invitation by a threatened local government or from an American initiative in response to a direct or indirect threat by the Soviet Union?[25] Presently the intervention force is not operational. Its preparation is to be spread over five years at a cost of $25 billion.[26]

The geographical scope of the Treaties binding the United States to Europe (NATO), to Australia and New Zealand (Anzus) and to Japan do not extend to the Middle East. Thus there is no permanent forum in which the United States can test with its allies its policies in the most sensitive area of the world. Apart from the bilateral diplomatic channels, the only transnational structure in which the Middle East problems are occasionally discussed are the unofficial summit meetings of the leaders of the seven larger OECD countries.

116

5. A Joint Approach to a Cluster of Risks

The energy situation in the last decade has become a major issue in international politics, involving much more than Euro-American relations.

There is no prospect in the next two decades for a massive substitution of coal and nuclear energy for oil, nor for the replacement of the Middle East in its position of major supplier to the industrial societies.

These societies are confronted with a cluster of risks. The first one is economic and concerns the oil supply and demand relationship and its impact on prices and economic growth. The second risk is financial and derives from the effect of higher prices on the current account balances of the oil importing countries, developed and developing, and on the international banking and monetary system. The third risk is related to the security of supplies which might be threatened by local subversion or warfare in the Middle East possibly kindled by some form of Soviet interference.

The United States energy policy is a key factor in regard to each of these risks. The American energy balance sheet is an important item in the oil supply and demand relationship. The dollar is the currency in which oil is purchased internationally and the financial surpluses of the oil producers are invested or recycled. The United States is the security warrant for the supply of oil from the Gulf to the OECD countries.

The three types of risks are interrelated. A strong domestic energy policy in the United States is required to meet the OPEC challenge. A strong American defense and diplomatic posture, backed by a common Western policy, is required to cope with the Middle East turmoil.

The three types of risks affect the United States and its allies in the Atlantic and in the Pacific Oceans. To face these risks in a world setting a concerted action of the United States, of Western Europe and of Japan is necessary and has so far been insufficient.[27]

There is no process whatsoever for regular multilateral consultation on Middle East problems. The only organized forum is that of NATO, with its geographical and substantive limits. The North Atlantic Treaty Organization does not extend beyond the Eastern Mediterranean. It is concerned essentially with defense. The International Energy Ageny (IEA) is in charge of collecting information and forecasting the evolution of needs and resources in the field of energy. It has set up an Emergency Sharing Plan in the case of energy shortage. It supports joint research projects. These actions are necessary but do not amount to a collective strategy. The seven nations summit meetings of the leaders of the advanced industrial countries are now taking place on a yearly basis, dealing with important economic and energy problems, but they do not discuss systematically broad geopolitical and security problems.

Thus there is no forum for the regular discussion of the sensitive and complex problems related to the Middle East. One approach to these problems might be the extension of the geographical boundaries of NATO, another the creation of a specialized international organization. Both approaches are open to serious objections, such as protracted negotiations for the amendment of an existing Treaty or the drafting of a new one and the lengthy ratification process by the Parliament of each participating country. A more flexible approach is preferable. It would consist in setting up a special forum for consultation on Middle East problems both on a current and a long term basis. This initiative would require no formal legislative approach and would involve only the agreement of the executive branches of the governments concerned.

Key questions arising would be those of membership, competence, administrative support and methods. The membership should be restricted to "those countries which are able and willing to accept concrete obligations within the troubled area. Participation would be linked to the capacity and responsibility for action".[28] The group should comprise the United States, Britain, France, Germany, Italy and Japan. It should be competent to discuss political and security questions as well as energy and economic questions related to the Middle East. In case of serious tension, it would be in charge of crisis management. Otherwise it would work out and continuously adopt a global long term strategy for the area. Such actions should be supported by a small permanent staff (of the type of the former NATO Standing Group). This secretariat would consult, according to the time and issue, with the proper levels of authority within NATO, the EEC and the IEA and draw when necessary on the experts of these bodies.

Would such a blueprint work? There is no clearcut answer to this fundamental question. Two remarks are relevant. The first is that summit decisions are taken and implemented when the participants show a political will. Short of a will, whatever the forum, no action ensues. A second remark concerns the ability for the Europeans -- assuming they are agreed between themselves -- to inject their views and their interests into the American desicion making process. It is a well-known difficulty -- experienced for decades in the Atlantic Alliance -- to confront the views of the leading country with those of its associates who do not carry the same weight in military and economic terms. If no complete agreement is reached between unequal partners, at least the information has been channelled in time, prior to the decision and at the proper level of responsibility. This is no small advantage compared to the present situation.

The United States, its major partners and also Japan should prepare for the requirements of a multi-alliance system dealing with a troubled and contested area and facing an empire.

Notes

1 BP Statistical Review of the Oil Industry, 1979
2 d°
3 Steam Coal, Prospects to 2000, OECD 1978, table D-3, p. 35
4 Uranium, Resources, production and demand, OECD/IEA, 1979, derived from table 1, p. 18
5 derived from Table 1 below
6 I. C. Bupp, The Nuclear Stalemate, in: Robert Stobaugh/Daniel Yergin (Ed.), Energy Future, New York, Random House, 1979, p. 125
7 Energy in America's Future, The Choices Before Us, A Study by Resources for the Future, Sam H. Schurr, project director, Johns Hopkins University Press, Baltimore, 1979, p. 417
8 Bank for International Settlements, 50th Annual Report, Basel 1980
9 OECD Economic Outlook n° 27, July 1980
10 Energy Policies and Programmes of IEA Countries 1979 Review, OECD, Paris 1980, p. 15
11 Robert Stobaugh and Daniel Yergin, Energy: an Emergency Telescoped, in Foreign Affairs, America and the World, 1979, p. 564
12 Ulf Lantzke, Expanding World Use of Coal, Foreign Affairs, Winter 1979–80, p. 357
13 Energy in America's Future, op. cit., p. 507
14 Mason Willrich, A Workable International Nuclear Energy Regime, Washington Quarterly, Spring 1979
15 Jacques de Larosiere, Managing Director of the IMF, at the US Council of The International Chamber of Commerce, New York, December 5, 1979
16 John Campbell, Les Etats-Unis et l'Europe au Moyen-Orient, Interets Communs et Politiques Divergentes, Politique Internationale, n° 7, Printemps 1980, pp. 165–172
17 Stobaugh and Yergin, Emergency, op. cit., p. 575
18 Shahram Shubin, Soviet Policy towards Iran and the Gulf, Adelphi Papers n° 157, Spring 1980, pp. 3, 4, 30, 36, 43
19 Adeed Dewisha, Saudi Arabia's Search for Security, Adelphi Papers n° 158, Winter 1979–80, pp. 28, 29
20 John C. Campbell, rapporteur, Oil and Turmoil, Western Choices in the Middle East, The Atlantic Council of the United States Policy Papers, Washington D.C, September 1979, p. 19
21 Abba Eban, quoted by George W. Ball, The Coming Crisis in Israeli American Relations, Foreign Affairs, Winter 1979–80, p. 244
22 Campbell, Oil and Turmoil, op. cit., p. 36
23 William B. Quandt, The Middle East Crisis, Foreign Affairs, America and the World 1979, p. 561
24 Le Monde, 15 June 1980, Une etape
25 Steven J. Warnecke, Energy and Raw Materials Security Issues, forthcoming Adelphi Papers, 1980, pp. 122–123
26 The Rush to the Gulf, International Herald Tribune, 23 September 1980
27 Robert J. Lieber, Organizing for Regional Economic Security: Energy and the Western Alliance, Colloquim on National Security, John F. Kennedy Institute, Tilburg, The Netherlands, 1980, p. 15
28 Karl Kaiser, et al., Western Security: What has changed? What should be done? Council in Foreign Relations, New York, 1981, V, 12

Foreign Trade Policy Interests and Decisions in the United States of America*

Trade Policy Interests

Harald B. Malmgren[1] has described the process of foreign economic policy decision-making in the United States as intricate, even as byzantine. Indeed, the amount of participating actors, as well as the pressing and competing responsibilities and authorities, is difficult to comprehend. The President, the Departments, the Congress, the International Trade Commission, and the interest groups of the business community, not to mention the particular companies, are all involved. The interplay and competition of all the involved roles in the political system is complicated not only by trade policy-oriented problems, but also by the institutional frictions within the political system. The delicate balance of power between President and Congress, to take an example, is one factor in trade policy formation which has its impact independent of substantive issues.

This complex constellation of institutions and authorities can be made intelligable with a model of the political system based on systems theory.[2] This model allows for the classification of decision-making processes from the demand on the political system to the allocation of values. By means of differentiating between demands as input, the conversion in the political system and the allocation of values as output, an analysis is possible which goes behind descriptions of institutions or events. The relevance of the involved particular roles can be thereby accentuated and their position determined. By looking at the regularities in the selection of trade policy demands, conclusions about the general chances of certain categories of demands will be possible and trends will be discovered.

The demands of economic interest groups in general are categorized as "free trade" or "protectionist". This only makes sense if the terms are separated from the definitions of the classic theory of liberal economics. Otherwise there are no free traders apart from economists. When defining "free trade" as oriented towards freer trade than the status quo and in analogy "protectionism" as oriented towards increased protection, these categories can be made operational. This is in any case valid for demands, in other words, the output in the political system. For the output, decisions and allocations of values, further questions are necessary. The demands of the American business community are exclusively national affairs, they refer exclusively to the system United States of America. The American decisions, however, refer also to the trading partners of the United States, in other words, they have transnational consequences. Since the international trade system never knew pure free trade but always protection, the most interesting question is whether the trade policy of the United States aims at an increase in the multilaterally agreed forms of cooperation in international trade, or if there is an increasing tendency towards unilaterally imposed protection.

For the 70's the trade policy network in the United States can be analyzed by example of the Trade Act of 1974. This important piece of legislation has given rise to new regulations for the trade policy of the U.S.A. The internal decision-making process may be analysed by means of the bargaining of the Trade Act, a bill proposed by the Nixon Administration, from its modifications in Congress to the final decision of President Ford on January 3rd, 1975, to sign the Trade Act into law. The Trade Act of 1974 has given a regulative framework for new internal trade policy allocations as well as the basis for the most important American attempt to reform the trade policy environment in this period: the multilateral trade negotiations in Geneva (the so-called Tokyo Round).

The complex decision-making process, which took place during the trade reform, makes it possible to go beyond the case study and to come to some structural findings on the trade policy decision-making system. On the basis of the Trade Act, a series of separate decisions were made as well as the second most important decision in the decade: the endorsement of the United States of the results of the Tokyo Round with the signing of the Trade Agreements Act of 1979 into law.

Foreign and domestic policy in their mutual interdependence turned out to be one issue area. The trade policy of the United States towards Western Europe, in this regard defined as the European Community (EC), is included in its most important aspects. The main point of the Tokyo Round of the General Agreement on Tariffs and Trade (GATT) was the agreement between the United States and the EC. The two relevant environments of analysis, the European Community and the United States of America, are brought here together. In the American decisions internal as well as external demands and interests came together.

The demands of the free trade-oriented groups of the American economy, cover a broad spectrum with one common denominator: the reduction of trade restrictions. This meant for the 70's the authority for the executive branch to negotiate liberalizing multilateral trade agreements with the main trading partners. Art I 8.3 of the American Constitution requires that this authority of the President be granted by a mandate of Congress. With this demand the free traders aimed at multilateral cooperative regulations within the GATT system. The European Community, as the most important trading partner of the United States after Canada, was included. The multinational corporations and the powerful organizations of the business community, the Chamber of Commerce and the National Association of Manufacturers, comprised the most important

121

part of the free trade coalition. In their set of demands, freedom of economic action had highest priority. The reduction of trade barriers (tariff as well as non-tariff barriers, import and export restrictions) was a secondary goal in their list of demands. The vested interests of the multinational corporations in Western Europe led naturally to their interest in further liberalization of the movement of capital and trade with this region. They perceived the Common Market as a present anf future important area of activities because of market-oriented economic and political systems and political stability. Protectionism can only be a barrier for multinational transactions.

The second powerful block within the free trade coalition is agriculture. The farm groups are primarily interested, within this context, in the unrestricted export of their products. Since the EC, with its Common Agricultural Policy (CAP), is a protectionist creation within the area of agriculture, the U.S. farm lobby, especially the American Farm Bureau Federation, demanded the abolition of CAP — which meant the abolition of the core of the EC. In contrast to the American Farm Bureau Federation — which is dominated by agro-business, which aimed at using the advantage of American agriculture against the EC harshly — the National Farmers' Union favored a more cooperative trade policy approach. They recognized the special position of agriculture in world trade and therefore were in favor of gradually introduced restrictions which were in the mutual interest of American and European producers. The National Farmers' Union wanted to avoid ruinous competition with European farmers. The third important voice within the free trade coalition, but by far the weakest, was the consumer groups. Their demands included the reduction of import restrictions because they were perceived as causing increased price levels and limiting of choices for the American consumer.

The catalogue of demands of the protectionist groups included the whole spectrum of usual protection measures: tariffs, import quota, marketing agreements, and the preservation of the Buy-American Act and the American Selling Price System. The unions categorically opposed any reduction of existing barriers. The AFL-CIO demanded increased restrictions, with the accent on import quotas. This hard protectionist line found its expression in the union backed bills of Representative Burke and Senator Hartke. This trade policy of the unions in the United States was of particular importance because it reinforced the political influence of the protectionist groups. At the beginning of the 60's, the labor unions still were on the other side of the line; they supported the Kennedy Administration during the debate of the Trade Expansion Act of 1962.

The demands for protection of the various branches of industry differed according to their specific interests. As a rule, the smaller the industry, the more hard-line protectionist position was taken. The biggest protectionist, the steel industry, had mixed interests. They had to consider their export-oriented interests, which moderated protectionist activities in the 70's. The greater part of the steel industry demanded marketing agreements and asked for export subsidies. The traditional protectionist textile sector was more or less satisfied for the moment with the arrangement regarding international trade in textiles, known as the Multifiber Agreement (MFA); in the mid 70's the textile lobby therefore remained silent. The footwear producers and the benzenoid sector of the chemical industry insisted on the American Selling Price System. The consumer electronics lobby demanded sharpened anti-dumping and countervailing duty measures. The small protectionist group in the agricultural field aimed at the preservation of existing dairy and meat quotas. Vegetable growers and wine producers pressed for a new quota system for their products. Of relevance for the Common Market were especially the protectionist demands of the steel industry, the chemical industry, and the dairy and wine producers.

Most efficient were those protectionist branches which brought about an alliance between industry and labor unions. This coalition was not yet the rule during the 70's, although the tendency in this direction was on the rise. In general the protection demands of industry were less intensive than those of the unions. Industry was in most cases satisfied with the Orderly Marketing Agreements, whereas the AFL-CIO preferred quotas. The most important common demand of the protectionist groups was that against any shift of authority from Congress to the Executive Branch. This was a consequence of the general perception that protectionist interest had a better chance of success in Congress than with the Administration.

The Decision-Making System

The selection of diverging demands of interest groups takes place in a complex decision-making process, in which Congress, the Administration, and the International Trade Commission are involved. The Treasury Department, the Department of Commerce, the Department of Agriculture, the Department of Labor, the Department of State, and the Office of the Special Representative for Trade Negotiations within the Presidential Office play an important role on the side of the administration during the first steps of selection. In Congress, the Ways and Means Committee of the House of Representatives and the Finance Committee of the Senate are responsible. Final decisions take place on the floor of both Houses of Congress and in the White House.

During the drafting of the trade reform bill of the Nixon Administration, the Office of the Special Representative and the Council on International Economic Policy (CIEP) played important roles. The Treasury Department, more precisely George Shultz as Secretary of the Treasury, had a controlling function because of his position as the "economic Kissinger"[3] in this period. The general preferences of selection of the Treasury Department as regards trade policy demands can be illustrated by his decisions in cases of dumping complaints. Despite the fact that the amount of dumping investigations increased on the

123

basis of the Trade Act of 1974, the Treasury Department tried in general to weaken protectionist demands. His attitude of reluctance can be shown exemplarily with the most spectacular dumping investigation of the 70's. This case concerned, in 1975, the import of cars from eight countries including the most important producers of the EC (West Germany, Great Britain, Belgium, Italy). In spite of the fact that the most extensive anti-dumping investigation the Treasury ever had done had the result that 17 of the foreign car producers sold their products on the American market below the prices of the domestic market, the Department avoided countervailing measures and favored a compromise. The Treasury referred to potential conflicts with trading partners and tried to influence importers to increase prices during the period of the investigation. This behavior can be seen as typical for the pattern of selection of the Treasury Department. It is required to investigate complaints by the anti-dumping and countervailing duty law. When making decisions, however, political consequences are calculated. The attitude of reluctance of the Treasury Department is illustrated by the fact that most protectionist industries, for example consumer electronics, demanded time limits for the anti-dumping decisions of the Treasury on the basis of the Trade Act of 1974.

The Department of Commerce, in spite of its name, played only a secondary role in foreign trade policy compared to the Treasury Department and the Department of State. Commerce ranked behind Treasury for the domestic process, wheras in international affairs it had to act, as the other Departments, through the Office of the Special Trade Representative. Rarely did the Secretary of Commerce play a leading role in trade questions. He was usually a secondary participant in the Interagency Committees. One may justifiably say that the United States had the weakest commercial ministry of all major trading countries during the 70's.[4] Only with the intended reorganization of trade policy responsibilities in the Carter Administration in 1979 was the implementation of a new strengthened Department of Commerce discussed. With the results of the Tokyo Round and the field of export promotion the responsibility of the Department was to be enlarged. Since the Commerce Department in part perceives its role as an advocate of the American industry, its policy was seen as more receptive of protectionist demands than that of the Treasury.

The Departments of Agriculture and Labor also played secondary roles. They did, nonetheless, present the interests of their clientel, the American farmers and labor unions, on the departmental level. The Department of Agriculture clearly favored a policy of free trade, which corresponded with the export interests of U.S. agriculture. This put Agriculture in the role of the main opponent of the agricultural protectionism of the European Community. Since U.S. agriculture expected to gain new export markets as a consequence of the Trade Act of 1974 and the Tokyo Round, this issue became the keystone of the GATT negotiations in the view of the U.S.A. The demands for protection from the American labor unions found no support in the Labor Department in the radical version that the AFL-CIO favored, but they had a secondary effect in the renewed and liberalized Adjustment Assistance Program for workers. One could say that the demands of the unions were converted by the Department of Labor.

The Department of State and the Office of the Special Representative for Trade Negotiations are responsible for negotiations with foreign countries. The role of the Department of State was reduced after the World War II step by step. Stephen D. Cohen[5] described the State Department in the mid 70's as more of a participant than a leader in the area of trade. The President's Special Representative for Trade Negotiations, created in 1962, took over a great deal of the responsibilities of the State Department. This shift was the result of a congressional initiative. The reason for this was the perception in Congress that the Department of State did not represent American trade interests in a sufficient manner. The Department of State was seen as a fortress of free traders which neglected the American industry's interest in protection.

Bilateral negotiations with the EC as well as multilateral negotiations within the Tokyo Round were the responsibility of the Office of the Trade Representative. The intention of Congress, however, to weaken the free traders' position was not realized, because the Office of the Trade Representative adopted more or less the liberal line of the State Department. When drafting the Trade Bill of the Nixon Administration, the STR Office took the free trade-oriented recommendation from the report of the Williams Commission of 1971 as its base.[6] From now on, it was not the Department of State, but rather the Office of the Special Representative which was responsible for presenting the demands and interests of the foreign trading partners during policy formation between the different departments and agencies of the executive branch. Its proposals could not merely reflect the national consensus, but had to also take the possibilities of compromising on the multilateral level into consideration.

The Trade Act of 1974

The version of the Trade Reform Bill that the President sent to Congress in 1973 was heterogenious. There was no clear message in which direction trade policy should develop. The bill was offering an open world trade system, but this was restricted by the vague term "fair". At the same time, goals were included in the bill which aimed at the exact opposite of an open system. A key to understanding this contradiction can be seen in the fact that the offer of a system of freer trade only was meant for these cases in which the American interpretation of "fair" was fulfilled. To this end quantitative trade barriers, restrictions in the agricultural sector, and non-tariff barriers were intended to be reduced.

The contradiction in the message of the President to Congress can be explained by his dependence on the consent of the legislative branch. There was concern in Congress that the approach of the administration was too much in favor of free trade and too little in favor of Amercian interests. Therefore, the main accent of the bill did not lie in defying as much free trade as possible by means of a 5-year authority to increase or decrease tariffs without limits in trade negotiations. Furthermore, the President demanded the authority to enter into agreements on non-tariff barriers in the condition that be submitted to Congress ninety days in advance and that neither the House of Representative nor the Senate disapprove within this time limit. Such an expansion of authority meant an important shift in the balance of power between the President and the Congress, and was consequently greeted with great scepticism on the Hill. The administration had to prove therefore its necessity and allay fears that the authorities provided by the bill would only be implemented in a free trade direction.

The main purpose of the President's bill was a plea for further authority to allow trade policy initiatives which were not detail for detail under congressional control. The Trade Reform Bill represented a selection — with a free trade bias — of those elements within the spectrum of possibilities and restrictions of the American decision-making system. The attempt not to involve Congress in the details of trade policy — thereby increasing the President's freedom to manouver — has been an indicator of liberal selection from the 30's to the present day. Nixon basically had a leaning towards liberal ideas of world economic order in spite of the necessity for internal compromising. This approach is typical for the executive branch from the time of the Reciprocal Trade Program of 1934 on. With this bill the administration showed its bias towards those parts of the American business community which were interested in a freer trade system. The multinational companies in this regard assumed top priority.

The Ways and Means Committee of the House of Representatives, responsible for trade policy questions and tariffs, modified the administration's bill in its Report of October 10, 1973, in major points. It limited presidential authority to negotiate by upgrading the controlling function of Congress. The Committee intended that Congress play a more active role in trade policy. Nevertheless, the President was to be accorded substantial power to negotiate for the simple reason that Congress cannot directly deal with foreign countries, as the Chairman of the Committee Al Ullman[7] pointed out.

The Ways and Means Committee appraised its Report of the Trade Reform Bill as a compromise between free trade and protectionist measures. In actual fact, the trend of the Committee's Report was to lean towards more protection. Nevertheless, the hard core protectionists favoring the labor union line did not come to terms. The Report of the Ways and Means Committee reflected the intention to restrict the Executive's freedom to manouver and to underline congressional control, which worked to the advantage of the protectionists. In general, however, the protectionists found less support than expected. One explanation for this is the fact that during the summer of 1973 the United States has a more favorable balance of trade and a decreasing rate of unemployment. In September of the same year the U.S.A. had the highest trade balance surplus per month since March 1965 (783 million dollars); at the same time, the rate of unemployment sank from 5% to 4.5%.

In the House of Representatives the Trade Reform Bill (HR 10170) was handled under a modified closed rule which allowed only three amendments. This rule was quite important for the House vote. An open rule, allowing for any number of amendments, would have endangered the chances of the trade reform as a whole. The House approved HR 10170 by a vote 272 – 140 on December, 1973. Ironically the controversy about East-West trade contributed to the approval of the Trade Reform Bill in the House of Representatives. The linkage of the question of Jewish emigration from the Soviet Union with the granting of most-favored nation treatment overshadowed the main controversy of HR 10170, i.e., whether the relationship with the main trading partners should have a stronger accent on free trade or on relief. The vote, therefore, does not permit any clear conclusions to be drawn about the free trade or protectionist attitudes of the representatives. Anticommunist, pro-Israel, human rights policy and trade policy considerations all came together in the vote; neither "yea" nor "nay" can be interpreted as liberal or protectionist vote.

The pattern of selection in the Finance Committee of the Senate which found expression in its Report of November 26, 1974, essentially followed that of the Ways and Means Committee: the authorities demanded by the President should be restricted and put under stronger congressional control. The Finance Committee insisted on the constitutionally guaranteed active participation of Congress. It was not ready to accept veto procedures. There was evidence of the opinion of the Committee that trade relations in general had not developed favorably for the United States and that there was necessity for change. The position of the Finance Committee differed from the Presidential draft in its stronger consideration of the interests of those industries hit by imports, but differed only marginally from the Report of the Ways and Means Committee.

The Senate vote took place under cloture. This rule in the Senate guaranteed that the bill could not be killed by a filibuster and that non-germane amendments were excluded.

In the Senate great attention was also given to the question of granting most favored nation status to Communist countries, which in itself was a question of secondary importance in the context of the issue of trade reform. The floor vote was clearly positive with 77 to 4. The four "nays" of the Senators Hartke, Metcalf, Abourezk and McClure represented the small protectionist core. The small number of opponents of the trade reform should not, however, be misinterpreted; the fact remains that moderate protectionist amendments, such as that of McIntyre, generally received approximately 40% of the vote in the Senate. In this case, however, the majority of the Senate supported the offer of the Administration to liberalize world trade; on the other hand it firmly put an accent on the preservation of American interests, and modified the Trade Reform Bill accordingly.

After the Conference Committee had reconciled the different versions of both houses, the House of Representatives voted in favor of HR 10170 on December 29, 1974, with a 323 to 36 vote. The Senate passed the bill on the same day with a vote of 72 to 4. These votes show clearly that the overwhelming majority in both houses was in favor of the trade reform package, in other words, of trade liberalization in the framework of the Tokyo Round. This clear result raises the question of what happened to the protectionists in Congress in the final voting procedure. In the House of Representatives the amount of opponents decreased within one year from 140 to 46. One has to take into consideration, as noted before, that "yea" or "nay" cannot be simplistically interpreted as a liberal or protectionist vote. On the one hand, the Trade Act of 1974 was no pure liberal bill; on the other hand, even in the final vote, the human rights issues in East-West trade and the shift of authority to the Executive branch, which troubled the conservative constitutionalists, blurred the lines of controversy.

In any case, the final votes in Congress indicated a successful coalition formation in Congress, in other word, a skillful interplay of the Administration with key committee members. For example, the congressional supporters of the textile industry were "bought off" by the prospect of a new international Multi-Fibre Agreement which would be favorable to domestic textile interests.[8] Even the AFL-CIO, which vehemently attacked the Trade Act to the end, was not able to mobilize its usual pool of supporters in the Congress. The majority of Representatives and Senators with a pro-labor bias obviously considered the adjustment assistance measures for workers to be fully sufficient. This leads to the conclusion that there was no large, clear-cut group of members of Congress with a blanket protectionist position; rather, there are members in both houses who are willing, on a case to case basis, to support protectionist initiatives, if major interests of their constituency are involved. Their pro-protectionist attitude is on an ad hoc basis. But the conclusion that the Congress in this period had a majority with an orientation to free trade is not possible, either. The Trade Act of 1974 was a compromise allowing both directions of implementation. Implementation itself was to show which group in the coming years was more successful.

With President Ford's signature January 3rd, 1975, the Trade Act of 1974 became Public Law 93–618. It was subtitled "an act to promote the development of an open, non-dicriminatory, and fair world trade system. To stimulate fair and free competition between the United States and foreign nations, to foster the economic growth of and full employment in the United States, and for other purposes". For this purpose the Trade Act contains in VI Titles on 199 pages regulations for domestic trade policy decisions as well as for policy towards other countries.[9] The first title provided the President with the basic authority for multilateral trade agreements within the General Agreement on Tariffs and Trade. For the management of the negotiation process an extensive system of hearings, consultations, and advice was established which included the International Trade Commission, advisory committees of the private sector, and Congress. Ten members of Congress, five members of the Committee on Ways and Means, and five members of the Finance Committee were accredited by the President as official advisors to the United States delegation. This procedure meant the direct participation of the major American trade policy interests at the negotiating process in Geneva. The executive branch was no longer able to negotiate autonomously and then present the package of results to Congress for ratification, but was already committed in the state of negotiation with foreign countries to establish domestic consensus. The Office of the Special Representative for Trade Negotiations was now based on law, and no longer on Executive Order (No. 11075 of January 15, 1973). The former United States Tariff Commission was renamed United States International Trade Commission, was raised in its position and provided with new functions and authorities.

Title II regulated relief from injury caused by import competition. The determination of "injury" was dependent on an investigation and findings of the International Trade Commission. The Commission investigated upon the request of the President, the Special Representatives for Trade Negotiations, upon the resolution of either the Committee on Ways and Means of the House of Representative or the Committee on Finance of the Senate, upon its own motion, or upon the filing of a petition of a trade association, firm, certified or recognized union, or group of workers which is representative of an industry. This procedure again involved the private sector directly in the decision-making process of the political system.

The third title regulated relief from unfair trade practices. It included possible measures of the President in the event of import restrictions or export subsidies by foreign governments. The President was provided with the authority to impose duties or import restrictions as countervailing measures. Furthermore, the Anti-Dumping Act of 1921 and the Tariff Act of 1930 were revised. The Treasury Department now had to come to a positive or negative determination within six months.

Title IV regulated trade relations with countries not currently receiving nondiscriminatory treatment (communist countries). Title V established a general system of preferences for developing countries. Both titles had no direct impact for the Euro-American trade relations. Title V, however, was of relevance for the system of preferences of the EC with former colonies.[10]

The Trade Act of 1974 as a system of regulations established the new framework for the main sectors of trade policy. Primarily, partition of competences between President and Congress was clarified. The President was provided with certain authorities, but the Congress kept control. Each particular case remained open. Whether the decisions concerning details turned out to be protectionist or free trade-oriented, unilateral or multilateral, each had to be made in a new decision-making and bargaining process. The institutional regulations for those processes, however, had been made clear. There was no further need for legislative procedures.

The Trade Act of 1974 contains contradictions and ambiguities. The main contradiction consists in the fact that further liberalization of the international trade system and free competition on the one hand, and national prosperity (interpreted as economic growth) on the other, are not generally harmonious. These goals, however, are not necessarily mutually exclusive. The expected national benefit for the U.S.A. could not be seen in all sectors and branches and therefore required regulating interventions. Both sides of this contradiction of goals could hardly be excluded from the Trade Act because there is no general solution. United States trade policy must take both internal interests and the international trade order into account. The ambigquity, which makes it possible to implement the Trade Act both in a national/unilateral manner and in a international/ multilateral manner was described by Wilbur F. Monroe as trade policy "in transition".[11]

The Implementation in the Ford and Carter Era

The analysis of decisions on the basis of the Trade Act of 1974 elucidates the influence of protectionists and free traders in the 70's. Each decision is the result of a separate political process with specific allocation outcomes. The synopsis of decisions over a five years period allows, it will be assumed, to determine a trend. Involved in the decision-making of the political system are the International Trade Commission, an independent agency, the President, the Congress, and in particular cases the Custom Courts, too. They were confronted with those interest groups which had made demands during the controversy around the Trade Act as well.

The International Trade Commission is only in a limited sense a decision-making body, since its findings and recommendations are binding neither for the President nor for the Congress; nevertheless, the results of the commission's investigations are politically relevant. The former Tariff Commission had no particular influence, but the International Trade Commission now was an independent agency between administration and Congress. Especially in the case of controversies between the executive and the legislative branch are its recommendations of importance. After the Trade Act was signed into law, the amount of investigations based on petitions to the International Trade Commission increased tremendously. The majority of complaints, however, resulted in negative findings. This included important cases as, for example, the automotive sector, which suffered a crisis in 1980. Nevertheless, a certain amount of petitions for import relief resulted in positive recommendations. The EC was involved in many pending cases; it was hardly effected, however, by any positive recommendations.

The presidential decisions on the basis of recommendations of the International Trade Commission showed a reluctant and appeasing attitude towards demands for protection. President Ford in 1976 imposed only in one specific case unilateral import restrictions. This decision was fostered by the influential position of the complainants, the steel lobby, consisting of 19 companies and the steelworkers union, as well as the parallelism with Ford's election campaign. In all other cases President Ford preferred weaker measures such as Adjustment Assistance or Orderly Marketing Agreements. The unilaterally imposed specialty steel quota did not, however, provoke a trade conflict with the deeply affected European Community. Parallelly in Western Europe there was a tendency towards protectionism for the steel sector, also.

President Carter more or less followed Ford's line. During his presidency, steel was also the main exception. In 1977 the steel crisis led to the trigger price system which de facto worked as a minimum price for importers. This factual price intervention was no liberal solution at all; however, it fits in the pattern of attempts to manage the issues below the level of "hard" tariff and quota measures. As in election year 1976, the steel lobby succeeded again in 1980 to win new concessions from the administration. After a short period of suspension of the trigger-price system, it was renewed and increased. This was again a unilateral measure, but it had been implemented together with consultations with the European Economic Community. It did not lead to a conflict, however, because in the Common Market, too, there was a tendency towards increased protection for steel.

President Carter, however, rejected affirmative recommendations of the Commission as well. The rule was that in those cases less powerful industries predominated, as for example the footwear industry or the honey producers. But influential industries, such as the well organized textile group, suffered from rejection as well. Carter vetoed on November 10, 1978, a bill that tried to exclude the textile industry and its products from any reduction of tariffs negotiated at the multilateral trade negotiations in GATT. This exclusion would have menaced the success of the Tokyo Round.

The most important decisions of Congress together with the implementation of the Trade Act of 1974 consisted in two non-decisions. The first one was not to revise the Trade Act up to 1979. The second one consisted in not overriding presidential decisions on import relief which rejected affirmative recommendations of the International Trade Commission. A further positive decision of Congress was necessary because of the delay of the Tokyo Round. On January 3, 1979, the waiver for the Secretary of the Treasury to impose countervailing duties on subsidized products expired. A high amount of exports from the European Community was involved, especially agricultural products. Therefore, an extension of the waiver was considered as a precondition of a successful termination of the Geneva negotiations. Both Houses gave their consent and thereby signaled their interest in the success of the Tokyo Round. The only relevant opposition against the extension of the waiver came from the apparel and textile lobby. This decision was of particular relevance for the EC. Approximately 1% of the total imports from Western Europe were involved. The amount of tariffs concerned was about 47 million US-Dollars.

The most important decision of Congress, however, had to be made about the results of the Tokyo Round. The package of trade agreements negotiated in Geneva represented the new regulation of trade relations with the main trading partners of the United States. In the Trade Act of 1974 Congress had accepted a time limit for the law-making procedure of the Trade Agreements Act of 1979. The Bill found overwhelming majorities in both Houses. The House of Representatives voted on 11th of July, 1979 with 395 in favor and 7 against. The Senate vote on 23rd of July, 1979 was 90 to 4. President Carter signed the Trade Agreements Act HR 4537 into law (PL 96—39) on the 27th of July, 1979. The only opposition was from 5 of the State of Wisconsin, where the dairy industry argued vigorously against the increase of the cheese quota, because this would favor European competition. By this decision, the attempt to regulate trade relations with Western Europe and with other main trading partners on a cooperative base within the GATT framework was judged by Congress as successful. The fact that there was hardly any protectionist opposition indicates that the relevant interest groups had been satisfied or expected benefits from the results of the Geneva Round. Powerful protectionist key industries, such as steel and textile, had won concessions and had been appeased with the plan to reorganize the trade responsibilities on the departmental level. The shift of responsibility for import relief procedures from the Treasury Department to the new upgraded Department of Commerce awoke expectations that this new Department would act more supportively. Agriculture calculated with high increases in exports, the multinational corporations and the consumer groups saw their interests ensured in liberalization.

The Trade Act also contains the possibility of judicial review of relevant trade policy decisions. This includes the possibility for companies and unions to ask for judicial review of anti-dumping decisions of the Secretary of the Treasury and findings of the International Trade Commission on unfair trade practices. In this regard two spectacular cases occurred, where the Customs Courts played a major trade policy role. The first issue was around the question if the refund of indirect taxes was an export subsidy according to Section 303 of the Anti-Dumping Act as amended in the Trade Act, and if the Treasury Department therefore had to impose countervailing duties. The Treasury announced in January 1976 that according to its interpretation, this was no "bounty or grant". The Zenith Radio Corporation commenced an action before the United States Customs Court in New York. Zenith argued that the refund of consumer taxes together with the export of Japanese electronic products would be a subsidy. The Customs Court's sensational decision of 12 of April, 1977, was in favor of Zenith.

Trade relations with the EC were involved by this judicial decision because in a second case before the Customs Court, the United States Steel Corporation had commenced an action arguing that the refund of the value added tax constituted an export subsidy. The EC Commission in Brussels expected a trade war in the case of a decision in favor of the United States Steel Corporation. Steel exports alone amounted to an eventual countervailing duty volume of one billion US-Dollars. Additionally, if other protectionist groups referred to this example, more or less all Euro-American trade would be affected. The Carter Administration was conscious of the danger of this decision of the Customs Court for world trade. Approximately 70% of total American imports of manufactured products would be involved. The Treasury Department appealed to the United States Court of Customs and Patent Appeals in Washington. This decision of July 28, 1977, was in favor of Treasury's appeal. Thereupon Zenith appealed to the Supreme Court. Its decision of June 20, 1978, finally rejected the appeal of Zenith and confirmed the Treasury Department's decision. By this, the court action of the U.S. Steel Corporation lost its ground, too.

The picture of the power relationship between free traders and protectionists shows for the 70's the traditional pattern in the United States which dates from the mid 30's. The political system decided, moreover, with a preference towards freer trade. The interests of the successful participants in the economic system have the best chance to be met. The demands for protection of weaker and less competitive parts of the U.S. economy increased, however, during the period of analysis. Because those industries include influential branches such as steel, textile, chemical, footwear, and consumer electronics, supported by union demands for protection, these interests had their resonance in the political system. Despite the intensity of demands for protection and the normally loud articulation in public, their actual influence ranked behind the interests for liberalization. This line was successfully promoted by the main organizations of the business community, such as the Chamber of Commerce, the National Association of Manufacturers, and the most relevant representatives of the farm block, the Amercian Farm Bureau Federation and the National Farmers Union. Against this coalition the trade unions and the protectionist industries fell back.

The liberal preference of selection predominated in the executive and in the legislative branch. It can be expected to remain relatively stable for the near future. The main promoters of this pattern of selection were the President, the departments and the independent agencies. Within these institutions, a consent for free trade demands and reluctance and appeasement towards demands for protection prevailed. In Congress demands for protection found more resonance in the relevant committees; however, there was a tendency towards channeling and weakening. The political impact of regional and sectoral interests in protection increased. Nevertheless, demands for protection only in exceptional cases had chances for a majority. The main condition for congressional decisions was the formation of coalitions. Up to now the chances for the free traders to established successful coalitions by a majortiy of votes have been better than those of the protectionists. Every single trade policy decision was the result of a bargaining process. The protectionists have won points in this bargaining during the 70's. The free traders preserved their albeit weakened dominance.

Multilateralism as a Measure of Control Between Foreign Policy Goals and National Interests

American trade policy decisions have to accommodate on the one hand internal wants and demands and on the other hand to those from the international environment. In our case the main question is in how the political system in the United States took Western European trade policy demands into consideration. The behavior towards the European trading partners has basically three instruments at its disposal: unilateralism, bilateralism or multilateralism. The first instrument means unilateral decisions from the United States which neglect European demands or takes them only marginally into consideration. Bilateralism is defined as coming to an agreement only with one partner, for example the EC, and to neglect the interests of other countries. The EC is seen as one entity in this regard because the foreign trade responsibility rests with the commission in Brussels and no longer with the national governments. Multilateralism is defined as an attempt for solutions which aim to include the interests of all participants. In the trade policy area, the General Agreement on Tariffs and Trade is in general used for this purpose. All three of the possibilities of behavior may include elements of a strategy of cooperation or conflict. In practice, however, unilateral trade policy means conflict, bilateralism is identical with cooperation with one partner and conflicts with others, whereas multilateralism means the highest extent of cooperation with as many trade partners as possible.

The United States of America after World War II had a preference for multilateral conference diplomacy in trade policy towards industrialized states. Up the 30's, protectionism and unilateralism had dominated. The turning away from this course occurred together with the Reciprocal Trade Agreements Act of 1934. With the new reciprocal approach, tariffs became a matter of intrastate negotiations. The main instrument used in this period was bilateralism. After the Second World War the General Agreement on Tariffs and Trade with its 23 founding members in 1947 marked the shift to multilateralism. This multilateralism, however, up to now was an exclusive one for the Western industrialized states. Unilateralism still dominated the behavior towards developing and communist countries. In the 7 multilateral rounds of negotiation in the GATT, the U.S.A. always played a protagonist role. Most important were the Dillon Round, the Kennedy Round, and the Tokyo Round, which was concluded in 1979.[12] Whereas the first six rounds of trade negotiations concentrated on tariff reductions, the Tokyo Round primarily dealt with non-tariff barriers.

The preference for multilateralism, however, did not exclude the use of unilateral actions by the United States. Despite agreements within the framework of GATT, unilateral measures have been imposed. This, however, was the exception, not the rule. The most striking example was the so-called "Connally shock". In August 1971, the United States imposed a 10% duty, initiated by the Secretary of the Treasury John Connally, because of an increasing deficit in the trade balance. This drastic unilateral decision provoked concern on the side of the main trading partners of the U.S., especially in Western Europe, that this measure would be an indicator for a trend of turning away from the multilateral approach. Those expectations have not been confirmed in the 70's. Nevertheless, the possibility that the U.S. might again take unilateral steps if its interests are not sufficiently realized with the multilateral line were threatening in the background. In spite of all confirming statements of American administrative spokesmen that the U.S. is still following the multilateral line, in Europe distrust remained virulent. This is due partly to the fact that the complicated trade decision-making system is not easily comprehended by foreigners, and therefore, statements of particular decision-makers are miscalculated in their importance, or the chances of implementation of a unilateral policy are overestimated. Occasionally the U.S. government reinforced European fears when asking for major concessions in negotiations by pointing out the protectionists' demands from the private sector and from Congress. Negotiation tactics called for flirtation with unilateral alternatives. The instrument of unilateralism in this regard was used as a covered or open bargaining chip.

The political system in the U.S.A. is confronted in foreign trade policy with multiple issues of control. Domestic and foreign market interests have to be considered. In addition, in our case the interests of the European trading partners must be taken into consideration because the area of trade policy is a sectoral issue area in Euro-American relations. On the domestic side, the protectionists want to see the influence of foreign competitors rolled back, at the same time the American exporters, especially the multinational corporations, want to see freedom of manoeuvering for export trade, especially for "intra-company trade", without limitation by governmental intervention to be preserved or even increased. Furthermore, there are interests of the EC, for example, the Common Agricultural Policy, which contradict strongly with American interests. The political system in the United States — in our case the government as responsible set of roles — has to make its decisions between interests of the EC and the domestic interest groups, in other words, it has to compromise and to control. This inevitably causes contradictions in the pursuit of goals and also problems of control. The prevailing concept in the United States for the World Trade Order, at least as regards the system of industrialized states, favors open markets. Decision-makers in the U.S.A. assume optimal benefits for their own country and all other participants. The benefits for all, however, are not visible in all sectors of the economy. In general, the position of the U.S.A. in the world trade system, compared with the EC and especially Japan, in the last two decades has fallen, U.S. trade performance has declined.[13] The interests of the losers in international trade under the auspices of freer trade are not neglectable. They create a necessity for regulation, i.e., allocations for their favor. The doctrine of liberal economic theory, however, condemns those interventions as wrong and globally inefficient; for political reasons, however, intervention has been proven necessary in all Western countries. The approach to adjust by the death of inefficient and no longer competitive industries has proved to be politically unacceptable, especially if foreign competition is involved.

If the so-called "dying industries" include branches of the size of steel, the strategy of "laissez-faire", recommended by economists, is not to be taken seriously by decision-makers. Those recommendations may serve as a value-oriented background for preferences, but decisions have to follow the realities of factual interests. In the U.S.A. decisions followed a general trend of granting adjustment assistance. This meant in practice correcting allocations of values in favor of demands for protection without fulfilling these demands entirely, in order to weaken them and to appease politically. The economic and political costs of adjustment assistance were calculated as less dear than the costs of open protections, which hardly would have been accepted without retortion from the side of the EC. It can be assumed that the picture of an open "beggar-thy-neighbor-policy", which would mean an escalation of closed markets on both sides, and the historical experience of the 30's with all its disastrous consequences for economic growth still has a deterring effect. The Western industrialized countries try to prevent developments in this direction through affirmative measures, not the least among which number the annual economic summits of the heads of state. The crisis in the economic system of the market-oriented countries has demonstrated the difficulties of global control. The governments' attempts at global control, which did anything but bring about final solutions proved, however, that the trade system of this group of countries is manageable and has capacity to control. The result of the Tokyo Round confirms this interpretation. Also the fact that a recession with substantial disruptions in trade between industrialized countries did not occur in the 70's testifies to this interpretation.

Control and regulation, however, developed into a highly complex process due to the fact that the necessity to compromise between all participants increased. The United States' leading role as the protagonist of the liberal world trade system, which it had assumed in the first two decades after the Second World War, was weakened in the 70's because of its declining trade performance. With the rise of the Common Market, a trade block materialized which caused fears in the U.S. for its own export chances. The decline of the hegemonic power of the United States in the economic field had the consequence of a loss of the capacity to control the Western trade system. The capacity for control of the leading Western power declined whereas the capacity of the other participants, especially the EC, grew, but not in equal proportion to the losses of the U.S.A.

The United States tried in the 70's to continue to play its leading role under more restricted conditions. Furthermore, it pushed in favor of liberalization of the World Trade Order. Again in the Tokyo Round it took the initiative. In this round of trade negotiations, however, the U.S. attempted far more intensively than ever before to push through changes in its own interest. With respect to the competitive sectors of the American economy, the free trade approach was preserved, even expanded upon. This pattern corresponds with the American tradition after World War II and with the interests of the export-oriented branches of industry and of the multinationals. At the same time, intensified efforts were mounted to protect the non-competitive branches by means of rules for international trade which caused as little restriction of trade as possible. Additionally there was a stronger accent on concessions of the EC in the agricultural sector because of the necessity to increase the chances of export for American agro-business in order to keep this group on the course of free trade. Agriculture was a necessary partner of the export-oriented industries in the U.S., since its support was needed to preserve the free trade majority. The American government in this regard tried to increase its domestic capacity for control by asking for concessions from its trading partners. Part of the domestic demands for protection, corresponding to the fact that free trade interests caused analogous conceptions of the order of world trade, were passed on the trading partners. In other words, the United States tried to increase its capacity for control of the Western trade system at the costs of the EC and Japan. At the same time, the domestic capacity for control in favor of the free trade coalition was to be preserved and even improved.

Both attempts of the political system of the United States in the 70's proved successful. Domestically, the capacity of control of the political system was improved in the trade policy area by a tranfer of authority in favor of the executive branch.[14] The Trade Act of 1974 and the Trade Agreements Act of 1979, despite all their ambiguities, reflected this trend. The main change in this period consisted in the improved integration of Congress and business groups in the trade policy decision-making process of the executive branch. A system of advisory committees assured the consideration of all interests. This led on the one hand to a more complicated decision-making process, but on the other hand to acceptable compromises for all participants and the improvement of capacity of control of the executive branch. On the level of advisory committees it became far easier to deal with interest groups and to confront them with the necessities of the cooperative trade policy towards Western European partners and to influence them in this direction.

The participation of members of Congress, that is, of the leading personalities of the relevant committees, also improved at least the position of the executive branch. Senators and Representatives, for example, in direct confrontation with the delegations of trading partner countries at the negotiations in Geneva could not help but to go beyond the regional perspective of their constituencies or the strictly national perspective of Congress. Since most members of Congress try to avoid congressional decisions over particular trade interests which would inevitably hurt parts of their constituency, Congress accepted — despite all of the fears about the balance of power between Congress and President — the elevated position of the executive branch. To some extent, Congress tried to deal with this problem by boosting the position of the International Trade Commission, an independent agency. The complaints of interest groups had to be formally investigated by the commission on an "objective" level. This freed Congress and the administration from the necessity of detailed comments. Finally this process helped to improve the capacity of control of the political system since interest groups now had to prove injury and the International Trade Commission worked as a filter against extreme protectionist demands. This procedure facilitated the administration's preference to operate with appeasing compromises. For example, in such a politically striking case as the complaint of the American automotive producers in 1980, the commission's negative findings avoided congressional or governmental decisions, which under the pressure of election campaigns probably would have had a more protectionist outcome.

The results of the Tokyo Round also turned out to be successful for the United States. The Geneva compromises were seen as mutually benefiting. But the United States came out ahead of EC. The trade system of the Western industrialized countries withstood the immanent and permanent conflict between competition and cooperation and proved its elasticity. American trade policy towards Western Europe consists therefore in favoring further liberalization together with the instrument of multilateral agreements, as long as aim and means are useful to win concessions from the EC, which serves to balance the deterioration of the position of the U.S.A. in the trade field. A shift towards increased protection and unilateralism cannot be excluded, but is in the immediate and near future not very probable. Some measures in this direction were ascertained, but with no clear trend. The European trading partners of the United States will have to make the greater contribution to negotiation in the future if this course is to be continued. The attempt of U.S. decision-makers to pass on protectionist demands to the trading partners probably will continue. The EC will, in the process of compromising, have to furthermore concede more than will be granted. Multilateralism proved once again to be a useful instrument of control for American trade policy.

Notes

* This paper is based on the author's study: Amerikanischen Handelspolitik gegenüber Westeuropa. Von der Handelsreform zur Tokio-Runde, Campus Verlag, Frankfurt/New York 1980, 230 pp. The more than 400 empirical notes of the study cannot be repeated in the paper; therefore, the paper's notes are restricted more or less to quotations. The most important source for the study had been the Hearings before the Committee on Ways and Means and the Committee on Finance. U.S. 93/1 Congress, House, Committee on Ways and Means, Trade Reform, 15 pts., Washington GPO 1973, 5317 pp. and U.S. 93/2 Congress, Senate, Committee on Finance, The Trade Reform Act of 1973, Hearings, 6 pts., Washington GPO 1974, 2976 pp. U.S. 96/1 Congress, House, Committee on Ways and Means, Subcommittee on Trade, Hearings, Multilateral Trade Negotiations, Washington GPO, 1979, 761 pp. U.S. 96/2 Congress, Senate, Committee on Finance, Subcommittee on International Trade, Hearings, Trade Agreements Act of 1979, 2 pts., Washington GPO 1979, 710 pp.

1 Harald B. Malmgren, The United States, in: Wilfrid L. Kohl, Economic Foreign Policies of Industrial States, Lexington, Mass. 1977, p. 37.
2 The model is based on David Easton, A Systems Analysis of Political Life, New York 1965.
3 Wilfrid L. Kohl, The Nixon-Kissinger Foreign Policy System and U.S.-European Relations: Patterns of Policy-Making, in: World Politics, vol. XXVIII, October 1975, No. 1, p. 34.
4 Stephen D. Cohen, The Making of United States International Economic Policy. Principles, Problems, and Proposals for Reform, New York 1977, p. 54.
5 Cohen, p. 45.
6 United States International Economic Policy in an Interdependent World. Report to the President submitted by the Commission on International Trade and Investment Policy, Washington, July 1971.
7 Congressional Quarterly Almanac 1973, p. 840.
8 Robert E. Baldwin, The Political Economy of Post-War U.S. Trade Policy, The Bulletin 1976−4, New York University Graduate School of Business Administration, p. 28.
9 U.S. 93rd Congress, House and Senate, Trade Act of 1974, Public Law 93−618, HR 10710, Washington GPO 1975, p. 99.
10 More than 50 developing countries now under the convention of Lome have a special relationship with EC including preferential tariff treatment.
11 Wilbur F. Monroe, International Trade Policy in Transition, Lexington, Mass. 1975, p. 111.
12 Cf. Gerard and Victoria Curzon, The Management of Trade Relations in the GATT, in: Andrew Shonfield (Ed.), International Economic Relations of the Western World 1959−1971, Oxford 1976, pp. 168−188. John W. Evans, The Kennedy Round in American Trade Policy. The Twilight of the GATT?, Cambridge, Mass. 1971, and Harald B. Malmgren, International Economic Peace Keeping in Phase II, New York 1972. General Agreement on Tariffs and Trade, The Tokyo Round of Multilateral Trade Negotiations, Report by the Director General of GATT, Geneva, April 1979.
13 Cf. Study of U.S. Competitiveness, Office of Foreign Economic Research, Bureau of International Labor Affairs, Department of Labor, Washinton, D.C. 1980.
14 Cf. the discussion on effective management of trade policy in the executive branch and the question of centralization. I. M. Destler, Making Foreign Economic Policy, Washington, D.C. 1980, Chapter 13.

John M. Kline

Multinational Corporations in Euro-American Trade: Crucial Linking Mechanisms in an Evolving Trade Structure

Storm flags are flying in Euro-American trade relations at the beginning of the 1980's. The major Western industrialized nations are making painful adjustments to spiraling energy costs, recurring inflation, sluggish productivity and slower overall economic growth projections. These troubles manifest themselves in renewed protectionist tendencies, as multilaterally incompatible policies of national export stimulation and import restriction are debated. In the United States, important aspects of foreign investment policies – both inward and outward – are also on the public agenda along with more traditional import/export issues. The challenge of resolving these interlinked policy issues in a manner consistent with multilateral accommodation and cooperation will require a careful new analysis and approach to defining the role of multinational corporations (MNCs) in Euro-American trade.

For three decades MNCs have been perceived as challengers to governmental economic policy control, first in Europe and now more recently in the United States. Past MNC growth sometimes failed to provide the type of national benefits needed to assuage certain domestic political concerns. While offering many market-oriented benefits in terms of product choice, availability and price, the inherent "foreignness" of MNCs seemed to increase risk and uncertainty on more politically sensitive production issues of plant ownership, employment and expansion. These concerns naturally appeared first on the European side of the Atlantic during the early postwar years, stimulating the development of European MNCs to counter American influence and carry forward national interest objectives. Many of these concerns are evident now in the U.S. debate over the reformulation of current national trade and investment policies.

The different bases for U.S. and European policy development stemming from the postwar period can explain much of both the cooperation and the conflict which has marked trans-Atlantic trade and investment relations. Even more important, the current evolution of national policies and attitudes toward foreign investment and MNCs may now hold important clues to the future development of general Euro-American trade relations.

Changes in the international economic equation, which have essentially equalized the competitive standing of the U.S. and European nations, also have begun to alter the political value base upon which many past policy differences were founded. These changes are especially likely to impact the United States, which emerged from the period of postwar economic dominance with a trade policy pegged to broad systemic concepts, an investment orientation adapted from free trade flow principles, and virtually non-existent policy regarding the role of multinational corporations.

Economic pressures at home and tougher business competition abroad are now forcing the U.S. to reevaluate its trade and investment policies. At the same time, the expanding use of transnational business arrangements such as co-development, co-production, joint equity and joint marketing systems adds a new and challenging dimension to the task of defining a coherent government approach to the role of MNCs in national policy objectives.

A critical time is approaching in the United States where a broad array of policy issues are being reassessed, with most indications pointing toward a shift from broad international principles to more specific national interest applications. This change will involve a shift from primarily an overseas marketplace view of MNC importance to greater emphasis on home production political values, thereby bringing policy-makers on both sides of the Atlantic closer together than ever before in their basic orientation to international companies.

While these developments could enhance the prospects for nationalistic, beggar-thy-neighbor competition, they might just as well lay the basis for a more realistic and equitable trading relationship in the Atlantic area. The renewed protectionist pressures which so concern current analysis could prove to be a temporary transition phase in a broadly evolving trade structure. Multinational corporations can play a key role in determing the direction of this evolution through their cross-national linking mechanisms which now may be more capable of meeting both economic marketplace and production oriented political needs. Governmental policy-makers, on the other hand, must face up to the central challenge of developing national and multilateral policy positions which will encourage a positive and reinforcing use of MNC linkages within a cooperative Euro-American trading system.

An Historical Perspective

Traditional views on the role of multinational corporations in Euro-American relations were formulated during the first two decades following World War II. This period was distinguished by unbalanced relationships in many areas, including the perception of MNCs as synonomous with dominant American influence. While there is much valuable literature already documenting the nature of postwar economic relations, a brief review of these years is advisable to provide the historical perspective necessary to more accurately evaluate the role of MNCs in current trade policy developments. In particular, it is important to focus in on the different origins of American and European policies toward foreign investment and MNCs as they bear on trade policy values.

141

United States attitudes toward MNCs developed over the years through an *ad hoc* decision-making process that applied broad economic standards in piecemeal fashion to functionally related MNC issues. Although there are many components to this patchwork pattern, the most important early standards involved non-discriminatory (MFN) free trade; national treatment for foreign investors; tax neutrality (foreign tax credit and "deferral"); and the extra-territorial application of antitrust and export control regulations.

The first three policy areas of trade, investor treatment and taxation all reflected an emphasis on macro-level, market-oriented principles within which MNC operations were to fit. This approach also implicitly assumed an overall identity between corporate and U.S. national interests. The extra-territorial enforcement principle established a functional check on that identity of interests to make certain that U.S. domestic principles did not get distorted by the vagaries of foreign influences and temptations.

Some accounts offer a sinister or at least more economically aggressive interpretation of U.S. intentions toward postwar Europe. While one would assume that U.S. corporate motivations were not altogether altruistic, a persuasive case can be made that official U.S. policy at the time stemmed from a more benign extension abroad of a domestic U.S. policy consensus based on economic growth, productivity and efficiency objectives.[1] Thus the fundamental thrust of U.S. policy decisions relating to MNCs simply sought to apply abroad the market-oriented value standards which seemed to work so well at home, essentially treating overseas business activities as if they were an extension of the U.S. domestic market.

Decision-makers in the U.S. could afford to focus on this macro outreach area of MNC policy because in-place domestic productive capacity was booming and both export sales and U.S. investment abroad seemed to further established postwar reconstruction goals. The possible impact of trade and investment policies on the American home economy were of much less concern since the trade component of GNP was relatively small, import dislocation was minimal, the dollar was strong and foreign investment in the U.S. consisted mainly of companies which had long ago blended into the American economic scene.

United States trade values were therefore systemic in nature and their application to MNCs was primarily determined by functional responses to conditions encountered abroad rather than a directed policy based on domestic economic necessities. This approach to international economic policy tended to obscure rather than define the interaction between foreign trade and investment, submerging them under broad free market principles in a way that the specific role of MNCs as linking mechanisms embodying both trade and investment activities was never sufficiently addressed. In terms of the approach and objectives of U.S. policy, there was essentially no difference between domestic and foreign market activities.

The roots of a divergent perspective on MNCs in relation to trade and investment policy took hold in Europe during this same time period. At first Euro-

142

pean policy options were severely constrained by the physical demands of reconstruction and the policy thrust contained within U.S. assistance mechanisms. Both public and private economic resources were needed to meet first-line necessities of the populace and to stave off the threat of further communist penetration.

As recovery progressed and a bi-polar military stand-off developed, European leaders began to perceive policy choices rather than political or economic imperatives. Galvanized by Jean-Jacques Servan-Schreiber's popular description of *The American Challenge*, their concerns shifted from the political threat from the East to the actual economic penetration from the West. This reaction to the continental spread of U.S. MNCs helped determine European policy not only to foreign investment at home, but also to the development and expected role of their own MNCs in world commerce.

It is dangerous to over-generalize about a "European" policy during this period of time — or perhaps during any time period. Certainly there were important distinctions between national policy approaches and even different policy stages within a given country. For example, France generally was more restrictive than Germany in its control over foreign investment, but even French policy shifted from broad investment denials to individually bargained access. Nevertheless, some policy generalizations may be risked if structured as broad contrasts with American policy development.

First, European motivations focused more on home-based production-end issues. Concern over the spread of U.S. MNCs stemmed not from an anlysis of their influence on market factors (product price, choice, service, etc.) but rather from political unease over who was to control European productive resources, both actual and potential. Heading the list of factors motivating the European policy response were several interrelated concerns: fear of U.S. industrial dominance as American investment tended to locate in the "commanding heights" of the economy; the threat of long-term technological dependence was the leading edge of key industrial sectors fell into foreign hands; and the loss of national control over the kind of economic planning deemed essential for domestic political stability and sociocultural integrity.[2] These types of concerns obviously relate to market-oriented factors further downstream in both a time and a process sense, but the origins of policy sprang more from dissatisfaction with the nature of the productive facilities rather than their actual market output.

The second significant difference in policy development was that this European reaction led to a more planned and directed policy response which incorporated an integrated view of trade and investment activities. While there were again differences in national application, most European nations gravitated toward the French planning mode and aimed at the promotion of corporate "national champions." To achieve the size and economies of scale thought necessary to compete successfully with American MNCs, these designated corporate challengers were slated to become trans-European from the start and globally competitive when mature. In short, governmental trade and investment tools involving import restraints, restricted investment sectors, mergers, subsidies, public procurement and other similar policies were consciously utilized to build European multinational corporations.

Viewed against this historical backdrop, European trade policy values can be seen to focus on home country conditions, where political control over domestic production factors was critically important and dictated a more purposeful and directed approach to the use of market forces both at home and in a broader trading system. Multinational corporations played a central role in both policy formulation and execution — the former aspect occurring when foreign MNC penetration stimulated countering trade and investment policy decisions and the latter when specific trade and investment tools were used in an interrelated fashion to encourage European MNC development and to define the national interest objectives these MNCs were to serve.

Rather different characterizations can be drawn regarding the wellsprings of American trade policy values. Possessing a prosperous domestic production base, trade policy objectives centered on responding to overseas conditions. Policies were pursued which sought to replicate abroad those domestic market principles which were seen to bring economic prosperity, political stability and a better standard of living. Multinational corporations were perceived as playing a generally beneficial but not central role in advancing these objectives. Little in the way of specific policy initiatives beyond verbal encouragement was taken to structure or integrate MNC trade and investment impacts within the broader operating construct of systemic free market forces.

These historically different foundations of postwar trade and investment policies established the basis for a divergent perspective on and application of trade policy values as they apply to MNC operations in the Atlantic area.

MNCs and Multilateralism

Developing from these divergent perceptual foundations, and considering in particular the early European reaction against U.S. MNC influence, it is perhaps surprising that the record of Euro-American trade relations involving MNCs has been one of general multilateral cooperation with confined specific conflict. A system of multilateral economic cooperation emerged early, primarily operating through the General Agreement on Tariffs and Trade (GATT) and the Organization for Economic Cooperation and Development (OECD). Most MNC-related conflicts tended to be limited to bilateral settings, primarily those involving the functional application of U.S. trade policy values to U.S. MNC operations.

The major threat of unilateralism involving MNCs at the systemic level was probably the European "national champion" policy, itself a response to the singular thrust of U.S. MNC penetration. The discriminatory potential of this approach was somewhat restrained, however, by multilateralizing influences stemming from the formation and growth of the European Economic Community (EEC). The EEC held forth broadening opportunities for national companies to organize for transnational markets. It also partially offset the restrictiveness of national actions taken against U.S. MNCs, since companies could usually avoid such measures by locating in a less restrictive country while still remaining within the Community Market system. In fact, American MNCs often proved to be more responsive to EEC integrative initiatives, such as regional investment measures, than many European national companies.

The United States government, in the meantime, also supported EEC development, primarily on the political-security grounds of building a strong contributive ally. It may be somewhat more problematic if such support would be as forthcoming today for what was an exclusionary trade device if viewed from the U.S. domestic perspective. The internal European position of many U.S. MNCs probably helped calm any such misgivings, however, and there was little offsetting U.S. domestic concern at that time regarding the effect of those MNC investments on the home country economy. Thus on balance, the role of MNCs during this period tended to support multilateral and integrative economic activities.

Serious trans-Atlantic friction involving MNCs did arise, however, from unilateral American application of extraterritorial antitrust and export control regulations. These actions became identified with the multinational corporate vehicle and served to reinforce European concerns regarding the national integrity of their economic institutions. Europeans found it particularly irritating when they were asked to treat U.S. MNC subsidiaries in a non-discriminatory, national treatment manner, only to be told that for certain issues that subsidiary must be considered a U.S. subject first rather than a French, German or British citizen. These cases were also the hardest to cope with for an MNC, which generally had little room for maneuver once the political battle lines had been drawn.

The logic of American extraterritorial law application is easier to understand within the context of a general systemic approach to trade and investment policy. These regulations were simply a functional application of the domestic policy values that the U.S. was seeking to replicate abroad. The absence of a specifically defined U.S. policy toward MNCs created no offsetting pressure to address subjects like differing jurisdictional claims which arise when trade and investment interaction occurs within an MNC business instrument.

Fortunately the occurrence of such conflicts, while still far from rare, has diminished in recent years. European political and economic strength has increased to the point where it can effectively counter U.S. initiatives in most individual cases. Nevertheless, the U.S. policy thrust has changed very little, as witnessed by the recent extraterritorial extension to U.S. subsidiaries of such items as the Foreign Corrupt Practices Act and regulations on compliance with international boycotts.

Euro-American relations have also been marked by a series of specific trade disputes, ranging from chicken wars to trigger price mechanisms. The role of

MNCs has generally not been the central element in these conflicts, however. While they may defend particular advantages accruing from favored sectoral tariffs or government procurement policies, MNCs have been among the strongest political supporters of liberal trade policies. Within the U.S., MNCs have been particularly important since the Burke-Hartke legislation in the early 1970's in opposing unilateral restrictive measures which threaten established multilateral trade policies.

Overall the goal of cooperative Euro-American trade relations appears to have been aided during the postwar period by MNC activity, which can adapt to and benefit from a relatively open trading system. Multinational corporations are generally more supportive of multilateral cooperation than unilateral government action, if for no other reason than a desire to avoid being sandwiched between competing political sovereigns.

The last decade did mark the beginning point, however, for a reexamination of U.S. liberal trade policy values. When the MNC "export of jobs" argument gained prominence in the Burke-Hartke debate, it cast doubt on the previously assumed beneficial impact of overseas investment on the domestic U.S. economy. This issue then set the stage for a serious reassessment of U.S. policy as it relates to fundamental changes occurring in the international economic system.

The Current Policy Debate

Over the past decade there have been some important changes in the historical backdrop to Euro-American trade policy and its relationship to multinational corporations. The unbalanced Atlantic relationship is now more equal. European postwar recovery objectives have long since fallen before the onslaught of both national and European Community progress. With the recovery and growth of domestic industry and increasingly effective bargaining leverage over U.S. MNCs, the goal of reasserting control over national economic decision-making has been largely achieved. Most European nations even appear to have survived relatively well the energy price spirals which could have proven disastrous at an earlier time period.

The concept of national or trans-European corporate champions has met with mixed success in terms of both economic viability and national interest fulfillment. There can be no doubt, however, that in many major industries European corporations now compete on an equal basis with U.S. MNCs, as illustrated in the relative rankings below. Finally, the spread of these European MNCs abroad has added a new dimension to Euro-American relations, ever to the extent of posing a "European Challenge" in the U.S.[3]

The United States, on the other hand, suffers from the shocks of the '70's. The phrase "sound as a dollar" took an ironic twist after August, 1971. Despite devaluations and floating exchange rates, the nation's trade deficit plummeted to over $30 billion annually toward the decade's end just as the trade

European and U.S. MNCs in Selected Sectors*

RANK	COMPANY	COUNTRY	TOTAL REVENUE (MILLIONS)
AUTOMOTIVE			
1.	General Motors	United States	$66,311
2.	Ford Motor Co.	United States	43,514
3.	Fiat Group	Italy	18,121
4.	PSA Peugeot-Citroen	France	17,114
5.	Volkswagen Group	West Germany	16,753
6.	Renault	France	16,101
7.	Daimler-Benz AG	West Germany	14,931
8.	Chrysler	United States	12,002
CHEMICALS			
1.	Hoechst Group	West Germany	$14,774
2.	Bayer Group	West Germany	14,186
3.	BASF Group	West Germany	14,128
4.	EI du Pont de Nemours	United States	12,572
5.	Imperial Chemicals Inds. Ltd.	United Kingdom	11,389
6.	Dow Chemical	United States	9,255
7.	Union Carbide	United States	9,177
8.	Montedison Group	Italy	8,224
9.	Rhône-Poulenc Group	France	7,940
10.	Naamloze Vennootschap DSM	Netherlands	6,356
ELECTRICAL EQUIPMENT			
1.	General Electric	United States	$22,980
2.	N.V. Philips Lamp	Netherlands	16,568
3.	Siemens Group	West Germany	15,065
4.	Cie Générale d'Électricité	France	8,310
5.	AEG-Telefunken Group	West Germany	7,752
6.	R.C.A.	United States	7,455
7.	Westinghouse	United States	7,332
8.	Thompson-Brandt Group ·	France	7,052
9.	Texas Instruments	United States	3,224
10.	Singer	United States	2,598
BANKING			
1.	Citicorp	United States	$10,904
2.	Bank of America	United States	9,450
3.	Banque Nationale de Paris	France	7,241
4.	Barclays Bank Group	United Kingdom	7,173
5.	Crédit Lyonnais Group	France	6,964
6.	Deutsche Bank Group	West Germany	6,634
7.	National Westminster Bank	United Kingdom	6,496
8.	Crédit Agricole	France	6,307
9.	Chase Manhattan	United States	6,079
10.	Sociéte Générale Group	France	5,600

*Information for the ranking drawn from listings of the 100 largest U.S. MNCs and the 100 largest foreign companies, *Forbes* (July 7, 1980): 99–108; *Business Week*, March 17, 1980, pp. 84–116.

147

component of U.S. GNP was doubling. Once proud domestic industries face serious import dislocation while U.S. MNCs abroad encounter stiffer foreign competition and more leveraged governmental demands. To add seeming insult to injury, Arab, Japanese, and European interests also appeared to be using the devalued American dollars to buy up undervalued U.S. productive resources.

This somewhat exaggerated picture is actually a rather accurate reflection of U.S. public perceptions which frame the current policy debate. Within the pending U.S. policy agenda, there is real potential for a value role reversal in Euro-American trade relations, with the U.S. becoming home production oriented, utilizing its MNCs as more specific national interest sales leaders. Europe, on the other hand, may be pulled away somewhat from MNC production end goals by the global market imperatives now facing its own MNCs.

The growing tension between old trade policy values and current economic pressures appears greatest in the United States, which is the primary focus of this analysis. Generalized systemic trade principles are under challenge as they appear increasingly insufficient to either safeguard or advance U.S. domestic interests. This change is most evident in the expression of nationalistic sentiments which fuel protectionist trade fears. The same attitude is also causing a new look at foreign investment policy, where a reassessment of inward investment flows may ultimately affect U.S. policy toward outward investment as well. Overall, there is less of a "fit" between the traditional, generalized U.S. policy approach and specific trade problems now facing the country.

Evidence for these developing U.S. policy changes can be garnered from diverse sources, including public opinion surveys, congressional activities, governmental program initiatives and interest group position-taking. Since the mid-1970's the proportion of American perceiving the U.S. as becoming more economically dependent on other countries has grown to nearly two-thirds of the population. Over this same time frame, there has been an increase in the percentage of Americans favoring restrictions on imported goods, ranging between 68% to 81%.[4] Taking these two changes together, one could interpret the growing protectionist sentiment as a reaction against interdependence and a reassertion of historical American withdrawal policies which favor national self-sufficiency. A further analysis of the data, however, suggests that this time around there is something more at work than simple isolationist tendencies.

Mr. Alvin Richman, a Senior Public Opinion Analyst of the U.S. Department of State, found that: "The desire to increase import restrictions does not necessarily connote opposition to foreign trade per se. The groups most desirous of tighter restrictions are also among those most favorably disposed toward the idea of trade — executives/professionals, those earning $25000 or more annually, males and Westerners."[5] Thus some of the change in U.S. trade sentiments may come not from isolationism, but from a more directed and activist desire to achieve a "better trade deal." Certainly the group favoring this posture would probably have a different orientation than isolationists to the role of MNCs in trade relations, although both groups will seek a change in broad U.S. free trade policies.

Public attitudes toward foreign investment also appear at odds with official U.S. policy positions. In June, 1979 the following question was asked in a Roper poll:

Foreign companies can invest in the United States, and American companies can invest in foreign countries in a number of ways — by buying up companies, by buying stock in companies and by building and operating plants. This benefits the companies that invest in other countries by expanding their business, and benefits the countries they invest in by providing greater production and more jobs in those countries.

We'd like to know whether you are in favor of or opposed to foreign companies investing in the United States . . . or don't you have any feelings one way or the other about it.

Even with such a beneficially worded preface, the question elicited a plurality of respondents opposed to foreign investments in the U.S. (44% opposed; 34% favor, 17% no feelings one way or the other; 5% don't know). An earlier Harris poll also documented similar attitudes, revailing a pattern of public opposition to different forms of inward investment which parallels in historical reaction in other countries — the greatest opposition to natural resource investments and corporate acquisitions, with less (although still a majority) of those surveyed opposed to new productive investments by foreign MNCs.[6]

The public mood is complicated further by the ambivalent reaction to U.S. investment abroad, the measurement most closely associated with attitudes toward U.S. MNCs. A June, 1979 Roper poll found the public evenly divided on U.S. investments overseas (38% opposed; 38% favor; 18% no feeling one way or the other; 6% don't know).[7]

None of these surveys provide much support for traditional U.S. free trade and investment principles. There does appear to be some room for influencing public sentiment, since there is a steady proportion of nearly one-fourth of those questioned who have no set opinions of these issues. However, to either capture the support of this segment, or to pacify the groups pushing for a better U.S. deal, it will be necessary for the government to address a range of specific dometic impact issues. U.S. trade policies, and even inward investments, are now being measured against a rough, home-oriented benefit standard. "When the public evaluates arguments in favor of free trade or protectionism, the most persuasive argument for either policy is that it results in more — or fewer — jobs for Americans." The consumer price impact of imports is another top-rated factor which proved important to respondents.[8] Concerns such as these are not easily reached by appeals to international trade principles said to operate for the greatest good for all nations.

These broader value changes mirror the critical public evaluations of U.S. MNC impacts, begun in the early 1970's, which sought to measure MNC benefits in relation to specific U.S. economic sectors. That debate is still going on, as evidenced by the public's ambivalent feelings toward U.S. overseas investment and the continuing opposition of organized labor and certain other interest groups to MNC operations in general. The connecting link between the debate over U.S. MNC actions and the future course of more generalized trade policy is drawing tighter, and may now turn on the same U.S.-centered cost/benefit calculations.

While national interest considerations were undoubtedly a part of earlier policy decisions, the period of postwar economic dominance allowed U.S. policy-makers greater latitude regarding official support for broader trade benefit considerations. The tenor of domestic debate at that time was rather constrained and even somewhat altruistic. Changed world economic conditions have removed this luxury from the U.S. government shelf and dumped the country into a period where more sharply drawn self-interest distinctions will be both common and necessary.

Recent congressional activities reinforce the impression that the persuasive power of broad international economic principles is on the demise while stricter national benefit determinations are gaining prominence. A sampling of trade and investment actions turns up the following examples:

--While Congress turned away the Burke-Hartke bill in the early 1970's in favor of new multilateral trade expansion talks, it is generally accepted that such an effort to reduce global trade barriers would not be reauthorized today. Even though Congress recently approved a package of agreements resulting from the Multilateral Trade Negotiations (MTN), the clear emphasis in congressional hearings was on the need for vigorous enforcement of U.S. rights and aggressive pursuit of potential U.S. trade gains, rather than the need for further systemic trade reform – a topic still officially on the GATT agenda.
--Two U.S. programs which have been challenged, in the U.S. as well as elsewhere, as antithetical to U.S. support for free market trade principles are the Domestic International Sales Corporation (DISC) and Webb-Pomerene Export Associations. While Congress cut back the DISC, it refused to heed Administration calls for its elimination and is now moving to expand Webb Act authority into more widely applicable export trading company legislation.
--Numerous bills to restrict foreign investment in the U.S. have been discussed in Congress, ranging from moratoriums to outright bans on new investment. Certain limited restrictions have already been added on foreign banks by national legislation while state actions affect several types of inward investment. The concept of a cost-benefit review determination or other similar screening process is gaining new credence despite its obvious clash with the official U.S. "open door" position regarding both inward and outward foreign investment.
--The Senate rejected a U.S.-U.K. Tax Treaty provision which would have restricted U.S. state use of a unitary tax formula in favor of a more internationally accepted approach. Similarly, while the U.S. has pressed for a multilateral agreement to limit investment incentives and disincentives, it is far from certain that such an agreement would be approved by Congress if it limited the states' rights to either entice a foreign plant or discourage a corporate takeover bid.

A number of governmental programs and interest group actions also portend a more nationalistic economic posture. The Commerce Department's new International Trade Administration and Foreign Commercial Service boast that for the first time, the U.S. Government is acting as an American business advocate in specific projects abroad. This approach contrasts with the armslength formality traditionally observed between U.S. business and government where it was the latter's job only to assure a fair international trading environment within which the former would compete for business strictly on its own initiative and merits. Now the Commerce program has adopted a stance which is not based on some reference to implementing broad international trade principles, but rather justifies governmental involvement more simply as a want to improve the U.S. trade account.

The evidence stemming from interest group positions probably needs the least explanation. Organized labor support for a more restrictionist trade policy has grown even stronger with the new posture of the United Auto Workers, just as several automobile companies now feel compelled to back national necessity arguments over strict adherence to international free trade principles. While most business groups would not endorse protectionist trade policies, there is widespread backing for more aggressive U.S. trade action. For example, the "Gentlemen's Agreement" on export credit financing was perceived as the type of multilateral accord which only disadvantages the U.S., thereby occasioning wide business support for a "meet and beat" approach by Eximbank to competition in this field.

International economic changes during the 1970's have thus created pressures in the U.S. for a more specifically directed foreign economic policy. In some respects this situation has parallels in the period when European policies were formulated, at least regarding the diminished power of international policy themes like anti-communism or free world trade expansion. The impression arising from the evidence of U.S. attitude changes clearly seems to point in the direction of a more nationalistic policy, politically premised on the importance of such factors as domestic employment, retention in the U.S. of leading-edge technological advances, suspicion of incoming foreign investment and the need to "reindustrialize" the home economy. Whether these pressures evolve into a negative, protectionist trade posture or more outwardly aggressive but positive trade competition could be strongly influenced by the role multinational corporations will play in linking the trans-Atlantic community together by addressing both its economic and political needs.

MNCs as Linking Mechanisms

Some potentially important but as yet unmeasured changes are underway which add a new dimension to the role of MNCs as transnational linking mechanisms. A series of governmentally directed or inspired inter-MNC business arrangements are being forged in areas such as military armaments, civil aviation and motor vehicles through devices like co-development, co-production, joint equity and joint marketing agreements. Many of these changes relate specifically to the altered trade policy conditions described above. The future development of these arrangements and specifically their relationship to governmental policy could have significant impact upon the trans-Atlantic trading structure and the role of MNCs as a supportive element behind multilateral cooperation.

Research studies, public debates and very often governmental policies have addressed MNCs primarily from a narrowly-defined, national gain-or-loss perspective. This approach focuses on the organization concept of an MNC parent firm headquartered in one country with subsidiaries abroad that function simply as directed arms of the parent – ready, willing and able to do its bidding.

It is of course, but a short step from this perception to the analogous view of MNCs acting as arms of the home country, doing that nation's bidding abroad. As we have seen, such a view both underlay European perceptions of U.S. MNCs and led them to structure a "national champion" policy based on precisely the same assumptions. This type of conceptualization tends to cast MNCs as biased actors in a trading relationship between nations where everything is played out as a zero-sum game. Integrative and linking aspects of MNC activities, both actual and potential, are thereby minimized or even discouraged.

In reality, of course, MNCs have never been limited to unidimensional parent-subsidiary ownership, although early American patterns were heavily weighted in this direction. There are a wide variety of business patterns to choose from, ranging from branches and wholly-owned subsidiaries to licensing and franchise agreements. Recently a new dimension has been added to some of these devices through the more direct involvement of governments in structuring co-development/co-production arrangements and the broader response of other private sector business schemes to changes in governmental trade policy values. The direction and utilization of these inter-MNC linkages as they relate to political trade pressures could help determine whether trans-Atlantic relations will move toward competitive trading blocks or a more progressive economic relationship.

One of the most obvious growth areas for these new arrangements is the field of military armaments, particularly the production of aircraft. Naturally this area exhibits more direct and influential governmental involvement than most economic sectors, but for that very reason it may allow a clearer look at these linkages and the public considerations they involve. Developments in this area have an important carry-over impact as well on related production outside of the defense field.

The early record in NATO military aircraft evidences reliance upon rather straight-forward national development and direct purchase agreements. This approach became increasingly unsatisfactory, however, for many of the same reasons that led to the general European reaction against U.S. MNCs, i.e. concerns about industrial dominance, technological dependence and control over national political/economic decision-making.

Direct international purchases of nationally developed aircraft is probably the most economically efficient method of production which also meets the military goal of NATO standardization and interoperability. National development activities, however, became concentrated mainly in the U.S. and, to a lesser extent, the U.K. and France. This production distribution pattern relegated most countries to only a buyer status, making direct purchase agreements more politically unpopular in these countries due to its negative impact on domestic employment, balance of payments and foreign industrial/technological dependence. Alternative options were then explored to essentially compromise market-end goals of final price and NATO standardization with these more home production-oriented considerations.

AIRCRAFT PROCUREMENT PROGRAMS BY TYPE

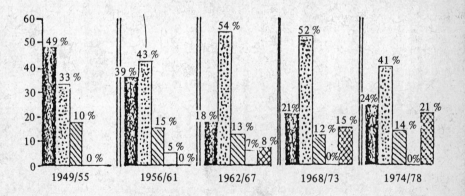

SOURCE: Adapted from data in Norman Asher and Janice Lilly, "Types of Weapon Programs and Their Implications for NATO Standardization on Interoperability," Institute for Defense Analysis, July, 1978.

153

A relatively recent innovation in this direction has been the use of cooperative development schemes between two or more countries, with at least eleven such instances occurring since 1962. These arrangements have linked the U.S./France, France/FRG; Canada/U.S.; Italy/U.S.; U.K./France; U.K./FRG/Italy; and FRG/Netherlands/Belgium. The trend in European military aircraft procurement programs over the last three decades demonstrates the growing importance of cooperative developed projects at the expense of national development programs. The utilization of co-development and co-production programs to give more countries a "piece of the pie" became especially critical as the pie grew smaller (fewer procurement programs) but more expensive (higher development costs).

While having important implications within the military field, these changes both symbolize and reinforce the importance of domestic-based economic factors in broader Euro-American trade values. The cooperative schemes also provide a pattern for more direct governmental involvement in transnational business, since these production arrangements are pieced together through intergovernmental negotiations and many of the contracting corporations are owned or heavily supported by their national governments. This increased government participation in business can in turn impact on the nature of MNC linkages, leaving less room for MNC maneuver and action — except where the MNCs may be governmentally-connected entities.

The nature of trade in military aircraft can also carry-over more broadly to other economic sectors through commercial product spin-offs and the impact that success or failure in this area may have on corporate strength needed to remain competitive in other product sectors. One of the clearest examples of carry-over influence occurs in the closely related civil aviation industry. While the governmental role is not quite as dominant as in military aircraft, many of the lessons learned there are being used now to structure trade competition in civil aviation.

In order to mount a challenge to U.S. domination of the civil aircraft market (for all the employment, technology, balance of payments, etc. factor discussed before), several European nations formed new transnational business alliances to produce first the Concorde and now the more highly successful Airbus. Having been burned by management problems raised by excessive political direction in the Concorde project, participating governments sponsored the creation of a separate new company to handle Airbus production once the officially determined national roles had been agreed upon. Thus this co-development/co-production venture established linkages involving a full range of private, government-sponsored and government-owned entities.

In a related development, even industry leader Boeing, now faced with a challenger capable of offering a "family" of competitive aircraft models, is apparently ready to explore new transnational linking mechanisms. For the first time the company has tied itself through risk-sharing sub-contracting arrangements to aerospace companies in Italy and Japan. This development seems to

154

involve not only economic development considerations, however, but perhaps even more importantly the changing climate concerning trade policy values. "Boeing seeks insurance against a wider outbreak of economic nationalism that could inhibit its overseas sales. As (President of Boeing Airplane Co.) Ernest Boullioun says, "If we were to bleed off all of the aerospace production, we'd get a backlash that would cause more trouble than sharing to a degree."[9] These new co-production links, reportedly totaling up to 30 percent of 767 and 777 airframe components, are designed to help head off such a trade policy "backlash." Thus governmentally-sponsored business arrangement are being matched by private company initiatives, with both developments being tied to the pressures of political trade policy values.

Another industry experimenting with new transnational business arrangements is motor vehicles, most specifically automobiles. Some linkages follow the simple parent-subsidiary straight-line relationship, like the establishment of Volkswagen of America, Inc. Other developments introduce more complicated arrangement, such as Renault's expanding interest in American Motors Corporation, where assemblage, distributorship marketing, financial and technological support and future co-development projects all appear to be involved.

Many other transnational schemes are appearing within Europe, between Europe and the U.S., and also with Japan. Some of these linkages have provided for co-development/co-production (Fiat-Peugeot, Renault-Volvo, Nissan-Alfa Romeo); marketing and distribution agreements (British Leyland-Honda; VW-MAN; Renault-Mack); component agreements (Fiat-Ford, Renault-Alfa Romeo, Fiat-Saab) and stock ownership (Chrysler-Mitsubishi, Ford-Toyo Kogyo; AMC-Renault).[10]

The presence of these arrangements can add a new dimension to MNC linking mechanisms in the automobile industry. As political pressures push companies from traditional import strategies toward full subsidiary establishment, these mechanisms can provide many more economically sound stopping points along the way, while maintaining the benefits of international flows of components and technology. Much as Boeing's "sharing-out" of production is aimed at maintaining market access, so the utilization of various levels of joint production or marketing arrangements could hold the potential for ameliorating if not altogether avoiding political objections to foreign import patterns.

A recent letter from Japan's Minister of International Trade and Industry to the U.S. Trade Representative demonstrates how these ideas relate to current political difficulties in the U.S. automobile industry. While noting the recent U.S. International Trade Commission ruling refused to recommend action against auto imports, Minister Rokusuke Tanaka pledged:

Japan also tends to play a responsible role in maintaining the world free trade system and at the same time we remain sensitive to the problems the U.S. auto industry is facing, particularly the problem of unemployment.

The Japanese government will continue its effort to encourage the Japanese auto industry to make economically viable investment in the U.S. and realize economically viable co-production activities with the U.S. auto industry.

155

The Japanese auto industry will expand the planned purchases of U.S. automotive parts in order to help create future job opportunities in the U.S.[11]

These three industry examples are meant to stimulate debate in this area rather than offer any hard and fast conclusions as to their more general representative nature. It is difficult to evaluate just how widely such inter-MNC connections may be spreading in various industries because data is not centrally collected or analyzed on such a basis. A careful gleaning of reports in trade journals and specific industry newsletters allows one to draw a general picture, but it will only reflect at best a rough snapshot in time whose images are blurred by unsystematic collection methods and the unavailability of much commercially sensitive information. An orderly system to gather and evaluate this type of information, perhaps through a centralized OECD office, would give public policy-makers valuable tool for their upcoming trade policy decisions.

It is nevertheless apparent that MNCs are fully capable of playing an increasingly varied role in trans-Atlantic trade relations — through direct foreign establishment or a variety of cooperative business arrangements; subsequent to or in advance of specific intergovernmental agreements; and with private, governmentally-connected or state-owned participants. The choice between various MNC forms of business can sharply affect physical trade flows and trade balance measures which are central to changing political values. Thus the nature of these MNC linkage patterns could play an important role in determining the future of Euro-American trade relations.

Evolving Policy Choices

The challenge for Euro-American relations during the 1980's will be to structure a mature trading system which meets both political and economic needs through an integrated approach to trade and investment policy issues. There is no turning back the clock to earlier days when broad free trade principles provided a satisfactory framework for European recovery and a sufficient guide to U.S. economic power. National and international economic changes have altered this relationship in a way which demands a more specific and equitable trading structure in terms of both opportunities and responsibilities.

The interrelationship between foreign trade and investment forces has never been closer, largely due to the linking mechanisms of multinational corporations. Europe has had experience dealing with all different sides of these forces and has developed an integrated view of foreign policy objectives as they relate to national economies. Both large trade adjustments and inward investment issues are relatively new for the U.S. A satisfactory response to these developments will require a level of policy integration and specificity very different from traditionally broad U.S. trade principles. The most immediate challenge then is probably to U.S. foreign economic policy, which must evolve a more refined and defined approach to advancing U.S. national interests, without allowing the pendulum to swing once again to the extremes of protectionist trade measures.

There should not be undue hesitancy on either side of the Atlantic about U.S. movement toward more specific and even outwardly aggressive policy positions. Measurement of U.S. trade and investment policies against a more explicit self-interest standard is probably overdue in international terms; it is also a necessary move to respond to domestic concerns which, if ignored, will turn U.S. policies much more surely toward an inwardly directed, protectionist trade posture.

Trans-Atlantic attention should focus instead on forging new Euro-American understandings on trade and investment policies as they relate to the role of national governments in transnational business arrangements. While in the past MNCs have been perceived as placing national "sovereignity-at-bay," the danger now is more that governments have gained too much explicit control over MNCs. Through governmentally negotiated production and marketing arrangements, public ownership or subsidization, as well as trade and investment policy tools, national governments can directly structure MNC economic activities far more specifically than was previously possible. Multinational corporations could play a crucial role in supporting multilateral cooperation if policy-makers on both sides of the Atlantic encourage the integrative, linking aspects of MNC activities, rather than focusing primarily on their utility as instruments of unilateral national gain.

Notes

1 See Charles S. Maier, The Politics of Productivity: Foundations of American International Economic Policy after World War II, in: Peter J. Katzenstein, Between Power and Plenty, 1978.
2 See Jack N. Behrman, National Interests and the Multinational Enterprise, 1970 and Raymond Vernon, Big Business and the State, 1974.
3 See: The European Challenge, in: European Community, July-August 1978, and Roy Eales, Challenge in Reverse, in: The Economist, October 1978.
4 The difference depends upon whether the survey question indicates that import restrictions would increase prices paid by consumers, with knowledge of the price impact lowering support for restrictions. For the poll data, see: Alvin Richman, Public Perservations of World Trade, a report prepared for the League of Women Voters Education Fund, 1980.
5 Richman, Public Perceptions of World Trade, p. 10.
6 U.S. Department of State, Public is Wary of Foreign Investment in the U.S., a Briefing Memorandum, September 6, 1979.
7 Ibid.
8 U.S. Department of State, Punlic Attitudes Toward Foreign Trade, a Briefing Memorandum, August 27, 1980.
9 Louis Kraar, Being Takes a Bold Plunge to Keep Flying High, in: Fortune, 25 September 1980.

10 Information gathered from a variety of news accounts, industry publications and other public sources.
11 Letter from Japanese Minister of International Trade and Industry, Rokusuke Tanaka to U.S. Trade Representative Reubin Askew, November 23, 1980.

About the Authors

Guy de Carmoy is a Professor at the European Institute of Business Administration, Fontainebleau, France

Joseph I. Coffey is Distinguished Service Professor of Public and International Affairs and Director, Center for International Security Studies, University of Pittsburgh

Ernst-Otto Czempiel is a Professor for International Relations Johann-Wolfgang-Goethe University of Frankfurt/M and a Research Group Director at Peace Research Institute Frankfurt

John M. Kline is Deputy Director, Karl F. Landegger Program in International Business Diplomacy, School of Foreign Service, Georgetown University, Washington

Gert Krell is a Research Director, Peace Research Institute Frankfurt

Harald Müller is a Research Associate, Peace Research Institute Frankfurt

Reinhard Rode is a Research Associate, Peace Research Institute Frankfurt

Proceedings of International Peace Research Association
Eight General Conference 1981

Egbert Jahn, Yoshikazu Sakamoto (Editors)
**Elements of World Instability: Armaments, Communication, Food,
International Division of Labour**

1981. 392 p., ISBN 3-593-32851-8

This book represents the main fields of present international peace research: arms race, militarism including intelligence services, disarmament and arms control, political economy of food, the social consequences of the new international division of labour, European détente policy, peace education, and as a new field of research: the world information order. The volume contains a selection of more than 90 contributions, from 35 countries, to the Eighth General Conference of the International Peace Research Association in Königstein, Germany in 1979. It reflects the tendency of peace research to concentrate its efforts more and more on problems of the relationship between the North and the South and the internal economic, social and political processes of the developing countries.

Table of Contents:
Part I: Political Economy of Food. O. Gonzalez Rodriguez (Norwich, U.K.): The Role of the Peasantry in the Development of Capitalism: The Case of Mexico; U. Oswald (Mexico): Ideological Penetration of the Peasantry through Productive Organisation; L. Herrera (Tampere, Finland): External Indebtedness in Latin America.
Part II: Social Consequences of the New International Division of Labour. L. R. Alschuler (Ottawa, Canada): The Struggle of Argentina within the New International Division of Labour; J. Olmedo de Garcilita (Mexico City): International Division of Labour and Industrialization. The Mexican Case, M. Naraine (Lancaster, Great Britain): Economic and Political Transformation in the Commonwealth Carribbean; T. Baumgartner, T. R. Burns (Oslo): Technology, Dependency and Social Relations, H. Elsenhans (Konstanz, FRG): Social consequences of the NIEO.
Part III: World Information Order. C. Aguirre-Bianchi and G. Hedebro (Stockholm): Alternative Communications in Latin America. R. Stanbridge (Uppsala, Schweden): Limitations on Press Freedom in South Africa; J. Becker (Frankfurt, FRG): Germany's Policy after the UNESCO Media Declaration of November 1978; A. P. Schmid (Leiden, Netherlands): Insurgent Terrorism and the News Media.
Part IV: World Military Order, Militarism and Disarmament. Y. Sakamoto and R. Falk (Japan, USA): A World Demilitarized: A Basic Human Need; A Varas (Chile): State Crisis, Arms Race and Disarmament in Latin America; P. Lock (Hamburg, FRG): New International Economic Order and Armaments; J. B. Adekson (Ibadan, Nigeria): The Five D's in Contemporary. Nigerian Civil-Military Thought (Defence, Development, Demobilization, Demilitarization and Democratization); G. Krell (Frankfurt, FRG): The Development of the Concept of Security; W. Agrell (Lund, Sweden): Military Intelligence and the Information Explosion; O. Wilkes, N. Petter Gleditsch (Oslo): Research on Intelligence or Intelligence as Research.
Part V: After Helsinki: Ideological Confrontation and Transnational Communication. H. Wiberg (Lund, Schweden): Détente in Europe; A. Boenisch (Berlin, GDR): Internal and External implications of Détente in Central Europe; E. Jahn (Frankfurt, FRG): Social Reform Policy and Détente Policy in Eastern and Western Europe; L. Brock (Braunschweig, FRG): Progress in East-West Relations. More Mutual Confidence in the Capability of Mutual Destruction?
Part VI: Peace Education. R. Burns (Bundoora, Australia): Problems of Legitimation of Peace Education: R. Steinweg (Frankfurt, FRG): Violence and Sensuousness. Theatreplaying as a means of Peace Education; E. Senghaas-Knobloch (Bremen, FRG): Rising Consiousness of Women and Politics against Violence; M. Gronemeyer (Bochum, FRG): The Ecology Movement – a New Field of Peace Education; N. Okechukwu (Ibadan, Nigeria): On Human Rights: Reassessment of the Concept in Africa.

Campus Verlag · Schumannstraße 65 · 6000 Frankfurt/Main 1

In the seventies, arms control, energy, and trade have been a source of conflict, not only in East-West relations, but also within the Atlantic Alliance. Since the United States play a prominent role in this alliance, one would expect that US foreign policy and its domestic roots have been widely analyzed and are well understood. That, however, seems not to be the case, as many articles and studies almost completely ignore the socio-political background of United States foreign policy towards Europe. This book focuses on domestic factors, and can thus provide explanations why the United States, in spite of all trans-atlantic rhetoric, have repeatedly taken decisions which neglect important interests of the Allies. The book contains contributions from American and European scholars about SALT II, Euro-American differences of interest in questions of defense and security, about US energy policy and its effects on Europe, about US trade policy, and about the position of American Multinational Corporations.

ISBN 3-593-32914-X